STUDIES IN IMPERIALISM

general editor John M. MacKenzie

When the 'Studies in Imperialism' series was founded more than twenty-five years ago, emphasis was laid upon the conviction that 'imperialism as a cultural phenomenon had as significant an effect on the dominant as on the subordinate societies'. With more than seventy books published, this remains the prime concern of the series. Cross-disciplinary work has indeed appeared covering the full spectrum of cultural phenomena, as well as examining aspects of gender and sex, frontiers and law, science and the environment, language and literature, migration and patriotic societies, and much else. Moreover, the series has always wished to present comparative work on European and American imperialism, and particularly welcomes the submission of books in these areas. The fascination with imperialism, in all its aspects, shows no sign of abating, and this series will continue to lead the way in encouraging the widest possible range of studies in the field. 'Studies in Imperialism' is fully organic in its development, always seeking to be at the cutting edge, responding to the latest interests of scholars and the needs of this ever-expanding area of scholarship.

Exporting empire

MANCHESTER
1824

Manchester University Press

Exporting empire

AFRICA, COLONIAL OFFICIALS AND THE CONSTRUCTION OF THE BRITISH IMPERIAL STATE, c. 1900–1939

Christopher Prior

MANCHESTER UNIVERSITY PRESS

The right of Christopher Prior to be identified as the author of this work has been asserted by him in accordance with the Copyright, Designs and Patents Act 1988.

Published by Manchester University Press
Altrincham Street, Manchester M1 7JA, UK
www.manchesteruniversitypress.co.uk

British Library Cataloguing-in-Publication Data is available

Library of Congress Cataloging-in-Publication Data is available

ISBN 978 0 7190 9929 8 *paperback*

First published by Manchester University Press in hardback 2013

This paperback edition first published 2015

The publisher has no responsibility for the persistence or accuracy of URLs for any external or third-party internet websites referred to in this book, and does not guarantee that any content on such websites is, or will remain, accurate or appropriate.

Printed by Lightning Source

To Helen and Les Prior

CONTENTS

LIST OF ILLUSTRATIONS

Table

Figures

ACKNOWLEDGEMENTS

The writing of this book was an enjoyable experience. Whilst I owe a good deal to many, I will confine myself here to thanking those people who had the greatest impact on the work. I am indebted to the following: Lucy McCann and all at Rhodes House, Oxford; Jane Hogan and all at the Sudan Archive at the Durham University Archives; all dealing with the Royal Commonwealth Society Collections at Cambridge University Library; Philippa Bassett and all at the University of Birmingham Special Collections; Helen Afi Gadzekpo and all at the Public Records and Archives Department in Accra; Jane Saunders and all at the University of Leeds Brotherton Special Collections, as well as the staff at Newcastle University Library, the National Archives at Kew and the British Library. I am grateful to the organisers and audiences of papers I presented at Durham University, Keele University, NUI Galway, SOAS, the University of Bergen and the University of Leeds for helping refine my thinking on colonial Africa, and to those at Sheffield Hallam University and the University of York for helping refine my thinking on the British Empire more broadly. The study also draws upon ideas from papers written for conferences at Lingnan University, the University of Bristol and the University of Glasgow. I would like to thank colleagues at Durham, Leeds and University College Dublin for creating fun and stimulating environments conducive to research and writing (this work was completed prior to my recent move to the University of Southampton). Whilst this study is a completely re-worked version of my PhD thesis, I must thank Justin Willis for the invaluable role he played in supervising the original thesis, and the AHRC for funding the research that went into it. I am also grateful to the British Academy for a Small Research Grant, and to the School of History at the University of Leeds for various School Research Support grants. Manchester University Press has made the whole process of producing this book remarkably smooth. The majority of this book was written in Durham, Leeds, Oxford, London and Dublin; the unfailing hospitality of the Barron family in Durham and Joan Tranter in Oxford are particularly noteworthy. Thanks go to Hester Barron, Shane Doyle, John Mackenzie, Stephan Malinowski, William Mulligan, Glyn Prysor, Andrew Thompson and Christopher Vaughan for their tremendously useful comments on various drafts of the manuscript; all errors are naturally my own. I owe a debt of gratitude to Olga Marsden and Linda Dixon. Seumas Spark provided a marvellous index. Jonathan Prior provided laughter and friendship. Cleo Barron displayed customary patience and provided support above and beyond what might be reasonably expected of anyone. This work is dedicated to my parents, Helen and Les Prior, for their unfailing love and encouragement.

LIST OF ABBREVIATIONS

ADC	Assistant District Commissioner
ADO	Assistant District Officer
BL	British Library, London
CO	Colonial Office
CSO	Colonial Secretary's Office
DC	District Commissioner
DO	District Officer
HMOCS	Her Majesty's Overseas Civil Service
IBEAC	Imperial British East Africa Company
ICS	Indian Civil Service
JC	Joseph Chamberlain Papers, Birmingham University
NA	National Archives, London
PRAAD	Public Records and Archives Administration Department, Accra
RHO	Rhodes House Library, University of Oxford
RNC	Royal Niger Company
SAD	Sudan Archive, Durham University
SPS	Sudan Political Service
WAFF	West African Frontier Force

GENERAL EDITOR'S INTRODUCTION

This book is partly based on memoirs and diaries, so perhaps I may be permitted to indulge in a reminiscence of my own. As a boy, I lived in Zambia (then Northern Rhodesia) and at the age of twelve in 1955, I announced my ambition to family and friends. It was to study to become a District Commissioner. The reason was of course obvious. In the world of my colonial town (Ndola), there was no question that the DC was the most important European around. His lifestyle seemed to be fascinating and important. Moreover, his son was a school friend of mine and I frequently visited the rather agreeable DC's house and talked to the great man himself, hearing stories of his relations with the local African chiefs. At that time, emulating such a career seemed the most natural thing to aspire to. Moreover, I was frequently regaled with stories of DCs in Kenya, where my father had worked in the 1920s and early 1930s, and at least one of those DCs had later become a governor (Sir Robert Armitage). When living in the remote Kakamega district, my father (somewhat to his Highland Scots shy embarrassment) was invited to dine with and play bridge with this local colonial potentate. It was the first time I had heard of the propensity of such officials to dress in dinner suits even in such out of the way tropical locations (my father possessed no such garment). At any rate, this indeed seemed to be an alluring pathway at a time when I was too innocent to peer into the future of colonialism. Some of its realities, not least racial discrimination, were all around me. But I personally admired Africans, loved their company and was sure that the less attractive sides of imperial rule would soon pass, not least if I was in charge!

However, I was soon disabused of such an ambition. By the early 1960s, at just the time when I was an undergraduate and no longer living in Africa, it was apparent that a wave of welcome acts of decolonisation was sweeping over East and Central Africa. Many years later, a distinguished imperial historian colleague and I, somewhat bizarrely while attending a conference in Tokyo, discovered that we had shared this youthful and wholly impractical ambition. To the great amusement of the other conferees, we made a public confession of this the following day.

'Confession' now seems like the right word. I moved swiftly from aspirant colonial administrator to a severe case of post-colonial guilt, which infused much of my work for many years, not least as I became increasingly aware of the vicious character of several white regimes in the region, particularly in apartheid South Africa and rebel Rhodesia (Zimbabwe).

Yet the personal connection with the colonies continued. Through my membership of the Royal Commonwealth Society in Northumberland Avenue, London, and my research in its magnificent library (now in Cambridge), I met many former colonial administrators. Once when attending a lecture by a celebrated historian of Africa in that building, I encountered a distinguished-looking elderly gentleman in the basement cloakroom. Commenting on the lecture, he suddenly said to me, 'The trouble with these historian wallahs ...'. As a junior historian wallah myself, I pricked up my ears, '... is that they believe what they read in documents. When I was a governor, I never ever told my Colonial Office masters the truth. I always told them what they wanted to hear. It was the only way to survive'. It was a salutary lesson about official papers that I have never forgotten.

I soon heard further interesting stories about document formation from that doyen of colonial administrators turned academic, Tony Kirk-Greene, a scholar whom I greatly admire. I think it was he who told me that at an early stage of his career he was instructed to write the district report for an area of Nigeria. When he asked his boss how he should go about it, he received the instruction, 'Just get out last year's report, repeat it, but make damn sure you change the date'. How much of this was tongue-in-cheek must have depended on the tone of voice. Later, I encountered many of the dying breed of former colonial officials in the Overseas Pensioners' Association (of which my father was a member), notably after they made the enlightened decision to use up some funds to institute a research project. In particular, I gave a paper at an excellent conference held under their auspices at the Institute of Commonwealth Studies in London in 2004. Its title, and that of the subsequent publication, edited by Terry Barringer, was *How Green Was Our Empire: Environment, Development and the Colonial Service*. None of those words implied guilt.

Through all these contacts, I knew that there was a mismatch between the people I met, so often dedicated, charming and thoroughly sympathetic, not least to the aspirations of colonised peoples, and the villains who haunted the pages of some modern scholarship. In many ways Christopher Prior's book helps to resolve this mismatch. A number of historians have written about colonial officials, their manner of recruitment, their *esprit de corps* (if it existed), and their predilections and prejudices when working in distant colonies. But none have used so many of the sources utilised by Prior, particularly letters, diaries and other materials available in some of the colonial archives built up in recent decades, as well as official papers and newspapers in London and Africa. Nor have any previous scholars covered so much ground, including colonies in both East and West Africa, as well as that extraordinary anomaly, the Sudan. Never before has there been such a comprehensive study of the 'mindsets' and 'mental landscapes' (as he calls them) of colonial officials, revealing much not only about their personal aspirations and professional ambitions, but also demonstrating the complexity of individual preferences and experiences, frustrations and desires. Among much else, he demonstrates the practical limitations under which colonial officials operated. Some areas of formal empire were scarcely even penetrated during the imperial period. Legislation and administrative orders were frequently entirely ineffectual beyond the immediate ambit of the boma or district office.

However, despite all these complexities, it is essential that such a study does not simply break down into a heap of broken shards. Out of it all, some kind of overall imperial pot has to emerge, but it must not be a crude and stylistically simple one. It is a pot where the complicated design, the detail, the decoration and the glaze nonetheless add up to an overall piece of ceramic – for which read interpretation – that conveys some understanding, often revisionist, of the imperial experience. Throughout, the relationship with indigenous peoples, which must never be forgotten in all such studies, is in the foreground. The great strength of this book lies in the fact that its author appreciates these points. Moreover, Prior poses four questions in his introduction and, in a valuable and symmetrical structure, sets out to answer them in his conclusion. All imperial historians, and indeed all former colonial officials owe him a debt of gratitude for setting about this task with such a perceptive and nuanced historical sense.

John M. MacKenzie

Introduction

This book examines what British colonial officials thought and why. It is concerned with those officials who served in Africa between the end of the 'Scramble for Africa' and the start of the Second World War. Colonial officials were the 'men on the spot' employed by the British government to administer a region of Africa. The nature of their job differed according to place and period, but as the need to 'pacify' African peoples became less of a pressing concern, officials took on an expanding range of roles that included tax assessor and collector, treasurer, town planner and surveyor, amateur ethnographer, overseer of public works, conflict mediator, superintendent of police, prison warden, judge and executioner. Their lives consequently intersected with those of Africans in a complex variety of ways. Whilst some of the concerns, prejudices and pressures of such officials are articulated in officials' memoirs and the novels of a small group of pre-1939 authors – of whom Edgar Wallace was the most popular, and Joyce Cary the most articulate – in contrast to historical works concerned with colonial governors, there are relatively few studies of the rank and file.[1] The earliest dedicated work on officials in Africa was Charles Jeffries' *The Colonial Empire and its Civil Service* (1938). However, this is an administrative history covering how the services were organised and officials' 'terms and conditions', such as salary and pension.[2] Robert Heussler's *Yesterday's Rulers* (1963) relies more on colonial officials' testimonies, but is primarily concerned with how officials were recruited, and contains very little on their actions once out in Africa.[3]

Older works could not benefit from the sources now open to scholars, particularly officials' private papers in the University of Oxford's Colonial Records Project, archived at Rhodes House. More recent work on colonial service has nevertheless focused on statistics and the mechanics of recruitment: how many officials joined the administrative ranks, where they were educated, and so on, rather than on their attitudes and mindsets.[4] In contrast with recent studies of the Indian Civil Service (ICS), in an African context, the only element of officials' mindsets to have received any sustained scrutiny is the impact of public school education on their sense of duty.[5] A. H. M. Kirk-Greene's *Symbol of Authority* (2006) builds upon a career spent studying the colonial state in Africa, but is primarily concerned with what officials did, rather than with what they thought of imperial rule, each other, and so on. At any rate, it only picks up the story in 1932.[6] Besides two popular history books, which provide interesting details but little analysis, the three works to have squarely addressed the matter of what officials thought are Lewis Gann and Peter Duignan's overarching, if rather brief and simplistic, assessment of late-Victorian and Edwardian officials, Heussler's essay on administrators in Tanganyika, and Henrika Kuklick's sociological study of those serving in the interwar Gold Coast.[7] Other works that examine different colonies invariably address officials' beliefs tangentially but are naturally more concerned with what this collectivity did than with what they thought.

This is nothing to complain about. How officials collectively impacted upon colonial and postcolonial Africa is an important matter that is fraught with politicisation and therefore needs to be negotiated with particular care. Nevertheless, a relative neglect of officials' attitudes means there are four pressing matters that the present study will seek to address. Firstly, how far were officials' ideas the product of their upbringing and education – both of which invariably occurred in the British imperial metropole – and how far were they the result of their African experiences? A great deal of work is still being done on the impact of empire upon British society, but how far were these metropolitan conceptions subsequently *re-exported* out to Africa via officials?[8] Some historians have focused briefly on officials' attitudes towards indirect rule, the system whereby local elites were to be seen as the rulers of their people, with officials working behind the scenes in a supposedly advisory capacity. Officials have been criticised for being too unimaginative and dogmatic in their implementation of indirect rule, treating the ideas passed onto them by superiors as if they were an untouchable 'canon'.[9] For one scholar, indirect rule became an 'unquestioned creed' in Nigeria.[10] In contrast, others have suggested that officials' mentalities were primarily shaped by what they experienced and learnt as 'men on the spot'.[11] Officials were pragmatists over anything else, perhaps both hostile to central authority decrees and anti-intellectual in their response to grand theories of governance.[12]

On the other side of the historiographical spectrum is Kathryn Tidrick. Building upon the aforementioned body of work examining the public school, Tidrick contends that colonial officials' defining characteristic was a tension between wanting to be loved and wanting to be good. Officials reconciled these as best they could by resolving to wield power 'responsibly'. Officials' internalisation of this conundrum is 'a tribute to the formative power of the [school] experience'.[13] Kirk-Greene has argued that, whatever his social background, each colonial official bonded so effectively with others because

> once he enters the post-Arnold world of public – and progressively of grammar – school into which he was likely to have been propelled from a middle-class ... family of professional parents, he has become socialized and homogenized in accordance with the prevailing code of expected behaviour, at once accepted internally and admired externally.[14]

This code, Kirk-Greene continues, emphasised 'the assiduous cult of the amateur, displaying modesty and decorum in triumph and resolute unemotion in adversity', and was 'an imperial virtue, sometimes learned at home, always inculcated at school, strongly encouraged at the university, and directly transferred into the [Administrative] Service'.[15]

Closely linked to this is the second matter to consider: selflessness and selfishness. Officials have been stereotyped as many things. They were the foot soldiers of economic exploitation and destroyers of indigenous polities,[16] or the glorious embodiment of an English eccentricity or public school stoicism.[17] Other explanations for their behaviour draw upon the diversity of the colonies they faced. For instance, officials' ideas about how to act might have been shaped by a sense of the 'maturity' of the colonies in which they worked, or by a sense of how far the peoples in their district were willing to countenance new ideas.[18] After all, it could be argued that one of the reasons officials in Northern Nigeria were so enthusiastic about indirect rule was because the peoples of the region were relatively willing to adopt it and required relatively little adjustment in order that they be judged ready for it.[19]

Nevertheless, it is an emphasis upon selflessness that has been the most pronounced feature of discussions of colonial officials' behaviour. As one would expect, selflessness was built into the mythology of imperial service in Africa throughout the period covered by this book. E. C. Adams' early twentieth-century doggerel about one 'John Theophilus Jones' in Northern Nigeria chastised the man who 'came out with the idea that he was the biggest thing that ever happened, and the boss of the show: That niggers were made to wait upon him; what other white men were for I don't know'.[20] Any deviation from this selflessness was marked out as the root of all trouble. Richard Oakley's reflection on his career as an official in northern Nigeria,

Treks & Palavers (1938), approaches the issue from a different angle. In it, Oakley argued that

> [an official's] job, viewed in its highest sense, as it should be viewed, is an altruistic work. It consists, not in what he can get out of the native, in labour or trade, but of giving something to the native himself namely, ideals and backbone, or of making the native do himself, even against his will, what is of benefit to his own race, as a whole, or to refrain from doing what is against those racial interests. This altruism is not a monopoly of officialdom or of any one department, but is present in all who have a right feeling towards the native ... a duty which a P[olitical] O[fficer] must ever have before his mind.[21]

Some historians have endorsed such images of selflessness by arguing that officials were dedicated humanitarians bringing democracy and development to lands that had previously known only the 'unrewarding gyrations of barbarous tribes'.[22] The poorly constructed, politically motivated nature of such arguments does not in itself render any claims of altruism inaccurate. There is certainly reason to assume that officials would have agreed that they were acting in a selfless manner. After all, they knowingly went to places where they would endure personal discomfort. In the case of Sudan, temperatures of 110 degrees Fahrenheit were not unknown.[23] Very little could counteract this (although one commentator felt it worth purchasing ice in West Africa, 'if only to hear, cooling in itself, the musical tinkle of a lump of ice in a long peg tumbler').[24] If a man was willing to dedicate his life to work in an environment where ice made him happy, one might surmise that he was first and foremost a selfless individual. It is therefore unsurprising that historians have largely accepted Oakley's claim, and the claims of many others like him. For instance, Robert Collins has argued that 'the heritage of the English countryside provided the basic desire "to serve" the Sudanese ... [a] genuine belief in the need to carry the "white man's burden" ... There can be no doubt that the members of the Service sincerely believed in their "mission" with a confidence and faith which the Sudanese never quite understood nor fully appreciated'.[25]

However, retrospective declarations of selflessness stand in stark contrast to a strong-selling 1913 guide to life in West Africa entitled *'Verb Sap.': On Going to West Africa, Northern Nigeria, Southern, and to the Coasts*, written by Alan Field, a retired official who had worked in Northern Nigeria. The guide suggested that 'An indictment of West Africa must here be made (with regret it is written), lest the reader should say he was not warned. It is a land of selfishness ... Surely exiles and pioneers should be the least selfish'.[26] Field went no further than this on the matter. Did Field pull away from full disclosure lest he be accused of being less than gentlemanly by airing specific pieces of dirty laundry about others in public? It is difficult to discern what really drove officials. They were, after all, raised in a social environment that prized selfless duty as imperial rule at its finest. For instance, a common complaint amongst District Commissioners (DCs) was that

> In the days before formal responsibility had been given to 'Native Authorities' [the system of indirect rule] to deal with disputes and minor criminal cases among their own people too much of a D.C.'s work consisted of dealing with matters which would have been settled more speedily, and no doubt more competently, by the village elders or tribal head well versed in local custom and the particular circumstances of the individual litigants.[27]

It is feasible that George Bredin, the author of these lines, was genuine in his belief that the overseeing of 'minor' trials by Sudanese elites was efficacious. Conversely, it is feasible that Bredin concealed a self-interested desire to avoid routine court work and instead undertake activities that were more varied and interesting. Of course, the two may have been inextricably linked, but the potential problems in using sources like Bredin's memoirs have yet to be satisfactorily dealt with by historians of the British Empire in Africa. It behoves us to investigate further in order to obtain a fuller account of the matter of selflessness and selfishness.

Thirdly, in their excellent introduction to *Colonial Lives across the British Empire* (2006), David Lambert and Alan Lester have noted that there remain significant gaps in our knowledge of how to link the 'local and particular (metropolitan and colonial)' with the 'general and universal (imperialism)'.[28] In addressing the issue of the formation of intellectual networks stretching across the empire (and indeed the point made above about how far metropolitan attitudes were redefined by local colonial experiences), a comparative analysis is evidently needed. It is therefore hoped that one of the virtues of this study is that, in drawing upon the experiences of colonial officials who served in Nigeria, the Gold Coast, Uganda, Tanganyika, Sudan, the Gambia, Sierra Leone and the British Cameroons, the work will be able to consider how far officials interacted with one another and created broader social and/or intellectual networks.[29]

Lastly, the study will address certain postcolonialist arguments about officials' faith in the imperial mission that have yet to be empirically tested.[30] Officials demonstrated confidence on the surface. In April 1931, Gold Coast official Alan Wilkinson gave a speech to chiefs at Akropong. Africa was, for Wilkinson, entering a time of great change ... Communications, motor roads, telephone. The spread of education. Changes of the same sort are going on all over the world ... These changes are seen most in Africa on the coast, in contact with Europe. They are now spreading inland. Change is not bad, but desirable ... But there is much good in some of the old customs, and it is desirable to conserve this and to combine it into the new ... What gives power is knowledge. The spread of knowledge is a very good thing.

Wilkinson stated he was confident that 'change' and 'stasis' could be combined in a coherent manner, and that any potential threat to social stability posed by change could be checked if due care was taken.[31] Wilkinson's speech was delivered at a meeting attempting to calm conflict between the people of Asankrangua and the Tufuhene, or local leader, of the Akropong area.[32] It is therefore obvious that Wilkinson's attempt to elucidate on the necessity of an interweaving of change and stasis, and his confidence that such an interweaving was possible, may have been borne of a need to publically emphasise stability and progress simultaneously, rather than of a belief in the truth of the statement.[33]

Certain postcolonialists have indeed suggested such proclamations masked profound uncertainty. For Homi Bhabha, imperial powers advocated a 'colonial mimicry', wanting those over whom they ruled to become a 'reformed, recognizable Other, *as a subject of differ-ence that is almost the same, but not quite*'.[34] This mimicry was 'constructed around an *ambivalence*'; the 'authority of that mode of colonial discourse ... is therefore stricken by an indeterminacy: mimicry emerges as the representation of a difference that is itself a process of disavowal'.[35] The British wished for the 'Other' to be both altered, in keeping with notions of the 'civilising mission', and, at the same time, for them to remain different – perhaps in line with a romanticised vision of the African as a Rousseauian 'noble savage' – in order that a space between 'them' and 'us' affirmed British claims to the role of coloniser. Bhabha is not the only one to make such claims, although he is the most verbose.[36] Was such tension an inherently omnipresent feature, defining officials' ideas about their role in Africa? Or is suggesting this to read present-day sentiments into the past? Or was ambivalence only the contingent outcome of certain contexts?

A few points of order are required before we proceed any further. Firstly, a variety of terms were used to describe British-held territories in Africa. As a result of the First World War and the stripping of Germany's colonial possessions, Britain administered Tanganyika as a League of Nations Mandate. In 1914, the union of the Colony and Protectorate of Southern Nigeria and the Northern Nigeria Protectorate saw the creation of the Colony and Protectorate of Nigeria.[37]

Uganda was a Protectorate, The Gambia was known as The Gambia Colony and Protectorate, whilst the Gold Coast and Sierra Leone were Crown Colonies. Sudan was a Condominium jointly administered (in theory at least) by Egypt and Britain.[38] For ease of reference, they will be referred to as 'colonies' generically, and as 'British Africa' collectively.

Prior to the First World War, there were changes in the London personnel responsible for administering British Africa. The Colonial Office had long overseen certain colonies such as The Gambia and the Gold Coast. In 1900, with the ending of the Royal Niger Company's charter, what would eventually be named Nigeria became a matter for the Colonial Office, rather than the Foreign Office. The Uganda Protectorate was similarly transferred in 1905. By 1913, only Sudan remained overseen by the Foreign Office, thanks to its special Condominium status.[39]

Officials for Colonial Office-supervised colonies were initially appointed under the patronage system, whereby the Secretary of State for the Colonies' private staff interviewed applicants. The Colonial Secretary invariably accepted the resultant recommendations. The most important amongst the Colonial Office staff was Ralph Furse, correctly called the 'father' of the modern colonial services in British Africa.[40] Furse increasingly controlled Colonial Office recruitment upon becoming Assistant Private Secretary (Appointments) to the Secretary of State for the Colonies in 1910, and from 1919 onwards in particular.[41] He oversaw a significant expansion of the colonial official corps, particularly after the First World War (see table 1). Furse's influence did not diminish when, thanks to the recommendations of the Warren Fisher Committee report, the patronage system was ended in 1930 and the process was formalised. Furse became the Colonial Office's Director of Recruitment, responsible for a recruitment committee, but Furse's superiors continued to rubber-stamp his appointment decisions.[42] Officials remained bound by rules and regulations that differed from colony to colony until 1932, when the creation of a unified Administrative Service began to ameliorate some of the disparities between the different conditions of service, and made it possible for officials to be transferred between colonies more easily.[43] This system then remained in place until the Colonial Service became the Administrative Branch of Her Majesty's Overseas Civil Service (HMOCS) in 1954.[44]

The aims behind Foreign Office recruitment for the Sudan Political Service (SPS) were very similar, although the application procedure was more rigorous.[45] After the Cambridge and Oxford University Appointments Committee (which were placement offices for graduates) had weeded out unsuitable applicants, two or three senior members of the SPS who were in Britain on leave would undertake a first round

Table 1 Numbers of officials in selected British African colonies, 1905–35

Colony	1905	1910	1915	1920	1925	1930	1935
Gold Coast	no data	31	38	71	72	73	70
Nigeria[a]	132	225	247	247	294	406	378
Sudan	25	35	64[b]	73	112	139	120
Tanganyika	n/a[c]	n/a[c]	n/a[c]	121	113	173	168
Uganda	no data	35	49	55	70	75	77

Notes:
[a] Combined figures for pre-unification Northern and Southern Nigeria until 1914
[b] Figure is for January 1916
[c] Administered by Britain from 1919 onwards
Sources:
The Dominions Office and Colonial Office Lists [1900–35]; Civil Secretary's Office, Sudan Political Service 1899–1929 (Khartoum: Sudan Government Press, 1930); Quarterly/Monthly Lists of the Sudan Government [1915–35]; Kirk-Greene, 'Thin White Line', 34–5

of interviews. The shortlisted candidates from these interviews were then re-interviewed in London by Sudan's civil secretary and five or six of the Condominium's provincial governors or their deputies.[46]

Colonial officials went by a number of different titles. They were most frequently called either District Commissioners (DCs) and Assistant District Commissioners (ADCs), or District Officers (DOs) and Assistant District Officers (ADOs). In Sudan, Inspectors became DCs in 1922. In Tanganyika, DOs became DCs in 1940. Upon amalgamation, Assistant Residents in Northern Nigeria became DOs. When individuals in particular colonies are examined, they will be referred to by their actual title but, for sake of brevity, when all from across Africa are looked at generically, they will be called DCs (even those who were actually ADCs or an equivalent) or, more frequently, simply 'officials'. 'Officials' will differentiate them from their immediate superiors, the provincial governors or residents, and those working in the central administrations. These will be collectively referred to as 'elites' and, when indicated, this group will sometimes include those working in London. 'Administrators' will be used to denote those who were not officials, but who instead worked as conservators of forests, agricultural officers, in public works departments, and so on.

As we shall see, there were different types of officials in Africa. The main groups examined will be termed 'military' and 'civilian' officials.

Unsurprisingly enough, the former group will refer to those men who became officials following service in the army, often having fought in the wars of 'pacification' at the very end of the nineteenth, and the very start of the twentieth, centuries. Invariably, these were men who had not been to university.[47] The latter group will refer to those men who were graduates. This group includes those who went to university, but whose career trajectory was interrupted by the Great War and consequent war service.

This book principally draws upon officials' letters home, diaries (both private journals and the 'semi-official' journals sent to governmental superiors, the completion of which was compulsory in the Gold Coast), reports they filed either annually or upon leaving an administrative region (which were known as 'handing over notes'), and memoirs. There are plenty of available sources because officials wrote frequently and at length. They were sometimes spurred on to write by their having tired of the narrow group of Europeans around them or their having run out of novels and newspapers to read, but most were keen to write to maintain links with the metropole and to better comprehend their working environment.[48] Memoirs written upon officials' retirement from service in Africa are the most important points of access that officials had with a public, because Clause 57 of the Regulations for His Majesty's Colonial Service stated that a serving official was not allowed to have any dealings with the press without the express permission of his governor or the Secretary of State, except publishing 'in his own name matter relating to subjects of general interest', that is, nothing political or administrative in nature.[49] As a consequence, works published by serving officials tended to focus on topics such as African flora and fauna and social customs, although some briefed the press anonymously, or made their voice heard through their contact with scholars such as Margery Perham.

Chapters One and Two will lay the ground work for the remainder of the book by considering what the metropole bequeathed to Africa. Chapter One will examine officials' backgrounds and what led them to apply in the first place. Historians have tended to suggest that a sense of duty and of Africa as a site of adventure generated enthusiasm for service in Africa. Chapter One will add a caveat to this by arguing that schooling failed to inculcate would-be officials with a sense of duty sufficient to overcome concerns about the esteem in which service in Africa was held. Instead, in the first decade of the twentieth century, young men preferred the kudos of service in India to the excitement of service in Africa, thereby demonstrating they were motivated by one of the mores (namely, social climbing) historians suggest actually motivated their escape from Britain in the first place. Until Ralph

Furse made the administrative services in Africa more appealing to ambitious young men looking for a reputable career, the officials appointed were often not those whom elites judged most suitable for the work.

Following the story through to those who were appointed, Chapter Two will examine the ideas to which young recruits were exposed in the metropole. It will consider the postgraduate training they invariably undertook immediately prior to departure to Africa, as well as British imperial culture more generally. It will argue that what defined the ideas to which they were exposed, whether regarding governance, race or the role of the individual in the collective experience of empire-building, was their imprecision. This encouraged officials to develop their own ideas as to what constituted normative modes of imperial governance.

Chapter Three will consider the ways that officials interacted with one another. Colonial elites were unable to establish the *esprit de corps* usually deemed a central feature of British colonial life in Africa. Officials rarely considered the world beyond their own colonies. In addition, each colonial service was fractured by disagreements powered by gossip and individualism. Convinced that they each knew best how to act in Africa, officials clashed with those who worked in different circumstances and different ways to themselves. Furthermore, although it was often a crucial means of maintaining morale, the very presence of other officials was simultaneously a constraint upon their freedom to act in the ways they wanted. This chapter attests to the relative failure of that prominent element within public schooling that attempted to inculcate in its students a normative sense of empire building as a collective experience. This has important implications for our understanding of British society and culture.

Chapter Four will examine shifts in what underpinned officials' sense of confidence. In the wake of Edward Said's *Orientalism* (1978), many studies have reiterated the cliché that, in a colonial context, 'knowledge equals power'.[50] This formulation is an attractive oversimplification. Military officials were less convinced of the virtues of what is here called 'knowledge collection' as an aid to governance than their university-educated counterparts, for whom this constituted a normative process.[51] Military officials laid greater emphasis on the use of force and prestige. Civilian officials felt the use of prestige a temporary expediency at best whilst they were in the process of seeking to understand African societies. These attitudes were due to the type of person the officials were before they left for Africa. Officials' African experiences were not sufficiently transformative to alter their beliefs in this regard.

Chapter Five will examine officials' attitudes towards economic, infrastructural and educational change. Rather than acting in accordance with inherent predispositions common to all officials as some scholars have suggested, their attitudes were instead largely determined by two different factors. Firstly, we have to consider the contingent nature of the power relationships in which officials were involved. Their attitudes were shaped by the belief that they knew best. They were consequently more likely to endorse those processes of change they thought were in their capacity to control than those they thought they could not. Secondly, a commitment or otherwise to change was shaped by personal self-interest, as opposed to some form of collective imperial interest, to a degree hitherto underestimated by historians. Change was welcomed in part when it offered an improvement to officials' own lives.

Chapter Six will examine officials' attitudes towards political change. It is frequently argued that, after the First World War, officials turned to indirect rule because it offered them a means of both preventing the crumbling of the tribal system and pre-empting increasingly vociferous anti-colonial nationalist demands. Some have suggested that indirect rule was a conservative doctrine that aimed to seal Africa off from broader global change for fear that its fragile social order would be destroyed.[52] The present study will argue that the extent of officials' concerns about the decay of the tribal unit in the face of imperial change can be overstated. Many officials believed African political structures possessed an ability to absorb and adapt to economic and social change. Instead, officials' own personal motivations played a significant role in accounting for their enthusiasm for indirect rule. It was felt that indirect rule had the capacity to make officials' own lives more in keeping with the ideal – a career as a leader, not an administrator – that had shaped their imperial vision since childhood.

Notes

1   E. Wallace, *Sanders of the River* (1911; Kelly Bray: House of Stratus, 2001); Wallace, *Again Sanders* (1928; London: Pan, 1961); J. Cary, *An American Visitor* (1933; London: Everyman, 1995); Cary, *Mister Johnson* (1939; London: J. M. Dent, 1995). Regarding colonial governors, see R. E. Wraith, *Guggisberg* (London: Oxford University Press, 1967); M. Perham, *Lugard: The Years of Adventure, 1858–1898* (London: Collins, 1956); Perham, *Lugard: The Years of Authority, 1898–1945* (London: Collins, 1960); H. A. Gailey, *Sir Donald Cameron: Colonial Governor* (Stanford, CA: Hoover Institution Press, 1974)

2   C. Jeffries, *The Colonial Empire and its Civil Service* (Cambridge: Cambridge University Press, 1938)

3   R. Heussler, *Yesterday's Rulers: The Making of the British Colonial Service* (Syracuse, NY: Syracuse University Press, 1963)

4   A. H. M. Kirk-Greene, *On Crown Service: A History of HM Colonial and Overseas*

Civil Services 1837–1997 (London: I. B. Tauris, 1999), pp. 15–38; Kirk-Greene, 'The thin white line: the size of the British Colonial Service in Africa', *African Affairs* 79:314 (1980), 25–44; N. Gardiner, 'Sentinels of empire: the British Colonial Administrative Service, 1919–1954' (PhD dissertation, Yale University, 1998)

5   C. Dewey, *Anglo-Indian Attitudes: The Mind of the Indian Civil Service* (London: Hambledon, 1993); D. Gilmour, *The Ruling Caste: Imperial Lives in the Victorian Raj* (2005; London: Pimlico, 2007); R. O. Collins, 'The Sudan Political Service: a portrait of the "Imperialists"', *African Affairs* 71:284 (1972), 293–303; J. A. Mangan, 'The education of an elite imperial administration: the Sudan Political Service and the British public school system', *International Journal of African Historical Studies* 15 (1982), 671–99; see also Mangan, *The Games Ethic and Imperialism: Aspects of the Diffusion of an Ideal* (Harmondsworth: Viking, 1986)

6   Kirk-Greene, *Symbol of Authority: The British District Officer in Africa* (London: I. B. Tauris, 2006)

7   V. Pakenham, *The Noonday Sun: Edwardians in the Tropics* (London: Methuen, 1985), ch. 3; C. Allen, 'Tales from the Dark Continent', in *Plain Tales from the British Empire* (London: Abacus, 2008), pp. 269–471; L. Gann and P. Duignan, *The Rulers of British Africa, 1870–1914* (London: Croom Helm, 1978), pp. 183–252; Heussler, *British Tanganyika: An Essay and Documents on District Administration* (Durham, NC: Duke University Press, 1971); H. Kuklick, *The Imperial Bureaucrat: The Colonial Administrative Service in the Gold Coast, 1920–1939* (Stanford, CA: Hoover Institution Press, 1979)

8   Examples include S. Ward (ed.), *British Culture and the End of Empire* (Manchester: Manchester University Press, 2001); C. Hall, *Civilising Subjects: Metropole and Colony in the English Imagination, 1830–1867* (Cambridge: Polity, 2002); A. Thompson, *The Empire Strikes Back?: The Impact of Empire on Britain from the Mid-nineteenth Century* (Harlow: Pearson Longman, 2005)

9   A. I. Nwabughuogo, 'The role of propaganda in the development of indirect rule in Nigeria, 1890–1929', *International Journal of African Historical Studies* 14:1 (1981), 66; M. Mason, 'The history of Mr. Johnson: progress and protest in Northern Nigeria, 1900–1921', *Canadian Journal of African Studies* 27 (1993), 202; see also J. Willis, 'Hukm: the Creolization of authority in Condominium Sudan', *Journal of African History* 46:1 (2005), 37

10   E. Isichei, *A History of Nigeria* (London: Longman, 1983), p. 380; see also Isichei, *The Ibo People and the Europeans: The Genesis of a Relationship – to 1906* (London: Faber and Faber, 1973), pp. 160–1

11   J. W. Cell, 'Colonial rule', in J. M. Brown and Wm. R. Louis (eds), *Oxford History of the British Empire: Volume IV – The Twentieth Century* (Oxford: Oxford University Press, 1999), p. 233. Another example of this type of work, albeit within an earlier context, is R. Price, *Making Empire: Colonial Encounters and the Creation of Imperial Rule in Nineteenth-Century Africa* (Cambridge: Cambridge University Press, 2008)

12   For anti-intellectualism, see S. Collini, *Absent Minds: Intellectuals in Britain* (Oxford: Oxford University Press, 2006)

13   K. Tidrick, *Empire and the English Character* (1990; London: I. B. Tauris, 1992), p. 216

14   Kirk-Greene, *Britain's Imperial Administrators, 1858–1966* (Basingstoke: Macmillan, 2000), p. 12

15   *Ibid.*, p. 13. This emphasis upon a metropolitan background ties in with Clive Dewey's work on the ICS; Dewey, *Anglo-Indian Attitudes*, *passim*, especially pp. 19–38, 103–85

16   A famous example of the latter argument is B. Davidson, *The Black Man's Burden: Africa and the Curse of the Nation-state* (London: Currey, 1992)

17   Heussler, *Yesterday's Rulers*, pp. 100–1. Of course, this stereotype is in part built on cultural works, such as Noël Coward's famous song 'Mad dogs and Englishmen' (1932)

18   After all, for one official, writing from Babara at the start of his career in Northern

Nigeria in 1911, 'there is no fear of open hostility here'; nevertheless, it would 'of course be absolutely impossible for me to do anything without their [the local Emirs'] help and if they took it into their heads to behave in a hostile manner I should have very [sic] small chance of getting out alive'. Whilst 'this country remains a Protectorate, and not a colony' he wrote elsewhere, 'we must put up with a certain amount of knavery and unless things are really bad one cannot turn a man out as there would be no better man to put in'; H. Miller-Stirling to E. Miller-Stirling, 7 February 1911, Rhodes House Library, University of Oxford (hereafter RHO) Mss.Afr.s.2051/52; Miller-Stirling to father, 16 February 1911, RHO Mss. Afr.s.2051/61

19 In Tiv it was resisted because it went against pre-colonial democratic procedure; D. Dorward, 'The development of the British Colonial Administration among the Tiv, 1900–1949', *African Affairs* 68:273 (1969), 316–33

20 E. C. Adams, 'John Theophilus Jones', in *Lyra Nigeria* (London: T. Fisher Unwin, 1911), p. 93

21 R. Oakley, *Treks & Palavers* (London: Seeley, Service, and Co., 1938), pp. 8–9; see also Kirk-Greene, *Symbol of Authority*, pp. 21–2, 28

22 Niall Ferguson is invariably brought out at this juncture; N. Ferguson, *Empire: How Britain Made the Modern World* (2003; London: Penguin, 2004), pp. 365–73. A bolder defence of empire, but of poor quality, is A. Roberts, *A History of the English-speaking Peoples since 1900* (London: Weidenfeld and Nicolson, 2006). The quote belongs to Hugh Trevor Roper; H. Trevor Roper, 'The rise of Christian Europe', *Listener* 70 (1963), 871–5, quoted in R. Reid, *A History of Modern Africa: 1800 to the Present* (Chichester: Wiley-Blackwell, 2009), p. 4

23 D. Newbold to W. B. Kennedy-Shaw, 11 September 1928, in K. D. D. Henderson, *The Making of the Modern Sudan: The Life and Letters of Sir Douglas Newbold* (London: Faber and Faber, 1953), pp. 27–9

24 A. Field, *'Verb Sap.': On Going to West Africa, Northern Nigeria, Southern, and to the Coasts* (London: Bale, Sons and Danielsson, 1913), p. 68

25 Collins, 'Sudan Political Service', 301

26 Field, *'Verb Sap.'*, p. 82

27 G. R. F. Bredin, Memoirs, 23 July 1983, Sudan Archive, Durham University (hereafter SAD), 815/12/5

28 D. Lambert and A. Lester, 'Imperial spaces, imperial subjects', in Lambert and Lester (eds), *Colonial Lives across the British Empire: Imperial Careering in the Long Nineteenth Century* (Cambridge: Cambridge University Press, 2006), pp. 4–5

29 It is the first five of these colonies that form the study's real focus. Kenya and Southern Rhodesia have been omitted because of their status as the home of white settlers. Even though it is appreciated that Tanganyika also contained some settlers – albeit far fewer than either Kenya or Southern Rhodesia – it was felt that the scope was broad enough already without having to make colonial officials' political battles with non-official whites a prominent feature of the work as well; regarding Kenya, see D. Kennedy, *Islands of White: Settler Society and Culture in Kenya and Southern Rhodesia* (Durham, NC: Duke University Press, 1987); D. Wylie, 'Confrontation over Kenya: the Colonial Office and its critics, 1918–1940', *Journal of African History* 18 (1977), 427–47

30 Now is not the place to get into a definition of what constitutes a postcolonialist scholar; this is addressed in a variety of works, including A. McClintock, 'The angel of progress: pitfalls of the term "post-colonialism"', *Social Text* 31/32 (1992), 84–98; S. Xie, 'Rethinking the problem of postcolonialism', *New Literary History* 28 (1997), 7–19

31 A. L. Wilkinson, 'Notes for speech at Akropong on 18th April 1931', RHO Mss. Afr.s.713/129–30

32 *Ibid.*, RHO Mss.Afr.s.713/134

33 *Ibid.*, RHO Mss.Afr.s.713/130

34 H. K. Bhabha, *The Location of Culture* (London: Routledge, 1994), p. 86; italics in original

35 *Ibid.*; italics in original

36 See also F. Cooper, *Colonialism in Question: Theory, Knowledge, History* (London: University of California Press, 2005), p. 154; Cooper and A. L. Stoler (eds), *Tensions of Empire: Colonial Cultures in a Bourgeois World* (Berkeley, CA: University of California Press, 1997); C. Lane, *The Ruling Passion: British Colonial Allegory and the Paradox of Homosexual Desire* (Durham, NC: Duke University, 1995), p. 15

37 When dealing with events prior to 1914, the book will refer to Northern and Southern Nigeria, but to northern and southern Nigeria after their amalgamation in 1914.

38 On day-to-day basis, these differences had relatively little impact upon the ways officials went about their work; Heussler, *Yesterday's Rulers*, p. 195; see also Newbold to F. Cottrell, 29 October 1933, in Henderson, *Modern Sudan*, p. 55

39 Gann and Duignan, *Rulers of British Africa*, pp. 60, 62

40 Kirk-Greene, 'Forging a relationship with the Colonial Administrative Service, 1921–1939', in A. Smith and M. Bull (eds), *Margery Perham and British Rule in Africa* (London: Cass, 1991), p. 62

41 G. Grindle to R. Furse, 23 January 1919, RHO Mss.Brit.Emp.s.415/1/2/2

42 Kirk-Greene, *Symbol of Authority*, p. 6

43 These are discussed in detail in Jeffries, *Colonial Empire, passim*

44 Kirk-Greene, *Symbol of Authority*, p. 8

45 Furse took a keen interest in how the SPS obtained its officials; see, for example Furse to Milner, 18 June 1919, RHO Mss.Brit.Emp.s.415/1/2/15–16; Furse papers, RHO Mss.Brit.Emp.s.415/6/7; Furse, *Aucuparius: Recollections of a Recruiting Officer* (London: Oxford University Press, 1962), p. 262

46 G. Bell, *Shadows on the Sand: The Memoirs of Sir Gawain Bell* (London: C. Hurst & Co., 1983), p. 14

47 Some had attended university, but most of these then rapidly gained promotion, therefore passing quickly beyond the remit of the present study

48 Miller-Stirling to father, 24 June 1910, RHO Mss.Afr.s.2051/38–9

49 'Permission to publish two articles on economic resources and native administration in T[anganyika] T[erritory]', National Archives, London (hereafter NA) Colonial Office papers (hereafter CO) 691/152/13/2; see also comments in 'Essay on Ahmadyyia [*sic*] movement in the Gold Coast by Mr. A. C. Duncan-Johnstone – permission for publication of', [c.1934], Public Records and Archives Administration Department, Accra (hereafter PRAAD), Colonial Secretary's Office (hereafter CSO) 18/12/33; Miller-Stirling to mother, 30 June 1910, RHO Mss.Afr.s.2051/41

50 E. Said, *Orientalism* (1978; London: Penguin, 1991); particularly important in shaping modern scholarly approaches to this relationship has been B. Cohn, *Colonialism and its Forms of Knowledge: The British in India* (Princeton, NJ: Princeton University Press, 1996)

51 The term 'knowledge collection' was chosen so as differentiate officials' endeavours from more academic ethnographic and anthropological study

52 M. W. Daly, *Imperial Sudan: The Anglo-Egyptian Condominium, 1934–1956* (Cambridge: Cambridge University Press, 1991), pp. 26–9; I. F. Nicolson, *The Administration of Nigeria 1900–1960: Men, Methods, and Myths* (Oxford: Clarendon Press, 1969), p. 239

CHAPTER ONE

The construction of a governing corps

I'm totally ignorant of these matters, but I can't see why our colonies should need third-class men with some capacity for organized sports.
Winslow, a Cambridge College Fellow in C. P. Snow's *The Masters* (1951)[1]

The best class of Englishmen don't come out to the colonies, and those who do are apt to be frightful bounders.
Lady Maud Cecil, Countess of Selborne[2]

This chapter will assess colonial officials' backgrounds, and the motives that originally drew them to Africa. Although works tackling the thorny issue of motives have been marked by a good deal of imprecision, historians have tended to argue that a desire for adventure and a sense of imperial duty, partly instilled by public schooling, were most important in convincing young men to work in Africa.[3] The desire for adventure and to serve the empire were certainly not absent. Much like their late-nineteenth century predecessors, young men saw overseas service as a means of escaping domesticity and the '9 to 5'.[4] As one SPS official put it, 'It is not given to all men to wander, but with some, more especially the men of our race, it is an abiding passion never to be quenched. To such men, after the shortest span of sedentary life, there comes a restlessness, a fever in the blood, a desire for some new thing. These men are not made for domesticity'.[5] Even after the First World War and the introduction of more sophisticated bureaucratic machinery, officials still derived great pleasure from being pioneers.[6] This was, in part, a residual effect of the gung-ho 'boys' own fiction' of an earlier era still consumed in vast quantities, as well as an interwar emphasis upon the continuing 'romance of colonisation'.[7]

It is harder to assess how far officials were truly motivated by a sense of duty. In sources created at the time they may have stressed a commitment to public service for fear that to suggest selfish reasons would have led to criticism from others. Retired officials may have emphasised a

commitment to public service in their memoirs in order to retrospectively validate their endeavours and to defend themselves against anti-
colonial accusations of exploitation. However, even though it appears
officials genuinely believed their work benefitted Africans, greater
attention needs to be given to more pragmatic concerns if patterns of
recruitment are to be understood. Graduates sought employment that
carried a social status consonant with their backgrounds. For most of
the Edwardian era, the low regard in which such men held the African
services meant they were reluctant to work there. Instead, London
elites had had to continue to recruit individuals they increasingly
felt unsuited to the role of administrator, such as ex-army men and
ex-Chartered Company employees. It was Ralph Furse who addressed
this issue most vigorously. Aided in his task by a broader cultural
environment increasingly focused on life as an official, Furse raised
the visibility and prestige of the services, and consequently oversaw a
sharp rise in graduate recruitment. As we shall see later in this study,
this process fundamentally altered the ways the colonial official corps
collectively conceptualised imperial governance.

Before an examination of the officials themselves, let us start with
a broader cultural observation. For one commentator writing of British
officials in West Africa in 1913,

> It must be acknowledged that until recent years the best class of men
> have not been attracted to the country. On the contrary, it may be
> asserted, without fear of contradiction, that, from its early history, the
> Coast as [sic] to a very large extent a dumping ground for undesirables.[8]

The press avoided naming individuals, tending to paint composite
pictures of official corps, but this statement was part of a broader
tendency.[9] In 1906, a *Daily Express* journalist lamented that 'Europe
does not send the flower of her capitals to the sun-scorched wastes
of Equatorial Africa'.[10] In comparison with fictional depictions of
'heroes', such as Allan Quatermain in Henry Rider Haggard's *King
Solomon's Mines* (1885), media portrayals of officials never constituted
a large proportion of British cultural content. Nevertheless, there was
a definite shift over time. By the interwar era, officials in Africa were
being paraded as exemplars of impeccable Britishness abroad.[11] In
1931, renowned journalist J. A. Spender suggested that as 'an example
of quiet competence, entire absence of pomp, vanity or self-assertion,
and loyalty to a common cause', there could be 'nothing better in the
world to-day' than the SPS.[12] Others made similar points with regards
to officials more generally.[13]

Why was there such a change in perception? After all, officials'
social backgrounds did not alter a great deal between 1900 and 1939.

As is suggested by their *almae matres*, the number of officials from the upper classes shrank after 1918.[14] However, the importance of this shift is minimal because, contrary to Heussler's claims, officials from the upper classes were always in a minority.[15] In refuting Heussler's suggestion that the post-1918 colonial services were 'elite' affairs, Gardiner has nevertheless gone too far in arguing that officials were 'conspicuous not by ... [their] social and national homogeneity, but by ... [a] diversity of family and national background'.[16] Certainly, approximately 7 per cent of officials recruited between 1919 and 1945 had been born in Scotland, 7 per cent in Ireland, and 2 per cent in Wales.[17] Therefore, those from Scotland, Ireland and Wales did not constitute a disproportionately high number of officials, minimising the significance of national background as an important determinant of recruitment patterns.[18] There was also diversity in England: 64 per cent of England-born officials came from the south, the south-east, London or East Anglia, but 29 per cent came from the Midlands or the north.[19] Nevertheless, recruits did not come from a particularly diverse range of backgrounds. Officials from lower-middle-class or working-class backgrounds were notable by their almost total absence. The overwhelming majority were sons of upper-middle-class professionals such as doctors, lawyers and parsons.[20] Although the information is harder to come by, it would appear that this also holds true for the pre-war years,[21] even for those officials who had previously worked in a military capacity.[22] Thus early criticisms of officials were not rooted in hostility towards social 'inferiors', but in disappointment that people from 'good' backgrounds had let Britain down.

In accounting for any change in metropolitan attitude towards officials, we instead need to turn to other elements of their background. In terms of motives, many young Edwardians seeking work in Africa were simply after money. This is quite clear from the testimonies of those who, on enquiring with London civil servants about positions in Africa, revealed they had no prior experience of the continent. Colonial Office staff frequently faced men who said they wanted to go to Africa because their current salary did not allow them to start or support a family.[23] This family issue seems to have been a particular problem for those in the army, but others had different financial concerns.[24] For example, prior to service in Uganda, Sydney Ormsby had been schooled in Switzerland and Germany before working as a surveyor, farmer and engineer in Canada and the manager of a fibre factory in Zanzibar.[25] Ormsby appears to have become an official in order to pay off heavy debts incurred from the failure of this factory.[26]

Others wished to maintain a pre-existing link with the continent. Some felt a sense of obligation to perpetuate a family tradition. Certain

[17]

well-connected fathers were able to use patronage networks to this end. Sir Richard Temple, the well-known Conservative MP and Governor of Bombay, was able to secure a post in Nigeria for his son Charles.[27] Imperial service in Africa appears to have been more of a family affair before the war than after it, although such sentiments did not die away entirely as a motivating factor.[28] Nevertheless, few upper-middle-class families had the level of access possessed by the Temples, so the importance of this factor in young men being able to secure employment in Africa must not be overstated.

As might be inferred from Sydney Ormsby's somewhat eclectic career, what is particularly noticeable about Edwardian officials is the diverse range of experiences they had had prior to becoming officials.[29] Many were already 'empire builders' who had become bored with, or failed in, their previous lines of work.[30] The Assistant Resident at Okene in 1911 had previously been a coffee planter in India and had fought in the Boer War.[31] Before arriving in Northern Nigeria, George Ormsby (no relation to Sydney) had worked in Borneo, India and Singapore, and had fought in China.[32] Approximately 10 per cent of officials who started work in East Africa before 1914 had come from employment in South Africa.[33] A greater number had previously worked for the Royal Niger Company (RNC) in Nigeria or the Imperial British East Africa Company (IBEAC) in Uganda. Perhaps most numerically significant were those who had already served in some form of military capacity, such as approximately 55 per cent of the officials who started work in the Gold Coast between 1900 and 1914.[34] These men had not been to university, instead invariably having already served in either South Africa or the Gold Coast itself.[35] Given their experiences in the military and commercial sectors, it is unsurprising that on average, SPS officials recruited between 1899 and 1904 were 30.1 years old.[36]

As a consequence, many of these officials saw their job as merely the latest in a series of non-metropolitan posts open to them. These officials did not conform to any imagined apex of altruistic Britishness. Some newcomers to the continent, raised on a steady late-Victorian diet of tales of imperial brilliance and selflessness, were struck by a discrepancy between preconception and reality. From Calabar in Southern Nigeria in 1900, new arrival Christopher Wordsworth wrote to a family friend that 'I think this place will amuse you ... Many [of the Britons] have had queer experiences and been all over the world and there are also some of the finest liars I have ever heard'.[37] It seems as if all officials who served in Africa prior to the First World War had at least one anecdote about a rogue who had no place in charge of a district.[38] For example, William Cockburn, nicknamed 'Rusty Buckle' because of his stint in the 2nd Dragoon Guards, worked as an Assistant Resident in Northern Nigeria between 1900 and 1914. Motivated by a dislike of central authority – he would avoid answering queries by readdressing them to the colony's outlying posts – Cockburn was a pathological liar.[39]

Of course, the very fact that such men were the basis for anecdotes means they were not indicative of all. Nevertheless, others gave cause for concern. In the first decade of the twentieth century, Whitehall was disappointed with its recruits. London was wary of those ex-Company men who became government employees, because of their low levels of education, and because they were thought afflicted by an ennui that had impeded the economic development of RNC- and IBEAC-administered territories.[40] Additionally, in the late 1890s, London had dealt with accusations that the Governor of Sierra Leone had used 'illegal and violent acts' in the enforcement of the Hut Tax, with 'grave errors' committed 'by the Colonial Officers from the Governor downwards'.[41] London was concerned that these men were given to unruly ways if not reined in.

The British found it difficult to establish colonial rule in Uganda in the later years of the nineteenth century. For instance, during attempts at conquering Bunyoro, the mutiny of Sudanese troops employed to fight Kabaleega and his Banyoro guerrilla warriors prolonged indigenous resistance, thereby jeopardising British endeavours in the northern lakes region.[42] Kenneth Henderson took part in one of the many punitive expeditions against the Nandi in the region. In 1900, he confided to his diary that the 'Protectorate could not, if they had tried, have succeeded in collecting a more ragged and extraordinary lot of officials, and a more disreputable crew of subordinates, than those to whom the running of the whole show out here ... is entrusted ... [The men were] the merest of rolling stones' who had been given jobs simply because they were 'on the spot when the posts they hold were created'.[43] Against such a frustrating backdrop, it is perhaps unsurprising that Henderson's dislike of officials was amplified. He was not, however, incorrect regarding the rather haphazard patterns of recruitment that prevailed. Some were recruited in London, others in Africa. Sydney Ormsby became an official in Uganda in 1903 merely because he happened to be working in the area as an ivory trader when the government was hiring.[44] Similarly, in 1893, Claud Cardew obtained a post in Chinde (which lies in Mozambique today, but was in Cardew's time a British Central Africa trading post) after leaving his previous job in the South Africa police 'purely "on spec" hearing that the country ... was in a state of "being opened up" and likely to turn out trumps'.[45] Such examples formed part of a broader trend.[46]

Elites believed matters needed to change. For example, Percy Girouard, Governor of the British East Africa Protectorate between 1909 and 1912, felt that employing whoever happened to be on hand in the East African colonies was to the empire's detriment.[47] Furthermore, whilst 'brute force' was prized in the years during and immediately after conquest, London increasingly felt that if budgets were to be balanced, those wholly given over to a boyish enthusiasm for adventure were cause for worry. Whitehall was increasingly won over to appointing university graduates.[48] In the case of Tanganyika, the shift repeated itself later on. There, military figures who had fought in the First World War campaigns in German East Africa were initially welcomed as officials for their ability to quell resistance during the transition from German to British administration, only to be replaced with graduates as London judged the mandate increasingly 'pacified' and no longer reliant on everyday coercive violence.[49]

Whitehall staff were nevertheless disappointed at the number of graduates who applied. Those ranked most suitable for service in Africa often rejected the ensuing job offers and went elsewhere.[50] In 1911, nine of the eleven applicants selected for East Africa did precisely that.[51] In 1908, there were ten vacancies for posts in Northern and Southern Nigeria. There were only eight applicants. Of these eight, one was ruled medically unfit, and two later turned down offers of employment. Of the remaining five, only three were deemed of a suitable standard. All three had military backgrounds.[52] Civil servants were understandably pessimistic about their ability to secure the services of those they judged the best of Britain's young men, and recruitment committees had to continue relying on those for whom their enthusiasm had dwindled.[53]

One reason for graduates' aversion to work in Africa is well known. Although the number of Britons in West Africa who died from malaria halved between 1903 and 1913, the region retained the resilient sobriquet 'White Man's Grave'.[54] Girouard praised the hard work of the men of Northern Nigeria in the introduction to a collection of letters written by Martin Kisch, who had become an Assistant Resident in 1908. For Girouard, Kisch proved that the service was suited to 'earnest, hard-working, and clever' young men. The impact of the book as an invitation to sign up was, however, rather hampered by the fact that Kisch had died of diphtheria four months after his arrival in the Protectorate.[55]

The understandable importance applicants attached to their health is indicated by the frequency with which they readily told Colonial Office staff they would work anywhere except West Africa.[56] In reality, non-Highland East Africa was not far behind in terms of deaths, suffering an average annual mortality rate of 13.6 per 1,000 European officials before 1914, compared to 17.1 in West Africa.[57] However, the East did not have the same reputation as the West, and consequently attracted more applicants with no previous experience of the continent.[58]

Although neglected by historians, in explaining the slow take-up of posts by graduates we also have to consider in more detail the ways that service in Africa was (or was not) discussed. It is beyond the scope of this book to satisfactorily address the contentious issue of how far Britons as a whole were empire-minded.[59] Nevertheless, it would appear that imperial culture was prominent enough to have the potential to inspire young men. Many officials later recalled how a sense of pride in the empire had been instilled at an early age thanks to schooling, Scouting and the novels of the likes of G. A. Henty, Rudyard Kipling and Rider Haggard.[60] Indeed, this cultural environment helped make it difficult for young men to imagine a world in which the British Empire did not exist.[61]

A question nevertheless remains as to how far these social and cultural forces converted any young boy's rather vague enthusiasm for empire into an adult determination to dedicate one's own life to working in the colonies as an official. After all, given that large swathes of British Africa had just emerged from open imperial warfare, conditions were tough. So tough, indeed, that there was a wave of resignations from the East African services between 1909 and 1911.[62] Letters from anonymous officials to Oxbridge publications kept undergraduates informed of the conditions.[63] More important as a disincentive, perhaps, was that the job was felt incommensurate with the maintenance of a 'respectable' upper-middle-class standing. Whilst John Buchan and others continued the work of Henty and his ilk in providing clichéd visions of imperial duty, the heroes depicted were explorers, a better breed of soldier, and adventurers, rather than colonial officials.[64] In spite of such visions, the continent was nevertheless unable to shake off the image that the majority working there were grizzled traders and soldiers who dropped their aitches.[65]

In an attempt to counteract this, Whitehall did offer officials a reasonable wage. Although new recruits had to spend between £100 and £200 on kit before their first tour, the annual salary of an Edwardian official in Southern Nigeria started at £300.[66] This was nearly identical to a metropolitan lawyer or parson's wage, but money went further in Africa than in Britain because officials paid little tax and were provided with free housing.[67] Nevertheless, in terms of marketing, London's efforts were limited. Some Colonial Office staff recognised they needed to do more in this regard. One minuted in 1908 that, 'If the candidates don't come to us, we must go to the candidates'.[68] London was not dynamic in this regard, which hindered the development of African service as an attractive employment option. The Colonial Office did work with the Cambridge and Oxford University Appointments Committees, although their involvement appears to have been rather limited.[69]

So, irrespective of how far the continent was viewed as a source of excitement, London was faced with two problems. The service was not particularly visible, and when it did attract notice, British Africa's reputation meant graduates frequently did not feel the salary was worth it. This helps explain why, on joining the Colonial Office, Furse was concerned about the low regard in which graduates held the tropical African services above all other problems he felt he faced.[70] In the first years of the twentieth century, a desire for both physical and social self-preservation won out over any general sense of imperial duty.

In retrospect, Ralph Furse liked to portray himself as the scourge of the 'prehistoric dinosaurs' in the Colonial Office.[71] Whilst his 'Young Turk' demeanour generated animosity in certain quarters, Furse met with great success in changing the status quo.[72] He kept abreast of potential recruits through a trusted group of Oxbridge informants, and then worked hard on a one-to-one basis to secure the services of those he thought the most promising.[73] Formalising this process in 1926, Furse developed a network of twenty to thirty dons apiece in Cambridge and Oxford.[74] Besides acting as Furse's informants, these dons were walking propagandists for life in the colonial services. Promising candidates could be tracked throughout their undergraduate years whilst being nurtured in the belief that a career in Africa was better than work in industry or the city.[75] Furse felt his informants 'would attract the notice and rouse the curiosity of like-minded friends or admirers younger than themselves; also of some tutors. In time this might well have a snowball effect'.[76] Interwar officials often later admitted that they had had no intention of applying for an African service until their college peers or respected superiors had alerted them to the work and their potential suitability for it.[77] It would there-fore seem that this effort to market the post of official to those still at university and, indeed, to market it as a respectable profession, was crucial in converting a general enthusiasm for empire into something capable of dissolving opposition to the particular role of official.

Those who had worked in Africa tended to retrospectively draw a sharp distinction between pre- and post-1918 officials. They were retired military men before, and Oxbridge graduates after.[78] University education did indeed increasingly become *de rigeur* after the Great War. Approximately 68 per cent of officials recruited between 1919 and 1945 graduated and then went immediately into training and on to Africa.[79] The majority of the remainder were graduates that joined after two or three years in business, teaching or, particularly in the case of those appointed soon after the Armistice, the armed forces.[80] By 1930 a degree was an essential prerequisite for the job.[81] As a result of this, the majority of officials appointed between the wars were aged twenty-four or under, a considerable decrease on the pre-war average.[82]

That officials later recalled that the Great War was a turning point in the composition of the colonial services was also partially validated by the fact that the conflict created the vacancies that could be filled by a new wave of graduates who viewed the continent as a suitable work destination. Military officials became increasingly scarce after the First World War, with the aforementioned exception of Tanganyika.[83] In July 1914, there were seventy-five officials on the ground in Sudan. By April 1920, forty-one were still working in Sudan, but only twenty-eight remained ordinary officials, with the others promoted to senior posts.[84] The majority of this group of forty-one held fast in Sudan. As of April 1924, thirty-seven of the forty-one remained in the SPS. However, they were now both largely removed from the ordinary work on the ground and marginalised numerically. As one might expect, twenty-eight of this pre-war group of thirty-seven now held senior posts, with eighty-three of all ninety-two SPS officials having been recruited after the Armistice.[85]

Additionally, it is worth noting a broader cultural shift that took place. The idea of the colonial official as a figure to be emulated was a distinctly interwar phenomenon. Edgar Wallace's tales of officials striving nobly against West African superstition and 'savagery', such as *Bones of the River* (1923), *Sanders* (1926) and *Again Sanders* (1928), were eagerly consumed in vast quantities. Over 50 million copies of Wallace's works were printed, making him the biggest name in interwar fiction by a considerable distance.[86] This popularity was enhanced by Zoltan Korda's film *Sanders of the River* (1935), which portrayed officials in glowing terms as noble 'Keepers of the King's Peace'.[87] Those with less sensationalistic tastes were catered for by Joyce Cary's works about officials in Nigeria, such as *Aissa Saved* (1932) and *Mister Johnson* (1939). Furse's agents' interwar claims that work in the colonial services was prestigious were produced just as cultural works started to emphatically proclaim that officials were virtuous and highly regarded 'righters of wrongs'.[88]

Nevertheless, that the number and type of applicants started to change just before the Great War demonstrates the immediate impact of Furse's efforts, and the pre-eminence of his actions in comparison with other factors.[89] In 1913, sixty-three people applied for six posts in Northern Nigeria.[90] This is obviously a distinct contrast to the

Figure 1 Sanders and Bosambo: Leslie Banks and Paul Robeson in *Sanders of the River* (1935)

situation in 1908 noted above. Additionally, between 1912 and 1914, two thirds of recruits came direct from university. Of these, 93 per cent had been to Oxbridge.[91] Furse altered things rapidly.

Consequently, this corps, already relatively homogenous in terms of its social background, was now also increasingly homogenised in terms of social experience. In recruiting from universities, London reduced the amount of global experience possessed by officials, instead choosing men who often viewed service as the basis for a long-term career. Declarations of one's peripatetic background became less frequent as time went on.[92] Furse did pioneer recruitment from the old White Dominions, although such officials were few in number and tended to work in departments other than the administrative services.[93] This was about as esoteric as it got in the interwar period. Recruiting committees increasingly had the luxury of choice as the 1920s progressed, and candidates whose personal backgrounds were as varied as those of pre-war officials were usually rejected as unpredictable.[94]

Before establishing himself as a famous traveller and travel writer, Wilfred Thesiger worked for the SPS between 1935 and 1939. Thesiger had been born and raised in Addis Ababa. Whilst most future officials spent their university holidays enjoying southern England's delights, Thesiger attended Haile Selassie's 1930 coronation and explored Abyssinia's Danakil desert.[95] Family links, an acquaintance with key senior figures in the SPS and his articles in *The Times* recounting his Abyssinian experiences helped Thesiger secure the post of ADC in Darfur. Thesiger initially impressed London officials, but he was in fact someone who viewed a career in the SPS as a short-term means of ensuring his being in North East Africa, an attitude missing from his more careerist contemporaries, whom he derided as 'conventional'.[96] Thesiger was hostile to all appendages of modernity, and when posted to Darfur, he was uninterested in administrative duties and eulogised the 'savage' African lifestyle.[97] Thesiger later recalled that, 'I knew that I was not really suited to be a D.C. as I had no faith in the changes which we were bringing about. I craved for the past, resented the present, and dreaded the future'.[98] As he correctly guessed, both Furse and senior SPS officials soon realised Thesiger was a bad fit for imperial duty.[99] The occasional troublesome official such as Thesiger reminded London of the importance of recruiting those with unspectacular graduate backgrounds if it was to avoid a re-emergence of its pre-war concerns.

In the late 1920s Furse complained that, even if interest in colonial Africa as a career destination was growing, all of the territories were still seen as part of a 'single estate'.[100] The complaint was rooted in the belief that not enough was done to educate Britons in the detail of African life.[101] As the famous explorer and elite colonial administrator Harry Johnston grumbled in 1919, 'our public schools still placidly contemplate Africa as the chief employment for the more adventurous of their pupils, yet still teach them nothing about Africa'.[102] As we shall see in Chapter Two, Johnston was largely correct. Whilst the prestige of the services rose across the board in the interwar period, patterns of recruitment were nevertheless shaped to a significant degree by applicants' rudimentary conceptions of the different colonies. Officials were not, in the main, drawn to a colony because it was poor or felt in the most need of help. When applicants decided to serve King and Country, they invariably strove to do so in a manner that would reflect most highly on themselves. There was a clear pecking order to the services. Nowhere in Africa had the prestige of a post in the ICS, although the SPS was ranked above all others on the continent, followed by the Nigerian service.[103] A minority of officials later argued that they had not put much thought into where they had applied, but this pecking order directly shaped the actions of the majority.[104] Young men who had applied unsuccessfully to the ICS then looked to places such as Africa, but it does not appear they acted the other way around until the 1930s. It has been suggested that this change in the 1930s was because young men started to realise that the ICS was no longer the basis for a lengthy career.[105] However, given that many in Britain did not yet believe that India was headed towards independence in the near future, it is perhaps more accurate to suggest they avoided the subcontinent because they did not want to work in a place where nationalist activity would most heavily threaten their own authority.[106] After India, officials chose the SPS over offers of work both elsewhere in East Africa and in West Africa.[107] The SPS was the first service to make a substantial transition to graduate recruitment. The process began in 1901, accelerating significantly after 1905.[108] By the time that fear of the West African climate had started to recede in the interwar period, Nigeria was the most requested posting of all territories overseen by the Colonial Office.[109]

There are a number of reasons for this hierarchy. An early preference for the ICS can be partially explained by India's prominence in domestic visions of empire. Although the White Dominions were of increasing importance in shaping a British imperial identity from the late nineteenth century onwards, India most embodied that which was not 'Greater Britain'.[110] As a consequence, the subcontinent was the best-known route to working in the empire. In addition, to be in the ICS was to be part of a well-established and well-respected service. In fact, India's time as the site of the type of adventurous conflict loved by schoolchildren had passed. The Battle of Plassey, Tipu Sultan and the Indian Mutiny were history, replaced with the zealous but less exciting administrative reforms of Curzon, Minto, *et al*. In contrast, the occupation of Kumasi, which ended the long series of wars against the Asante, as well as Lugard's conquest of Northern Nigeria and, to a lesser extent, Gordon's exploits in Khartoum, were still within

[26]

living memory. The prestige of the ICS evidently trumped the fact that Africa was the part of the empire viewed as the biggest potential site of adventure.

Of all African services, the relative attractiveness of Sudan as a destination for graduates was nevertheless in part because it was the region of British Africa most closely connected with imperial glory. Gordon besieged at Khartoum by the Mahdi was (and, indeed, remains) the best-known of the three military engagements noted above.[111] The race against time of Wolseley's relief expedition, Gordon's death in 1885, and questions about Gladstone's culpability for this seized the nation.[112] Britain knew few specific details about Sudan, but Gordon's archetypal display of muscular Christianity and Kitchener's conquest of 1896–99 remained central to metropolitan conceptions of the Condominium throughout the Edwardian and interwar periods.[113] The visibility of the SPS was enhanced by the fact that, in contrast to the Colonial Service, senior Edwardian SPS members seized the initiative. They visited universities and talked to prospective candidates, encouraging the best and developing personal links in advance of any call to interview.[114]

That the transition to civilian recruitment began in Sudan before all other parts of Africa also owed something to an attractive tour-leave ratio, a relatively early retirement age (forty-eight), and a starting annual salary of £420, at the time the best in British Africa.[115] Recruiting committees consequently had greater choice and were able to select more, and better-qualified, graduates. This prestige then became self-perpetuating, as others wanted to join these graduates. In 1937, one young man chose the SPS in the face of simultaneous offers of posts in Nigeria and Uganda. He wrote in his diary that he had refused these 'on account of the known superiority of the Sudan Political Service which, in my view, is shortly becoming in the XXth century what the ICS was in the XIXth'.[116] Indeed, a civilian takeover of the Edwardian SPS was only prevented by Khartoum's enduring belief that 'unsettled' southern Sudan had to be administered by men with military experience. This meant that of the sixty-one Inspectors in Sudan as of March 1914, thirty-three had previously served in the Egyptian Army.[117] Unsurprisingly, Furse was envious of the success with which the Foreign Office had built up the reputation of the SPS.[118]

Although not as popular as Sudan, Nigeria attracted more attention than its West African neighbours, particularly after 1918. Nigeria was known as the place where governmental innovations concerning 'traditional' African life were first conceptualised and put into practice.[119] For *The Times*, Northern Nigeria was a 'part of the Colonial Empire which must always figure largely when British policy towards African

[27]

peoples is under discussion and review', being, after all, 'the classical instance of the [indirect rule] system'.[120] It would appear that the chance to work within the system associated with Lord Lugard, then the best-known of all elite administrators in West or East Africa, was an opportunity to bask in reflected glory.[121] Once again, the self-interest of graduates played a large part in influencing their job applications.

Conclusion

Africa was selected as a place of work for a variety of reasons. Particularly in the years before the First World War, a desire to make money and pre-existing ties with the continent, be they familial or through previous employment, were important. However, the people motivated by these factors were not necessarily those London wanted. Officials from a military background had an important part to play in the 'pacification' of Africa, but when Whitehall turned its attention to making the new colonies pay their own way as quickly as possible, it preferred to employ graduates. Kuklick has suggested that the 'majority of [interwar] colonial officers would probably have preferred other careers'.[122] There is no substantial means of supporting this claim. However, just like their counterparts today, graduates with the luxury of different job opportunities selected those they felt benefitted them the most. Concerns about climate and social prestige limited the importance of a desire for adventure as the key determinant of would-be officials' actions. The clear existence of a pecking order in the administrative services demonstrates the importance of prestige and one-upmanship.[123] Scholars have to date neglected or marginalised the importance of the desire for a 'good' job, but this factor's prominence makes it hard to accept Kirk-Greene's argument that public school inculcated a selfless attitude above all else. London consequently had to overcome several barriers to alter the composition of the colonial corps. It was only when the job of colonial official became more attractive that the government was able to weed out what it saw as rogue public school-educated recruits and replace them with a different type of young man. Officials were still overwhelmingly from the same social backgrounds as their predecessors. However, they increasingly viewed work in Africa as the basis for a long career, rather than what one simply did due to *noblesse oblige* or precedent, or whilst waiting for a better job to come along. Until that time, such promising men preferred the prestige and salary of the home civil service.

Notes

1   C. P. Snow, *The Masters* (Kelly Bray: House of Stratus, 2001), p. 22
2   Quoted in D. Cannadine, *The Decline and Fall of the British Aristocracy* (1990; London: Penguin, 1992), p. 442
3   See, for example, Gann and Duignan, *Rulers of British Africa*, pp. 200, 203–7; Collins, 'Sudan Political Service', 301
4   J. Tosh, *A Man's Place: Masculinity and the Middle-Class Home in Victorian England* (London: Yale University Press, 1999)
5   C. P. Browne, 'The wander years', [n.d.], SAD 422/14
6   See, for instance, Mrs C. H. B. Grant, notes, [undated], RHO Mss.Afr.s.141/367
7   A. Wright, *The Romance of Colonisation: Being the Story of the Economic Development of the British Empire* (London: Melrose, 1923), *passim*, especially pp. vii, 1, 92, 274, 367–8; R. Muir, *A Short History of the British Commonwealth: Volume II – The Modern Commonwealth (1763 to 1919)* (London: George Philip and Son, 1922), pp. 652, 659–60
8   Field, '*Verb Sap.*', p. 55
9   Furthermore, scandals concerning individual officials were rarely highlighted in the media; F. Bösch, '"Are we a cruel nation?" Colonial practices, perceptions, and scandals', in D. Geppert and R. Gewarth (eds), *Wilhelmine Germany and Edwardian Britain: Essays on Cultural Affinity* (Oxford: Oxford University Press, 2008), pp. 115–40
10 J. Henderson, 'Rulers of the Congo: motley crew who serve under the Free State flag', *Daily Express* (17 December 1906), p. 4. However, see Tidrick, *Empire and the English Character*, p. 204; Hesketh Bell to parents, 7 December 1910, British Library (hereafter BL) Add Mss 78721/188
11 'In the Nuer Country', *The Times* (20 December 1927), p. 15
12 J. A. Spender, '"Old Blues" oust the slaves', *News Chronicle* (16 February 1931), p. 8
13 H. Samuel, 'Sir Herbert Samuel on the Empire Conference', *News Chronicle* (2 October 1930), p. 6; H. Condenhove, 'On certain facets of the Central African natives', *Cornhill Magazine* 55 (1931), pp. 216–17, 220
14 Kirk-Greene points out that the great schools that attained prominence in the nineteenth century, such as Winchester and Rugby, increasingly replaced Eton and Harrow; Kirk-Greene, *Britain's Imperial Administrators*, p. 136
15 Heussler, *Yesterday's Rulers*, pp. 24–5, 35, 188; Civil Secretary's Office, *Sudan Political Service 1899–1929* (Khartoum: Sudan Government Press, 1930); J. M. Coote papers, RHO Mss.Afr.s.1383(1); Gann and Duignan, *Rulers of British Africa*, p. 185
16 Gardiner, 'Sentinels of empire', p. 256
17 *Ibid.*, p. 302. After 1921, 'Ireland' refers to both Northern Ireland and the Republic of Ireland.
18 Calculated using the population statistics given in C. L. Mowat, *Britain Between the Wars, 1918–1940* (Cambridge: Cambridge University Press, 1955), p. 225; J. Lee, *Ireland 1921–1985: Politics and Society* (Cambridge: Cambridge University Press, 1989), p. 512. This is, of course, very different to suggesting that, for instance, Presbyterianism did not subsequently influence the manner in which Scottish empire-builders went about their business; see A. Lownie, *John Buchan: The Presbyterian Cavalier* (London: Constable, 1995)
19 Yorkshire alone counted for 5 per cent of all officials during this time; Gardiner, 'Sentinels of empire', p. 306
20 Gardiner's own statistics confirm as much; *ibid.*, p. 294; Gann and Duignan, *Rulers of British Africa*, p. 185
21 Kirk-Greene, 'The Sudan Political Service: a profile in the sociology of imperialism', *International Journal of African Historical Studies* 15:1 (1982), 30–1; Kirk-Greene, *Britain's Imperial Administrators*, pp. 136–8; Mangan, 'The education of an elite imperial administration', 681

22 Gann and Duignan, *Rulers of British Africa*, p. 186
23 Colonial Office desk diary, 6 March 1911, RHO Mss.Brit.Emp.r.21; Colonial Office desk diary, 30 May 1911, RHO Mss.Brit.Emp.r.21; Colonial Office desk diary, 22 July 1911, RHO Mss.Brit.Emp.r.21; Colonial Office desk diary, 2 July 1914, RHO Mss.Brit.Emp.r.21
24 H. K. Sadler to Hawkin, 11 November 1910, RHO Mss.Brit.Emp.r.21; Colonial Office desk diary, 16 January 1911, RHO Mss.Brit.Emp.r.21
25 S. Ormsby, 'Application for promotion in the Colonial Service', [1908], RHO Mss. Afr.r.105/35; see also E. Richardson, Scrapbook, RHO Mss.Afr.s.580/2
26 S. Ormsby to H. Ormsby, 30 November 1896, RHO Mss.Afr.r.105/i; S. Ormsby to father, 15 May 1903, RHO Mss.Afr.r.105/9b
27 R. Temple to Goldie, 1 October 1901, RHO Mss.Afr.s.141/405. This is not, however, to marginalise Temple's evident administrative ability; C. L. Temple, *Native Races and their Rulers: Sketches and Studies of Official Life and Administrative Problems in Nigeria* (Cape Town: Argus, 1918)
28 Gann and Duignan, *Rulers of British Africa*, p. 6; Gardiner, 'Sentinels of empire', p. 93; Kirk-Greene, *Symbol of Authority*, p. 4
29 For one such example, see Colonial Office desk diary, 16 February 1907, RHO Mss. Brit.Emp.r.21
30 For example, see Colonial Office desk diary, 20 October 1904, RHO Mss.Brit. Emp.r.21
31 H. Mathews to parents, 11 January 1911, RHO Mss.Afr.s.783/1/1/8
32 G. Ormsby, 'The land of the Boxers: From Pekin to Kalgan', [n.d.], RHO Mss.Brit. Emp.s.287/5
33 Gann and Duignan, *Rulers of British Africa*, p. 185
34 Daly, *Empire on the Nile: The Anglo-Egyptian Sudan 1898–1934* (Cambridge: Cambridge University Press, 1986), pp. 82–4; Kirk-Greene, *On Crown Service*, p. 17; Kirk-Greene, *Symbol of Authority*, p. 11
35 Statistic calculated using the biographical details listed in T. Williamson and Kirk-Greene (eds), *Gold Coast Diaries: Chronicles of Political Officers in West Africa, 1900–1919* (London: Radcliffe Press, 2000), pp. 385–98
36 As noted below, the SPS switched to recruitment from universities earlier than other administrative services; the increased appointment of graduates after 1905 meant that the average starting age of SPS officials recruited between 1905 and 1914 inclusive was 24.6 years. Figures calculated using Civil Secretary's Office, *Sudan Political Service*, pp. 1–35
37 C. Wordsworth to G. Young, 24 July 1900, RHO Mss.Afr.s.1373/12
38 Including places not covered by this study, such as Egypt; J. Johnstone to Cromer, 27 July 1903, BL Add Mss 62124/8–15
39 M. C. Atkinson, *Nigerian Tales of the Colonial Era* (unpublished, n.d.), pp. 3–6, in RHO Mss.Afr.s.2065/1; *Annual Reports of Bende Division, South Eastern Nigeria, 1905–1912, with a commentary by G. I. Jones* (Cambridge: African Studies Centre, 1986), p. iv
40 'Correspondence respecting the retirement of the Imperial British East Africa Company', *Parl. Papers 1895*, lxxi (7646); M. Hicks Beach to J. Chamberlain, 11 February 1898, Joseph Chamberlain Papers, Special Collections, University of Birmingham (hereafter JC) 9/4/2A/4; Goldie, 'Memorandum on spirituous liquors for Nigeria', 10 February 1899, JC 9/4/2A/14; see also Lord Salisbury papers, RHO Mss.Afr.s.141/410–14; G. Portal to Rosebery, 1 November 1895, in 'Further papers relating to Uganda', *Parl. Papers 1893*, lxii (7109), p. 35; Colonel Colvile to Portal, 11 November 1893, in 'Papers relating to Uganda', *Parl. Papers 1893*, lxxi (7708), p. 1
41 D. Chalmers to E. Wingfield, 2 March 1899, JC 9/5/3/4
42 For a useful account of this, see S. Doyle, *Crisis & Decline in Bunyoro: Population & Environment in Western Uganda 1860–1955* (Oxford: James Currey, 2006), ch. 3; see also N. Malcolm, diary, RHO Mss.Afr.s.759/1–14
43 K. Henderson, diary, 29 June 1900, RHO Mss.Afr.s.1484/34; see also W. H. Williams, diary [1890–93], BL Add Mss 60344

44 S. Ormsby, 'Application for promotion in the Colonial Service', [1908], RHO Mss. Afr.r.105/35
45 C. Cardew to F. Cardew, 21 June 1893, RHO Mss.Brit.Emp.s.500/77
46 Gann and Duignan, *Rulers of British Africa*, p. 183
47 Kirk-Greene, *Britain's Imperial Administrators*, p. 62
48 'African Tropical Service Committee', [undated minute, probably 1908], NA CO 96/476; Minutes of fifth meeting of African Tropical Services Committee, 2 December 1907, NA CO 96/476
49 J. Iliffe, *A Modern History of Tanganyika* (Cambridge: Cambridge University Press, 1979), pp. 262–3, 325
50 See, for instance, the notes at the back of Colonial Office desk diary, [1907], RHO Mss. Brit.Emp.r.21; G. Tomlinson to mother, 26 February 1907, RHO Mss.Afr.s.372/41
51 Heussler, *Yesterday's Rulers*, p. 15
52 All three accepted the job offers; 'Administrative vacancies in West Africa', [April 1908], NA CO 96/476; see also Heussler, *Yesterday's Rulers*, pp. 13–14
53 See, for instance, Colonial Office desk diary, 20 February 1907, RHO Mss.Brit. Emp.r.21
54 A. Roberts, 'The imperial mind', in Roberts (ed.), *Cambridge History of Africa: Volume 7 from 1905 to 1940* (Cambridge: Cambridge University Press, 1986), p. 33 n. 8
55 M. Kisch, *Letters & Sketches from Northern Nigeria* (London: Chatto & Windus, 1910), p. ix
56 For example, see Colonial Office desk diary, 20 June 1904, RHO Mss.Brit.Emp.r.21
57 Gann and Duignan, *Rulers of British Africa*, p. 230
58 Minutes of first meeting of African Tropical Services Committee, 12 November 1907, NA CO 96/476
59 See, for example, B. Porter, *The Absent-minded Imperialists: What the British Really Thought about Empire* (Oxford: Oxford University Press, 2004); J. M. Mackenzie, *Propaganda and Empire: The Manipulation of British Public Opinion, 1880–1960* (Manchester: Manchester University Press, 1984); Mackenzie (ed.), *Imperialism and Popular Culture* (Manchester: Manchester University Press, 1986); Thompson, *The Empire Strikes Back?*
60 See, for instance, A. E. D. Penn, 'Distant drums', [February 1983], SAD 722/13/2
61 For example, into the interwar era, there remained the widespread notion that the Thirteen Colonies of North America had been lost as a result of a heavy tax and administrative burden upon settlers, rather than because colonies inherently developed a sense of independence and pressed for national self-realisation; H. Golding (ed.), *The Wonder Book of Empire for Boys and Girls* (London: Ward Lock and Co., 1925), p. 28; 'Keeping in touch with the empire', *Tanganyika Times* (16 January 1926), p. 2; D. A. Percival, 'Tropical African Service Course 1929/30: Lecture Notes', RHO Mss.Brit.Emp.s.364/1/30
62 Heussler, *Yesterday's Rulers*, p. 15
63 R. Symonds, *Oxford and Empire: The Last Lost Cause?* (Oxford: Oxford University Press, 1986), p. 12; these complaints were not limited to administrative staff; Anonymous, 'West African Medical Service', *British Medical Journal* (26 January 1907), p. 231
64 Buchan, *Prester John* (London: Nelson, 1910); J. S. Bratton, 'Of England, home, and duty: the image of England in Victorian and Edwardian juvenile fiction', in Mackenzie (ed.), *Imperialism and Popular Culture*, pp. 73–93
65 See, for example, R. Kipling, 'Fuzzy Wuzzy' (1892), in A. Rutherford (ed.), *War Stories and Poems* (Oxford: Oxford University Press, 1990), pp. 68–9; Adams, *Lyra Nigeria*
66 Field, *'Verb Sap.'*, p. 31; G. F. Sayers (ed.), *The Handbook of Tanganyika* (London: Macmillan and Co., 1930), p. 152
67 Jeffries, *Colonial Empire*, pp. 109–10; on metropolitan professional salaries, see P. Thompson, *Edwardians: The Remaking of British Society* (Bloomington, IA: Indiana University Press, 1975), p. 14

68 Quoted in Heussler, *Yesterday's Rulers*, p. 14
69 M. C. Curthoys, 'The careers of Oxford men', in M. Brock and Curthoys (eds), *The History of the University of Oxford: Volume VI – Nineteenth-century Oxford* (Oxford: Oxford University Press, 1997), pp. 506–7
70 Furse to Milner, 18 June 1919, RHO Mss.Brit.Emp.s.415/1/2/11
71 Furse, *Aucuparius*, p. 68
72 *Ibid.*, pp. 68–71
73 J. Daniell, diary, 7 August 1937, SAD 777/13/5
74 Furse, *Aucuparius*, p. 152
75 Furse to Milner, 18 June 1919, RHO Mss.Brit.Empr.s.415/1/2/15. The SPS had a similar system in place; Kirk-Greene, 'Sudan Political Service', 34
76 Furse, *Aucuparius*, p. 151
77 A. Sillery, 'Working backwards', RHO Mss.Afr.r.207/40; T. Letchworth, interview with Kirk-Greene, 7 May 1968, RHO Mss.Afr.s.2112/1. This is not, however, to say that this attitude was entirely absent prior to 1914; see C. Dundas, *African Crossroads* (London: Macmillan, 1955), pp. 8–9
78 See, for example, P. A. Clearkin, 'Ramblings and recollections of a colonial doctor 1913–1958', [1967], RHO Mss.Brit.r.4/1/54
79 Gardiner, 'Sentinels of empire', p. 278
80 *Ibid.*, pp. 322–3. Whilst 15 per cent of officials questioned are listed as not having been educated at university, this figure includes those who did not put a university down on their HMOCS questionnaire
81 Bush, *Imperialism, Race and Resistance: Africa and Britain, 1919–1945* (London: Routledge, 1999), p. 57
82 Gardiner, 'Sentinels of empire', pp. 278, 282
83 See, for example, Daly, *Empire on the Nile*, pp. 271–2
84 Figures calculated tabulating names taken from *Monthly Return of Senior Officials, Sudan Government, and British Officers Temporarily Employed in Sudan Government Service, Showing Appointments & Stations on the 1st July, 1914* (Khartoum: Sudan Government Press, 1914) and *Quarterly List, Sudan Government, Showing Appointments and Stations on the 1st April, 1920* (Khartoum: Sudan Government Press, 1920)
85 *Quarterly List, Sudan Government, Showing Appointments and Stations for the Quarter Beginning 1st April, 1924* (Khartoum: Sudan Government Press, 1924)
86 Including, admittedly, thrillers not concerned with Africa; W. W. Dixon, 'The colonial vision of Edgar Wallace', *Journal of Popular Culture* 32:1 (1998), 122; M. Lane, *Edgar Wallace: The Biography of a Phenomenon* (London: Heinemann, 1938), pp. 72, 94
87 Z. Korda (dir.), *Sanders of the River* (1935); K. Dunn, 'Lights … camera … Africa: images of Africa and Africans in Western popular films of the 1930s', *African Studies Review* 39:1 (1996), 149–75; see also Nicolson, *Administration of Nigeria*, p. 64
88 Paul Robeson sings as much in Korda (dir.), *Sanders of the River*.
89 There had already been some upward movement in interest prior to Furse's appointment. As recorded in the Colonial Office Assistant Private Secretary's desk diaries, the number of enquiries the Colonial Office received about service in Africa rose from twelve in 1904 to twenty-seven in 1907; Colonial Office desk diary, [1904], RHO Mss.Brit.Emp.r.21; Colonial Office desk diary, [1907], RHO Mss.Brit. Emp.r.21. Self-educated men such as Donald Cameron were rare across the period; Kirk-Greene, 'Sudan Political Service', *passim*
90 One of the successful six was Joyce Cary; M. Mahood, *Joyce Cary's Africa* (London: Methuen, 1964), p. 5
91 Furse to Amery, 1 April 1920, RHO Mss.Brit.Emp.s.415/1/2/39; see also Gann and Duignan, *Rulers of British Africa*, p. 203
92 For one such pre-war declaration, see Dundas, *African Crossroads*, pp. 1–2
93 Masterton-Smith to Clifford, 11 January 1924, NA CO 323/916/87–91; Gardiner, 'Sentinels of empire', pp. 302, 304

94 T. D. Cranston to Acting Colonial Secretary, Gold Coast, 30 July 1938, PRAAD CSO 26/4/63; Jardine to M. Macdonald, 18 May 1939, PRAAD CSO 26/4/63

95 W. Thesiger, *Arabian Sands* (1959; Harmondsworth: Penguin, 1964), pp. 18–22; A. Maitland, *Wilfred Thesiger: The Life of the Great Explorer* (2006; London: Harper Perennial, 2007), ch. 8

96 *Ibid.*, p. 127; Thesiger, *The Life of My Choice* (London: Collins, 1987), p. 202

97 Maitland, *Wilfred Thesiger*, chs 3–4, 7

98 Thesiger, *Life of My Choice*, p. 202

99 *Ibid.*, p. 209; see Furse's annotations on his 'Quarterly list of the Sudan Government: 1st January 1936', RHO Mss.Brit.s.415/6/7/3; Newbold to Moore, 25 May 1939, in Henderson, *Modern Sudan*, p. 112; Maitland, *Wilfred Thesiger*, p. 127

100 Furse, untitled memo, 27 April 1929, RHO Mss.Brit.Emp.s.415/4/1/12–13

101 Furse, *Aucuparius*, p. 138

102 H. H. Johnston, 'The Africa of the immediate future', *Journal of the African Society* 18:71 (1919), 182; see also editorial, *Morning Post* (26 December 1905), p. 4

103 The pecking order has been noted before, but its full implications for our understanding of would-be officials' motivations has not; Kirk-Greene, 'Sudan Political Service', 21–2

104 Letchworth, interview, RHO Mss.Afr.s.2112/2

105 A. Ewing, 'The Indian Civil Service 1919–1924: service discontent and the response in London and Delhi', *Modern Asian Studies* 18:1 (1984), 33–53; Kirk-Greene, 'Sudan Political Service', 33

106 For metropolitan conceptions of India at this time, see C. Bridge, *Holding India to the Empire: The British Conservative Party and the 1935 Constitution* (London: Oriental University Press, 1986); J. Darwin, 'Imperialism in decline? Tendencies in British imperial policy between the wars', *Historical Journal* 23:3 (1980), 657–79; see also G. W. Morris and L. S. Wood, *The English-speaking Nations: A Study in the Development of the Commonwealth Ideal* (1924; Oxford: Clarendon Press, 1930), pp. 252–3

107 Daniell, diary, 6–8 August 1937, SAD 777/13/55

108 For biographical details of these recruits, see Civil Secretary's Office, *Sudan Political Service*, pp. 17–19

109 According to the returns of HMOCS questionnaires, in the interwar period, 26 per cent of all Colonial Office-appointed officials had originally listed Nigeria as one of their destinations of choice; Gardiner, 'Sentinels of empire', p. 68

110 C. Dilke, *Greater Britain* (London: Macmillan, 1868); Thompson, 'The language of imperialism and the meanings of empire: imperial discourse in British politics, 1895–1914', *Journal of British Studies* 36:2 (1997), 147–77

111 Johnson, 'The death of Gordon: a Victorian myth', *Journal of Imperial and Commonwealth History* 10 (1982), 285–310

112 R. Shannon, *Gladstone: Heroic Minister 1865–1898* (London: Penguin, 1999), pp. 344–51

113 J. Kenrick, memoirs, [undated], SAD 815/4/3; R. C. Mayall, memoirs, [1940], SAD 851/7/5; A. C. Parker, memoirs, [c.1930s], SAD 294/2/2. This was an attitude strengthened by popular fiction, such as A. E. W. Mason's *The Four Feathers* (1902).

114 R. Davies, *The Camel's Back: Service in the Rural Sudan* (London: J. Murray, 1957), pp. 14–15

115 Kirk-Greene, 'Sudan Political Service', 34

116 Daniell, diary, 31 December 1937, SAD 777/13/19; see also Daniell, diary, 8 August 1937, SAD 777/13/5

117 *Monthly Returns of Senior Officials, Sudan Government, and British Officers Temporarily Employed in Sudan Government Service, Showing Appointments & Stations on the 1st March 1914* (Khartoum: Sudan Government, 1914)

118 Furse to Milner, 18 June 1919, RHO Mss.Brit.Emp.s.415/1/2/16; Furse, untitled memo, 27 April 1929, RHO Mss.Brit.Emp.s.415/4/1/12–13

119 Some of whom will be examined in Chapter Two.

120 'Through Northern Nigeria', *The Times* (16 February 1934), p. 15; 'Indirect rule in Africa', *The Times* (27 November 1930), p. 15
121 Lugard could not, however, compete with Cromer in Egypt or Milner in South Africa.
122 Kuklick, *Imperial Bureaucrat*, p. 153
123 On one-upsmanship, see H. Callaway, *Gender, Culture and Empire: European Women in Colonial Nigeria* (Basingstoke: Macmillan, 1987), p. 186

CHAPTER TWO

An imperial education

This chapter will consider the metropolitan attitudes and ideas about Africa and empire to which officials were exposed. This exposure took two principal forms. Firstly, there was the formal training officials received. Secondly, there was British culture more broadly, with which they engaged both before and during their time in Africa. Thanks in large part to the development of more comprehensive training, officials' access to material concerning the governance of Africa increased during the period under consideration. Nevertheless, officials left Britain equipped with very little detailed sense of what their jobs would entail. Training only covered Africa in broad brushstrokes. In addition, the published material on imperial governance, and indirect rule in particular, to which new recruits had access was invariably written by prominent administrative elites who for a number of reasons were only prepared to brandish generalities. Furthermore, officials were often unwilling to engage with what they received. Training was at its most influential in very simple ways, such as when it helped normalise the belief that anthropological study was a routine component of imperial governance.

Contributions to the ongoing historiographical debate over how far Britain was an imperial society have not assessed the detail of the imperial content available to the British public as fully as they might have done. Historians have been more concerned with whether or not this cultural output constituted a critical mass capable of tipping Britain over into support for empire than with assessing the quality of the material. Britons were continually exposed to ideas of race and empire but, again, in the main, this exposure left inexact imprints. Uncertainty as to the precise role of race in the perennial 'nature' versus 'nurture' debate provided officials with an unclear message. Similarly, commentators discussing how Britons might best engage with their peers were unable to formulate a means of striking a balance between imperial governance as a route to self-realisation and self-fulfilment on the one hand, and as a collective endeavour in which all were united on the other.

In the early years of the twentieth century, officials were given a good deal of intellectual room for manoeuvre. No training existed until 1908, when the Colonial Office introduced a three-month course at the Imperial Institute in Kensington. Furse's later involvement in reforming this training meant he had a vested interest in claiming that the Imperial Institute 'course was a not very satisfactory piece of cramming and discipline was slack', but he was correct.[1] In spite of Colonial Office requests that absences from lectures be closely monitored, overworked and underpaid Imperial Institute staff were reluctant to add to their own administrative burdens by doing so.[2] Consequently, officials did not always take onboard what the Institute had to offer. One would later admit that it

> was not ... a very serious business and we all thoroughly enjoyed ourselves, even though some of us did not do a great deal of work. For example, one of our number managed to get no marks in one of the papers, mainly because he found the atmosphere in the bar of a nearby hotel more congenial than the stuffy rooms of the Imperial Institute.[3]

As for the content itself, those who did attend were given lectures on four topics: hygiene, government accounts and accounting, law and economics. There are good reasons for this. For example, ongoing fears about the 'White man's grave' and recent events such as an outbreak of plague in Accra in early 1908 make it entirely understandable that those devising the course felt hygiene was important. Nevertheless, training as a whole was light on any administrative content that extended beyond the 'nuts and bolts' of everyday life.[4] For instance, the accounting lectures were concerned with basics such as how to complete ledgers. The law lectures tackled procedural matters such as how to tell one type of crime from another, consider evidence and cross-examine. There is no indication that this training considered cultural contact or the implications of the introduction of Western legal procedures for African political structures.[5] Because the course was so short, those responsible for shaping the Institute's curriculum rejected the idea that officials should also be trained in the geography, history and constitutions of East and West Africa, believing that 'for the present it would be sufficient to supply selected candidates with a copy of the annual Blue book' and a list of works to read.[6]

Officials had access to more information than this. Those serving in West Africa invariably bought the government-issued *West African Pocketbook*. However, rather than information on the societies in which they would be working, this contained practical advice regarding disease prevention, cooking and other matters relating to personal health.[7] Even this was found wanting. It is unsurprising that, for one official new to Northern Nigeria in 1906,

> a vagueness as to our destination and the form our work would take was the chief feeling in the minds of [fellow Assistant Resident] Grier and myself. A copy of the Northern Nigerian laws, such as had been promulgated up to that time ... together with a curious little official effort, called the West African pocket-book, comprised my only literature on the country. The one has long since mouldered into dust upon some office shelf, the other, misleading me completely on most subjects, was very soon thrown upon the fire.[8]

After the First World War, training became more organised, particularly after 1926 with the introduction of the Tropical African Service (TAS) course, which then prevailed basically unaltered until 1945.[9] New recruits spent two terms (extended to a full academic year in 1928) at Oxbridge being trained by some of the most prominent imperial thinkers of the day. For instance, Beit Professor of Colonial History Reginald Coupland, noted academic Margery Perham and anthropologist Edward Evans-Pritchard were amongst those who taught at Oxford. The training received by SPS members was basically the same, although introduced earlier. Initially, officials were trained for one year at Oxford or Cambridge in Arabic, law, tropical medicine, surveying and, from 1908, anthropology. Training switched to London in the 1920s, and in 1930 SPS officials started on the same Oxbridge courses as their peers elsewhere in British Africa.[10]

Certain attitudes towards postgraduate training remained constant in spite of a change in the type of young men recruited. Regardless of the princely sum of £225 the government paid probationers undergoing training, some treated the whole enterprise as an extra year at university to be enjoyed before entering the world of work proper.[11] Thomas Letchworth later recalled that, during his training at Cambridge prior to starting in Nigeria in 1928, 'We did some tropical agriculture, and I understood nothing about it, all I can remember is "sorghum" and that meant nothing at all to us then'.[12] Letchworth also undertook some courses at the Imperial Institute, where

> Sir somebody-Stevenson [Sir Albert Stephenson] ... was teaching us the basic stuff about Colonial treasury work. Almost all of us took the very least notice of that, and I really think he had rather a poor do from everybody. But had we known a little better, of course, we would have taken much more interest and paid a great deal of attention to it, and saved ourselves a great deal of trouble in our lives later on. But I think that is rather symptomatic of our general approach to everything. One couldn't

have cared less, and we must have been most unsatisfactory material in every possible way.[13]

Nevertheless, it does seem that an increasing proportion of would-be officials took an interest in their studies after 1918. However, due to the range of topics to which officials were exposed, even eager students had difficulty absorbing details. Whilst at Balliol, one trainee wrote home to say that 'There are far too many subjects to concentrate on any particular one of them'.[14] In addition, some made the effort to attend lectures, only to feel their studies were of dubious relevance to the work undertaken in the field. Sometimes this was only felt after the training had happened, particularly when it came to the efforts recruits made learning Arabic. One new arrival into Sudan complained that as 'an understanding of the colloquial [Arabic] dialect goes, we might as well have been learning Chinese for the last year at Oxford'.[15] Others voiced frustrations in the middle of their training. After attending a lecture given by Perham on 'Cultural Contact and Native Administration in North America', one young probationer complained that 'We shall probably have to study uses of the small tooth comb among the Esquimaux next'.[16]

Officials who had already commenced work in Africa were the market for the other principal formal point of access to metropolitan ideas about governance and anthropology. This was the annual Oxford University Summer Schools on Colonial Administration, which began in 1937. In the early years, the schools were largely organised by Perham, who called them 'a sort of intellectual refresher'.[17] Over the course of two weeks each summer, talks were given by anthropologists such as Bronislaw Malinowski and Charles Seligman, and elite political figures such as William Ormsby-Gore, Secretary of State for the Colonies.[18] As with university training, however, the impact of the summer schools upon officials was slight. In 1937 there were roughly 800 DCs serving in The Gambia, Gold Coast, Nigeria, Uganda, Sierra Leone, Sudan and Tanganyika.[19] Approximately sixty-six administrative officials from Africa attended the 1937 summer school at St Hugh's College, Oxford,[20] but this figure included elites, and it would appear that a proportionally higher number of elites attended than DCs.[21] Irrespective of elite concerns about officials' levels of training, colonial governments' overriding concern was naturally that officials were in place on the ground, which meant they were only prepared to facilitate summer school attendance by making 'minor' adjustments to leave schedules and by meeting travel and lodging costs.[22]

At any rate, it was only the most ambitious who were prepared to take two weeks out of home leave to attend.[23] Nevertheless, even they do not seem to have fully engaged with the course. Douglas Newbold, a senior SPS figure in attendance at Oxford in 1938, thought that although the existence of the summer schools was 'heartening', there were only 'one or two young D.C.s from elsewhere in Africa with a crusading spirit'.[24] This may have been because the presence of so many officials' wives in Oxford proved a social distraction that disappointed the more intellectually-minded organisers.[25] Even when they attended, officials were faced with a majority of talks that did not concern British Africa at all, but other international matters such as recent events in Russia.[26] The lectures that did concern Africa rarely discussed 'the higher problems of colonial policy and the general uplift of primitive peoples'.[27] For instance, Perham's lectures provided basic information, such as when indirect rule was introduced across Africa, and the nature of the relationship between the colonies and the Colonial Office.[28] She suggested that the process of establishing colonial rule, which she defined as the introduction of indirect rule and technical departments, was coming to an end, and that more study was needed into what should happen next. Beyond that, there was very little else.[29]

There were further limits to officials' engagement with ideas about governance and Africa. Many simply avoided such matters when on leave. According to one elite SPS figure in Sudan, when back in Britain, 'So many just go home to drive sports cars to Brighton or gaze into a *bint*'s eyes in some cabaret dungeon at midnight'.[30] There is doubtless an element of snobbish exaggeration to the statement, although even senior officials were not beyond declaring their leave a success if it resulted in a reduced golf handicap.[31] Besides work on the links, diaries kept whilst on leave suggest that the theatre, restaurants and tennis impinged upon officials' horizons more than brushing up on Hausa history and grammar.[32]

Nevertheless, as we shall see later, despite their lack of engagement with metropolitan training, many – perhaps the majority – of officials took their jobs seriously when they were not on leave. Statements such as that noted above from Letchworth consequently add substance to the accusation that expressions of patchy interest and complaints about poor training opportunities were attempts at hiding something more fundamental: officials' lack of ability. New recruits may simply have not been up to the intellectual tasks set them by their tutors. After all, historians have invariably argued that Furse and others in charge of recruitment held that 'character' was 'antithetical' to intellect, and that London elites obtained what they wanted in this regard.[33] Officials were, supposedly, those not destined for jobs in the City or as metropolitan civil servants, being men of the sports field rather than the classroom. Sudan was, after all, known as a country of

'Blacks ruled by Blues'.[34] The idea that officials were equipped with the robust constitution necessary for work under a sub-Saharan sun, but were lacking in intelligence, can be tied in with the works discussed in the Introduction that suggest officials were rather 'dogmatic' or unthinking in the ways they applied indirect rule.[35] Collins believes the intellectual ability of SPS officials was of a type that 'tended to encourage conformity rather than creativity, [and] duty rather than initiative'.[36]

Furse certainly did not want to appoint those unable to sacrifice idealism for realism.[37] Nevertheless, Furse – an Oxford graduate who studied Classics, peppered his work with Ancient Greek *bon mots*, and named his memoirs *Aucuparius* after a friend told him the word referred to a bird catcher of classical antiquity – argued it was the 'all round men' who combined a love of books and the outdoors who made both ideal gentlemen and colonial officials.[38] It was always Furse's intention to make the colonies economically sound and politically stable, and he believed he needed to recruit intelligent, resourceful men to realise this. Comparing the dashing exploits of the trail-blazers in eighteenth-century India to the men who had balanced the Egyptian budget, there was no competition. 'Clive and the Lawrences', Furse later recalled, 'have never meant so much to me as Milner and Cromer'.[39]

Academically, the strongest officials in Africa were those in the SPS, whom Furse had not recruited. At least 10 per cent of SPS officials had been awarded Firsts at Oxbridge, which was higher than the average proportion of Firsts awarded across the Arts.[40] SPS officials frequently contributed articles of a high standard to *Sudan Notes and Records* and other government-approved publications.[41] Nevertheless, Furse also recruited some with a clear aptitude for academic work. Frederick Parsons served in Nigeria between 1932 and 1945 before becoming Lecturer in Hausa Languages at the School of Oriental and African Studies.[42] Numerous others filled the pages of the in-house colonial publications that came in the wake of *Sudan Notes and Records*, namely *Tanganyika Notes and Records*, *Uganda Journal* and *Nigerian Field Notes*. Some officials had technical interests. The Tanganyikan DO Frank Langland wrote the 'Bible' for DCs concerned with field engineering.[43] Whilst sometimes lazy, many officials were naturally inquisitive when faced with topics in which they were interested.[44] DCs turned their hands to a bewildering variety of endeavours, including intricately detailed tribal histories, and archaeological, linguistic and geological studies.[45]

That these were men naturally interested in the pursuit of knowledge makes it difficult to assess the extent that formal training in anthropology shaped their approaches to colonial governance. Kuklick and Douglas Johnson suggest it did not have much impact upon officials in the Gold Coast and Sudan respectively.[46] Johnson argues that the reports officials compiled in Sudan bore few traces of anthropological training until the 1930s. Prior to this, ethnographic work drew on skills and information gleaned from nineteenth-century travel writers, classical geographers and historians, and from assessing Arabic legal documents, rather than from fieldwork.[47] However, officials were generally not as 'wary' of anthropology as an academic discipline as Johnson suggests.[48] Whilst officials invariably agreed with Lugard that those in the administrative services knew Africans better than anthropologists did, it only tended to be the older elites who were actively hostile to anthropologists and their work.[49] A notable example of this is the obstreperous C. A. Willis, who was opposed to Evans-Pritchard spending time amongst the Nuer in the early 1930s.[50] In fact, in contrast with officials' attitudes towards other types of 'outsiders' such as missionaries, anthropologists did not attract the same criticism. Even if officials were not *au fait* with functionalism's theoretical intricacies, they felt the discipline was important. From Sillak in Sudan's Fung Province, James Robertson wrote that 'Very little is known about the manners and customs of many of these peoples. They are out of the beaten track [*sic*], and unless one has had some anthropological training one doesn't know what to look for'.[51] When in 1936 Furse asked one Tanganyikan ADC what should remain in the Oxbridge training courses, the official suggested the three 'essentials' were law, language and anthropology.[52] After all, officials' criticism of the anthropological training received at university had been levelled at the specifics of the course content, rather than the principles that underpinned such content.[53] The points made above suggest officials retained little in terms of specifics after the fruits of the inevitable pre-exam cramming had faded, but even if they had not originally fully availed themselves of such training, officials nevertheless later defended its value.[54]

An interest in anthropology did not simply appear fully formed upon the introduction of formal anthropological training. From the very first years of the twentieth century, there were DCs working in Africa who felt that 'everyone going to live among savage tribes – soldier, engineer, civil servant, or missionary – ought to go for a short course of anthropology before he leaves England'.[55] However, particularly given that very few future officials studied anthropology as undergraduates, it would seem that it was postgraduate training that helped normalise the subject as a 'valid' discipline.[56] Many only became aware of anthropology for the first time during their training. An awareness of the discipline was, after all, unavoidable. At Oxford in the late 1930s, one SPS probationer recorded having attended twenty hours of anthropology lectures in Michaelmas Term alone, at the same time as reading a number of respected anthropological studies, such as prominent Primitive Methodist missionary Edwin Smith's classic *The Golden Stool* (1926).[57] Cambridge's 'Primitive Thought and Religion' exam in Michaelmas 1929 contained questions about totemism, lycanthropy, ancestor worship, magic and the importance of tradition in 'savage life', whilst its 'Social Anthropology' exam for Lent 1930 asked officials about age grade systems, secret societies, endogamy, matrilineal descent and marriage by inheritance.[58] As we shall see in Chapter Four, it was graduates who were increasingly comfortable with studying those they governed in great detail, and it is consequently not unfeasible to suggest that a natural curiosity was sharpened by an exposure to anthropology as a formal academic discipline.

It is important to emphasise that the anthropological studies to which officials were exposed did not condemn imperialism as something harmful that destroyed societies.[59] Anthropological works instead placed an emphasis upon African societies' adaptability in the face of cultural contact. At the start of his 1920 study on the peoples of the Gold Coast's Northern Territories, A. W. Cardinall noted that Africans will 'in no long time ... neglect and forget these hampering fetters of old-age custom which in the following pages I have endeavoured to record'.[60] Despite describing the Kassena language in exhaustive detail, Cardinall displayed no despondency at the inevitable passing of the language. Feeling it an improvement that one day all in the north would speak Moshi, he considered Kassena an archival curio of 'very small importance', something to be preserved on the page for the day it no longer existed.[61] This is perhaps unsurprising, given that Cardinall was a colonial official, but there were plenty without an administrative past who said much the same.[62] Indeed, anthropologists often publically supported imperial activity, not least because they relied on colonial states for patronage, funding and access. One of the most visible interwar anthropologists was Diedrich Westermann, Director of the International Institute of African Languages and Culture. Westermann spoke warmly of the efforts of the British in Africa.[63] He had no commitment to a primitivism that stood in the way of administrative efficiency. Westermann was the great linguistic standardiser of the interwar period. Looking at the Gold Coast, Westermann advocated the merging of the two Akan dialects, Twi and Fante, and the standardisation of Akan, Ga and Ewe. Westermann believed that this would make imperial administration easier.[64]

The prominent anthropologists to whom officials were exposed also displayed little concern that the British were damaging Africa economically. Instead, a picture often emerged of robust African societies absorbing British demands. For Meyer Fortes, writing of the Northern Territories of the Gold Coast,

> Pax Britannica, by extinguishing pillage and slave raiding, has extended the economic frontiers of the tribe to the Mamprussi country, so that young men now have no hesitation in going to farm there. That this is a purely economic expedient compatible with the institutional fabric of the community, is shown by the fact that a settler will always eventually return to his patrimony and his ritual prerogatives when he succeeds his father; and this in spite of the greater ease and higher profits of farming in Mamprussi.[65]

It is therefore unsurprising that elites and the press alike were for the most part enthusiastic about anthropologists,[66] and that Edgar Wallace's fiction depicted anthropologists as the only type of European in Africa capable of rendering assistance to officials.[67]

In addition to a training that emphasised anthropology, officials were exposed to indirect rule, particularly after 1918. However, an important point curiously neglected by historians is that domestic notions of imperial governance were not particularly detailed. Proclamations arguing that Britain's presence in Africa was essential if Africans were to be 'raised to a higher plane' were, of course, commonplace, but it was harder to find material on how precisely this righteous entity was to be administered.[68] The lectures that probationers received on this point appear to have put forward few hard and fast conclusions. This is understandable, given that the lectures had to deal with so many territories that they had to cover basic facts rather than specifics.[69] For example, in order that the history component of the Cambridge University TAS course considered British rule across the empire, the development of indirect rule in all of Africa was covered in a single lecture.[70] At any rate, indirect rule as discussed in the metropole is perhaps best thought of as a series of attitudes, rather than as a doctrine. In essence, it meant the promotion of local 'elites', with Britons remaining behind the scenes but able to step in, were such elites to break 'acceptable' codes of behaviour, or were a situation to arise that was judged beyond their capacity to successfully manage. Indirect rule was hailed as a means of maintaining societal stability whilst simultaneously allowing for the reform of those aspects of African society felt abhorrent or no longer required if Africa was to be altered for the 'better'.[71] The British were to work 'behind the scenes' so that any changes they felt necessary would be more readily acceptable to Africans.

Lectures tackling indirect rule naturally highlighted the efforts of Lord Lugard in Nigeria.[72] After his retirement from active service on the continent in November 1918, Lugard remained a highly respected commentator on African affairs. This was thanks in large part to his 1922 work *The Dual Mandate*, the most famous guide to British rule in Africa. The work sold 2,300 copies before the Second World War, earning Lugard the tidy sum of £1,094 in royalties.[73] Lugard and his publishers were mindful of the status of *The Dual Mandate* as a textbook for officials, and post-1926 officials inevitably became cognisant of his work to at least some degree.[74] In one Cambridge Michaelmas exam for probationers in 1929, one of the many questions to reference indirect rule asked, 'What do you understand by the "Dual Mandate" and how far can the conception be applied to the economic development of African territories?'[75] Whether or not they believed in it, officials left for Africa with a belief that indirect rule and the contents of *The Dual Mandate* were the starting points for all debates on governance.

Scholars have tended to argue that *The Dual Mandate* (and indirect rule more generally for that matter) was essentially a legitimisation of a British desire to seal the continent off from global change.[76] However, Lugard's text is rather imprecise in its assertions. Lugard argued that three elements needed to be in place for an African society to possess a true 'Native Administration' governed by indirect rule: a Native Authority, a Native Treasury and a Native Court. The chiefly Native Authority was preferably to be elected by a community from amongst its own, although an outsider might be necessary.[77] Officials were to assess local customs to ensure the systems developed would not be rejected because they were too dissimilar to 'traditional' practices.[78] Chiefs were to be salaried. Tax was to be collected as a single annual payment – preferably an income or hut tax – assessed by district and village headmen supervised by an official, and collected soon after harvest, with chiefs and headmen receiving a proportion of the takings.[79] The eventual aim was for half of all tax revenue to end up in a Native Treasury, which would pay the salaries of court judges, police, clerks, and so on, with any remaining funds spent on infrastructural development.[80] When it came to civil cases affecting Africans, officials were warned that they should 'recognise native law, religion and custom when not repugnant to natural justice and humanity, or incompatible with any local ordinance'.[81]

Beyond this, however, Lugard was reluctant to go further in terms of specifics. Indeed, he felt it necessary for officials to start out with a 'rough and ready' approach symbolised by a 'lack of precision' in order that the process of establishing indirect rule could be modified to suit local customs.[82] The onus was upon officials to study and to supervise. Even setting to one side the obvious room for manoeuvre that phrases such as 'repugnant to natural justice and humanity' afforded officials, Lugard's masterplan was in keeping with his claim to Girouard that 'my systems ... [are] only in gradual course of development ... In the interests of the future I would beg you to make no *absolute pledge;* leave a loophole for the experience of the future. You will find that in every agreement made by me, every title of appointment and every settlement of every kind, that I endeavoured always to do this'.[83] Girouard was Lugard's successor in Northern Nigeria, so Lugard was evidently attempting to protect the system he had established from irrevocable alterations. Nevertheless, writing about a territory as diverse as Nigeria, Lugard had to stress flexibility and regional specificity. Whilst the introduction of indirect rule was borne of economic necessity, prominent commentators such as Ormsby-Gore and Perham argued Lugard's programme was correct because such flexibility allowed it to be adapted to suit an array of local conditions.[84] Lugard's lack of precision explains the subsequent struggles that took place over the meaning of indirect rule, whereby some pushed him to be more specific in ways that suited their own agendas. Upon hearing that Lugard was preparing a new edition of *The Dual Mandate*, the Governor of Tanganyika, Donald Cameron, felt it necessary to write to Lugard, saying, 'I venture to suggest that you should emphasise the side that the duty to develop the resources of a country like Tanganyika, for example, does not lie necessarily in handing over a part of the country to Europeans; that the intervention of Europeans is not essential ... People have used your book to show, or attempt to show, that the intervention of non-natives is essential'.[85]

The other most prominent commentators concerning colonial administrations in Africa were Cameron, Hugh Clifford, William Gowers and Charles Temple.[86] Like Lugard, each had experience as part of the colonial elite in Northern Nigeria. Whilst these commentators had strong opinions about what should be done in Africa, there were constraints upon their ability to add detail to Lugard's message. The men did not always get on. Clifford and Cameron disliked Lugard's micromanagement tendencies, which they felt had created an 'unsatisfactory' *ad hoc* secretariat system.[87] Lugard broke off letter-writing contact with Cameron in the 1930s over the latter's plans for law court structures in Tanganyika.[88] Professional and personal rivalries set Gowers and Cameron against one another.[89] These battles were nevertheless largely shielded from metropolitan public view, if not from those actually out in Africa.[90] As Governor of Northern Nigeria, Henry Hesketh Bell frequently complained about Girouard in his diaries, but he was (entirely understandably) impeccably polite about his predecessor in public.[91]

Of course, a need for politeness did not in itself prevent the emergence of serious intellectual difference, although given the respect Lugard garnered, it would perhaps have been unwise to have attempted to unseat him from his throne. Once again, however, the need to produce work applicable to all of British Africa placed the intellectual initiative in the hands of officials. It would be rather repetitive to systematically examine each commentator at length, but to illustrate this point, Cameron advised that in order to establish indirect rule, officials needed to

> discover what really is the form of authority that each unit of Native society acknowledges; what indigenous institution has in the past, according to their own law and custom, regulated their society; do they accept it freely and are they ready to continue to give it their allegiance? Recollect that the allegiance of a people to a tribal head freely given and without external cause is the essence of true Indirect Administration.[92]

The end aim was for

> just government according to civilised standards, together with the moral and material well being and social improvement of the people. We must seek an ordered and systematic development of Native institutions so that they may become more attuned to modern conditions and, what is more, gradually lead the Native Authorities to realise that this must be the aim.[93]

This was about as specific as advice published in the metropole got. Commentators (and others in the metropole more generally) provided only vague imperial schematics as to what might occur beyond the establishment of Native Administrations. There was, for instance, a common belief that 'the apparent antagonism between British imperialism and colonial or dominion nationalism was not an historical inevitability but a temporary and curable disorder'.[94] There was consequently very little impetus to look ahead and try to envisage a world in which the relationship between Britain and Africa had radically altered. The idea that nationalists would be capable of developing cogent popular nationalist parties was alien. Regarding a respect for authority, senior SPS figure Harold MacMichael set the tone in his *The Anglo-Egyptian Sudan* when he wrote that the Sudanese man was 'essentially feudal in his instincts. It is, for instance, useless to approach him with abstract ideas of Liberty, Fraternity, Equality ... He has his chief, secular or religious, and expects to have to obey him and to see authority upheld'.[95] This was an update of Charles Temple's earlier view that 'without exception, the African native lives as he walks, in single file. It is necessary for his mental contentment that he should look up to a superior to himself, whom he can trust to support him in time of adversity, and that there should be others his inferiors'.[96]

Consequently, according to Lugard, African self-determination was not even 'visible on the horizon of time'.[97] Towards the end of the 1930s, the furthest commentators were prepared to go was the suggestion that 'the ultimate object of British Colonial policy is the development of the various communities of the Colonial Empire into self-supporting and self-reliant partners of the British Commonwealth of Nations'.[98] However, in Africa's case, 'self-supporting' and 'self-reliant' could be understood as 'local political responsibility' (in other words, indirect rule) and 'a balanced budget' respectively. Africans' supposed limited ability for independent development neutralised the emergence of any radical conception of the Commonwealth.

To argue that imprecision prevailed challenges the argument that there was a move from a relativistic conservatism, embodied by Lugard, to a reformist developmental mindset, embodied by Lord Hailey's *An African Survey* of 1938. Hailey's lengthy work is credited with both helping consolidate, and being indicative of, a legislative atmosphere amenable to the Colonial Welfare and Development Act of 1940.[99] It is, however, important to emphasise that *An African Survey* was actually rather tentative. Hailey did write, 'it is clear that the scheme of indirect rule has not only its unsolved problems, but some noticeable points of weakness', mainly because a 'traditional' African authority was a less efficient agent of development than a nominated and trained chief.[100] Rather than espousing universalism, however, Hailey actually couched his work in distinctly Lugardian rhetoric, claiming that 'the character of the political or cultural institutions to be adopted must be related to the capacity of each unit for development rather than to any preconceived theory of the value of institutions of European civiliza-tion'.[101] Furthermore, he argued that it would 'be rash at this stage to attempt to pronounce a final judgement on the relative value of these different systems' of governance, because Native Administrations had not yet gained much experience of governance, making it difficult to tell how suitable they would be as local representatives of the Crown. He called for the matter to be studied further.[102]

The whole work is full of such caveats, stressing the need for a flexible approach to governance in Africa rather than critiquing Lugard. In essence, *An African Survey* amounts to a suggestion that indirect rule should not be applied dogmatically without thought for local conditions.[103] In 1935, the more radical – and relatively margin-alised – historian William Macmillan, who had given advice to Hailey during *An African Survey*'s formative stages, suggested that Hailey was so cautious of offending Lugard and other establishment figures that his report would 'say nothing'.[104] True to Macmillan's prediction, many did not see anything particularly revolutionary in Hailey's work.

Instead, they felt the principal innovations of *An African Survey* were that it was a work of many collaborators, and that it considered the colonies of all European powers operating in Africa.[105]

It is nevertheless necessary to address the possibility that Lugard *et al.* provided enough detail to sow seeds of irreconcilable tension in the minds of officials, between a relativistic maintenance of the 'noble savage' on the one hand and universalist reform on the other. It has been suggested that Lugard's memos are 'riddled with logical inconsistencies and contradictions' because his 'objective was to bring the "benefits of civilisation" with as little interference as possible in African laws and customs'.[106] Cameron's views are deemed 'paradoxical' because 'Tanganyika had to be trained in, yet protected from, the ways of the modern world through indirect rule'.[107] However, it is important to emphasise that elite commentators presented their readers with programmes that attempted to pre-empt claims of inconsistency. The very 'existence' of racial types provided a clear demarcation between moral universalism and cultural relativism. For Lugard, the aim was

> complete uniformity in ideals, absolute equality in the paths of knowledge and culture, equal opportunity for those who strive, equal admiration for those who achieve; in matters social and racial a separate path, each pursuing his own inherited traditions, preserving his own race-purity and race-pride; equality in things spiritual; agreed divergence in the physical and material.[108]

In *The Dual Mandate*, Lugard added that principles 'do not change, but their mode of application may and should vary with the customs, the traditions, and the prejudices of each unit'.[109] Cameron felt that a universalistic moral code should underpin and alter localised cultural forms. The aim was to change the 'content', but not the 'packaging', of African life.[110] Cameron saw no tension in local African rulers being educated by the British, having 'no doubt at all' that the latter would not damage structures overseen by the former. If chiefs were made aware that their positions were held on trust from the British, patient and tactful officials would be able to uphold the move to civility in a manner that would not undermine the stability of the empire.[111] Others such as Clifford were of a similar mind.[112] In accord with his Mendelian belief that it was of 'vital necessity' to maintain 'the purity of race-types', Lugard claimed Africans had to remain 'rooted' in Africa because the Europeanised African of the coast was less fertile and more susceptible to disease than the 'normal' African.[113] Go ahead of what Africans were felt to be racially capable, and their society would disintegrate, but not before then. Nature itself, it seemed, sanctioned change within racially prescribed limits.

Much has been made of the contempt Britons showed for the 'half-educated', 'coastal' African. The stereotype was prominent enough to serve as the 'bad guy' in popular novels by authors such as Edgar Wallace and Leslie Chatteris. Scholars often argue this prominence was a product of Britons' hostility to change in Africa.[114] Bhabha suggests that, in the ideological construction of the 'other', colonial discourse depended on fixity. Stereotypes were therefore repeated frequently in an attempt to reassert a feeling of authority undermined by the impossibility of imperialists ever creating an 'other' who was 'civilised' but nevertheless still recognisably 'other'.[115] However, even Lugard, who is often deemed to have been amongst the most conservative when it came to the applicability of Western education to Africa, suggested that the aversion to 'half-educated' Africans was on the basis that this education ran against the racial grain. He argued that it 'cannot be said with any vestige of truth that true learning and culture is despised by the white man when exhibited by a coloured man. It is the attempt to imitate unsuitable customs, dress – and even vices – and the absence of racial dignity which excites the white man's contempt'.[116] Not all European characteristics were deemed inappropriate for the African to assimilate. Instead, what was 'good' and what was 'bad' for the African to adopt was evaluated on a case-by-case basis. The 'natives' to be most admired were those who, by combining supposedly Western values with African courtesy, came closest to 'gentlemen', whilst cads were to be criticised the most.

As a consequence, in arguing that change *per se* was not detrimental to African stability, Lugard propagated a stable vision of Africa. Others concurred with this. In 1930, *Round Table* produced an article about education in Kenya. The article concerns a Kikuyu named Justin, who was a 'pioneer'. 'Born and bred in the squalor of Africa', it reads,

> he had acquired new knowledge and applied it, he had built a home which it was a pleasure to visit, squalor had utterly disappeared, and he had made no mistakes; there was nothing of Europe but what should be there, though some things were still wanting ... I realised the length of the road he had travelled and the magnitude of his achievement, for not only had he remade Africa, but he had spoiled nothing in the process.[117]

This is not the place to assess whether such sentiments were genuine. At this stage, all that matters is that the ideas available to colonial officials contained within them conscious efforts to pre-empt charges that they had been inconsistent in their discussions about education.

Officials nevertheless engaged with non-academic material more frequently than they did the works of Lugard and his peers. It is therefore necessary to turn next to other types of sources. In spite of early twentieth-century innovations in communications technology, officials in Africa accessed metropolitan ideas in much the same way as their nineteenth-century predecessors. It was not merely African publications such as the *Sierra Leone Weekly News* that rejoiced in the capacity for radio contact with Britain to break the 'monotony' of African life.[118] Recognising a market of bored officials, the BBC believed the wireless had the ability 'to keep us in touch with the isolated man in the back of beyond to whom any contact with this country would be a very good thing'.[119] However, the technology was rolled out relatively late on in the period under consideration. For instance, it was not until 1933 when the first wireless arrived in El Obeid in Sudan.[120] Furthermore, some wireless manufacturers treated the colonies as 'a dumping ground for out-of-date and faulty stock', whilst officials' attempts to listen to British radio programmes were sometimes frustrated by bad signals.[121]

In addition, officials got little beyond basic local information from colonial newspapers. The settler publication *Tanganyika Times* came close to replicating the trenchant tone of Kenya's non-official community, but this was in strong contrast to the newspapers produced by Europeans elsewhere in Africa.[122] For instance, the *Sudan Herald* contained little beyond adverts and local event listings. There were occasionally lightly pro-Tory editorials, but in one February 1921 edition, the closest the paper came to expressing a point of view was when it hoped that, following a recent agricultural show in Wadi Halfa, 'these local shows will be developed and encouraged', particularly considering the 'historic' quality of the beetroots on display.[123]

Barring the majority of spoken exchanges between officials, now invariably lost to the historian, letters, books and newspapers sent from home to Africa were consequently the most informative sources to which officials had access. Such sources' importance was enhanced by the eagerness with which officials engaged with them, for the simple reason that they naturally afforded an opportunity to reaffirm a link with a home and a Britain (re)imagined.[124] An unreliable postal service could provide a convenient excuse for a lack of home-bound correspondence, but officials' numerous and lengthy complaints when packages from Britain were not forthcoming or were delayed is testament to a pressing psychological need.[125] As one commentator providing advice on life in West Africa noted,

> The event of the week in a place where a postal service runs is generally the mail, and oh, reader, arrange that you get a good fat budget! Write to aunts, old loves, anyone and everyone, to get answers. And, above all, have a good bandobust [arrangement] about periodicals being sent to you.

The mail means more to exiles than the exiles themselves remember, when at home.[126]

Reading was a key leisure activity, particularly when on trek.[127] Boredom heightened many officials' obsessions with keeping up with what was going on in Britain.[128] As one official later recalled to a metropolitan audience,

> You live in the midst of such cloying and indecent plenty that, apart from selecting, you are actually able to reject books. Printed matter of every kind is spurned by you as tedious, as dry, as 'unreadable'! *Printed matter*, if you please, *unreadable*! Body of Bumpus, what is this?[129]

The jocular tone does not make the sentiment less genuine. Besides personal letters, virtually all had British publications sent out to them. Most popular of these was *The Times* or its weekly digest equivalent, followed by periodicals such as *Punch* and the *Spectator*.[130] In spite of delays in getting to hear from the outside world, most had a good awareness of home news. Beyond major events such as general elections, the General Strike of 1926 and the Wall Street Crash, officials gossiped about prominent British public figures and day-to-day political machinations.[131] Writing to his parents from Mwanza in Tanganyika, Francis Dowsett was not alone in commenting that 'everyone here talks more about England than anything else'.[132]

Andrew Thompson's point of clarification that empire meant different things to different sections of British society at different times is important, but unfortunately the paper trail does not allow a detailed reconstruction of all officials' interactions with the metropole.[133] Nevertheless, imperial culture was highly generalised in content. It might be argued that this was initially fed by a prevailing air of uncertainty. In 1906, one journalist noted that 'Africa remains Europe's puzzle and Europe's danger. England, France, Germany have their African problems ... Consequently and naturally ... of the opinions expressed [about Africa] there is infinite variety'.[134] More specifically, when it came to imperial governance, in October 1901 *The Times* noted that 'No attempt has been made to ascertain what are the special conditions of the administrative problem in Equatorial Africa, no attempt has been made to formulate the general lines of a well-considered policy in dealing with that problem, and no machinery has been devised for maintaining continuity of administration'.[135] Whilst indirect rule eventually became the starting point for all debates, the popular media said very little about how colonies operated, except during certain points of controversy such as the 'Nigeria Debate' of 1916 on the role of non-British commercial interests in the colony.[136] The minority of Britons on leave who actively sought out the latest news about Africa reveal that, even had they wanted detailed information, it was difficult to come by.[137]

This lack of detail extended to discussions of race. It is commonplace to argue that officials believed in the existence of race as a biological fact that helped explain why Britons were supposedly superior to Africans.[138] There were certainly ongoing doubts as to Africans' racial capacity for substantial political responsibility. It was, after all, felt that even Egyptians had made a mess of the partial independence they had obtained in 1922, in spite of the belief that they were higher up the racial pecking order than their sub-Saharan counterparts.[139] However, the precise role Britons felt race played in shaping a person in comparison with culture and upbringing was never fixed. The interwar period saw a rise in the belief that environmental and cultural factors determined certain societal attributes and attitudes, whilst eugenics became increasingly discredited, having attracted a flush of support before 1914.[140] This shift was nevertheless a continuance of a pre-war change, whereby race was not as fervent an issue as in the late nineteenth century.[141] A strict Social Darwinism was of less importance in shaping metropolitan thinking than has previously been assumed. Beliefs were flexible to a certain degree, and were heavily influenced by everyday political and social concerns.[142] For instance, the racial 'gulf' that the media felt existed between the British and Japanese decreased considerably in the wake of the Anglo-Japanese treaty of 1902.[143] The rise of cultural racism added a further complicating factor to British conceptions of others.[144] Whilst it was commonly believed that racial heredity accounted for the majority of human traits, the continued refrain was consequently that further investigation into the matter was required.[145] Even if one's racial heritage was held to be of predominant importance before the Second World War, a belief that cultural factors might also have a role shaped the idea that anyone was malleable to some degree. Thus, the continued existence of race as a biological 'truth' did not foreclose the possibility of Africans being changed. On the contrary, it was this mixture of 'nature' and 'nurture' that enabled the blend of change and stasis that underpinned what Lugard and his peers deemed to be internally coherent programmes of reform.

In anticipation of Chapter Five's focus on officials' perceptions of economic development in Africa, it is worth spending a little time on metropolitan ideas about industry. Martin Wiener's well-known argument is that a conservative hostility to industrial innovation powered by ruralism was an important check upon British economic growth.[146] This exaggerates both the numerical significance of the public commentators who expressed such ideas and the extent to which the public agreed with them. The chief exponents of the idea that through industrialisation Britons were losing what it meant to be British, such as William Inge, Dean of St Paul's from 1911, were in fact marginalised individuals whose doctrines were widely felt antithetical to British progress.[147] Attitudes towards industry epitomised a moderation long felt one of Britons' most prominent and likeable collective characteristics.[148] Criticisms of modern industry and commerce were not indictments of these activities *per se*, but instead arguments in favour of the moderation of such activities in order that they not undermine a culture's essential elements. That this was felt possible owes something to prominent commentators of the day, such as Arnold Bennett, who championed the appurtenances of everyday living as evidence of British innovation.[149] The notion that the products of industrialisation could be put to the service of the nation received a boost after the First World War, when machines were imbued with a romantic edge, courtesy of popular images that, for example, turned aviators into knights of the sky. A spiritualised technology was deemed able to perpetuate, rather than to undermine, pre-industrial attributes of the nation.[150]

However, whilst officials may not have emerged from an environment as implacably opposed to industrialisation as Wiener believes, they were not given guidance as to how they might harness any willingness to develop Africa economically, or indeed whether industrialisation was of benefit to Africa. Officials were not trained by anyone who dealt with such matters, and the available literature on the topic was scant. Officials could not move for commentators declaring that a generic economic development of Africa was removing the fetters of supposedly barbaric practices. Nevertheless, the closest the metropole came to providing officials with economic advice was with regards to agricultural trade, rather than industry, and even then such advice was the preserve of isolated preachers.[151] Ex-ICS official Charles Strickland is the key example of this. Strickland was committed to the introduction of cooperative societies, whereby small-scale farmers were advanced credit for the purchase of agricultural tools, seeds and the like, and were placed in charge of marketing their own produce as small communities.[152] However, given that he was concerned with the introduction of such societies across the empire, even Strickland could not provide much in terms of specifics particularly applicable to Africa.[153]

Metropolitan commentators also gave no firm guidance on how precisely Britons were expected to act when working as 'pioneers' on the frontiers of empire. Firstly, there were different ideas about how identity, masculinity and empire should intersect. On the one hand, there was the need to embrace the physicality of one's existence, with struggle and competition valorising the life of the individual by allowing the realisation of one's potential. Officials may have agreed with Curzon that life on the 'outskirts of Empire' would provide 'an ennobling and invigorating stimulus for our youth saving them alike from the corroding ease and morbid excitements of western civilization'.[154] On the other hand, there was a belief that centuries of a Burkean accretion of custom and practice had served to lift the West away from the apes and into the arms of the angels.[155] These layers of sentimental sediment included respect for crown and empire, the 'rules of the game', and the realisation that order and progress were needed. It was, after all, Britain's gradual evolution and (invoking Walter Bagehot) its populace's deferential respect for hierarchy that had supposedly allowed Britannia to perpetuate its global eminence, thereby avoiding the fate of the temperamental Mediterranean powers.[156] Amongst other mechanisms, schoolmasters encouraged team games, convinced that these acted as a form of social control (enabling young men to take out tensions in 'legitimate' struggles with one another) and social cohesion (reinforcing notions of camaraderie and fair play).[157] These games, commentators felt, were important because they made 'as much as possible of the side and as little as possible of the individual'.[158]

The metropolitan gentlemanly ideal was to strike a balance between these two competing elements, with a natural virility grounded and controlled by a moral code and an internalisation of self-restraint. Nevertheless, attempts at normalising behaviour ran up against the images of determinedly idiosyncratic imperial heroes to which officials were continually exposed. All British imperial heroes, from the supposedly quintessential muscular Christian General Gordon to the colder, martial General Kitchener, were recognised as individualistic, making their mark on the empire as a direct result of their *sui generis* qualities.[159]

The metropole was consequently unable to provide a clear vision of how to reconcile the desire to develop one's individuality as a means of self-realisation with the fulfilment of one's obligations to society. Of the many examples that could have demonstrated this, the one selected is the proclamations of Stanley Baldwin. Baldwin's ruminations on England and Englishness were carefully constructed acclamations of moderation that attempted to shepherd the Conservative Party into the world of universal suffrage and the mass media.[160] In an era where the relationship between individual and community was changing, Baldwin felt Britain's maintenance of stability and global pre-eminence was fraught with difficulty. He depicted the 'work in progress' project of democracy as resting on a knife's edge between falling into the 'licence' and 'chaos' of liberty on one side, or the 'tyranny' of conformity on the other.[161] Baldwin spoke of Britons' duties, rather than rights, with the act of service the means of reconciling the individual and the community.[162] Regarding the individual, he argued that Britons needed to cling to their 'diversified individuality', claiming 'we [must] never allow our individuality as Englishmen to be steamrollered'.[163] Regarding community, Baldwin placed schooling at the heart of English life for its being 'part of the binding force' that united all in a common purpose and a sense of duty.[164] How might these comfortably sit alongside one another? How much by way of personal preference was to be surrendered in the service of one's country? The problem was left unresolved. It might seem churlish to complain that Britons had no final answer to this, for the simple reason that modern society does not either. The fact remains, however, that there were significant gaps in the metropolitan advice given to officials about how they were expected to act.

Conclusion

Furse's efforts to change the training recruits received were not entirely in vain. Training exposed an increasingly intelligent corps of young men to anthropology for the first time. However little this exposure provided in terms of specific knowledge applicable to officials' own districts, as we shall see in Chapter Four, the normalisation of anthropology as a discipline helped alter the ways they went about their work in Africa. Nevertheless, recruits did not leave Britain armed with a precise idea about what their job entailed. Officials learnt to love the empire without learning how. This was due in part to the recruits, and in part to the training they received. Some attending postgraduate training courses were disinterested, but all of them were faced with a curriculum that was broad, and with content that was non-specific and placed the emphasis upon the intellectual endeavours of the official. The British Empire was relatively decentralised politically; in the African case at least, it was also intellectually decentralised. This was due in part to the need of those writing about imperial governance to maintain good public relations with one another, and in part to their attempts to make their ideas applicable to all of British Africa.

In addition, officials' training did not critique Lugard by embracing the developmental rhetoric that would shape the ethos of the post-1945 colonial state. However, that officials were exposed to imprecise ideas should not lead us to assume that officials registered in such ideas an irreconcilable tension between universalistic reform and a relativistic conservation of an African status quo. As for British culture more generally, beyond enduring enthusiasm for empire, little guidance was given as to both how officials were to act, and how far they were able to use race in understanding those whom they had to govern. Before we examine how such ideas (or, rather, the lack of them) were applied in Africa, it is necessary to turn next to officials' relationships with each other.

Notes

1 Furse, *Aucuparius*, p. 151
2 Antrobus to C. W. Daniels, L. W. Kershaw, E. Harris, W. R. Dunstan, 12 May 1908, NA CO 96/476; W. Golant, *Image of Empire: The Early History of the Imperial Institute* (Exeter: University of Exeter Press, 1984), pp. 23–4
3 R. Surridge, 'Salad days in Tanganyika', in Kirk-Greene (ed.), *Glimpses of Empire: A Corona Anthology* (London: I. B. Tauris, 2001), p. 283; see also Sillery, 'Working backwards', RHO Mss.Afr.r.207/41
4 R. L. Antrobus to W. J. Simpson, 31 January 1908, NA CO 96/476
5 'African Tropical Service Course: syllabus of lectures on procedure, evidence and criminal law', [Colonial Office memo, May 1908], NA CO 96/476; see also Dundas, *African Crossroads*, p. 11
6 Minutes of sixth meeting of African Tropical Services Committee, 12 December 1907, NA CO 96/476
7 The present author consulted the fifth edition of the work; *The West African Pocket Book: A Guide for Newly-Appointed Government Officers* (London: Crown Agents for the Colonies, 1920)
8 A. C. G. Hastings, *Nigerian Days* (London: John Lane, 1925), p. 2; see also Langa Langa [H. B. Hodge], *Up Against It in Nigeria* (London: Allen and Unwin, 1922), p. 8
9 Following the unification of the Colonial Service in 1932, the course was opened to cadets serving 'East of Suez' and renamed the Colonial Administrative Service Course; Heussler, *Yesterday's Rulers*, p. 133
10 Davies, *Camel's Back*, p. 9; D. Johnson, 'Political intelligence, colonial ethnography, and analytical anthropology in the Sudan', in H. Tilley and R. J. Gordon (eds), *Ordering Africa: Anthropology, European Imperialism, and the Politics of Knowledge* (Manchester: Manchester University Press, 2007), pp. 314–15
11 Jeffries, *Colonial Empire*, p. 136; Gardiner, 'Sentinels of empire', p. 72
12 Letchworth, interview, RHO Mss.Afr.s.2112/4
13 Letchworth, interview, RHO Mss.Afr.s.2112/6
14 W. Tripe to parents, 7 May 1929, RHO Mss.Afr.s.868/1/50
15 G. Bell to parents, 17 September 1931, SAD 697/4/15; see also Kenrick to parents, 24 January 1937, SAD 647/5/21
16 Daniell, diary, 18 October 1937, SAD 777/13/9
17 Kirk-Greene, 'Forging a relationship', p. 73
18 On Ormsby-Gore's attitude towards technology in the colonies, see A. Briggs, *The History of Broadcasting in the United Kingdom* (London: Oxford University Press, 1965), Volume Two, p. 380
19 In 1935, there were 808; see *The Dominions Office and Colonial Office List for 1935*, ed. A. J. Harding and G. E. J. Gent (London: Waterlow and Sons, 1935); *Quarterly List of the Sudan Government 1st January, 1935* (Khartoum: Sudan Government Press, 1935)
20 This is calculated as follows: a total of 155 officials attended, of whom 101 served in the six territories noted above. Coincidentally, 101 of all officials were administrative personnel, the others being from colony's departments of Education, Customs, and so on. Assuming an even ratio of administrative officials to non-administrative

officials irrespective of colony, this leaves sixty-six administrative officials from the six territories; *Oxford University Summer School on Colonial Administration: St. Hugh's College 3–17 July 1937* (Oxford: Oxford University Press, 1937), pp. v–vi

21 For instance, the seven members of the Gold Coast service attending the summer school in 1937 included the Assistant Secretary for Native Affairs and the Chief Commissioner of the Northern Territories among their number; Colonial Secretary, Accra, to Ritchie, 10 April 1937, PRAAD CSO 18/1/134; see also Colonial Secretary, Accra, to E. Swinton, 4 May 1938, PRAAD CSO 18/1/134

22 Colonial Secretary Circular 10/38, 21 February 1938, PRAAD CSO 18/1/134

23 Bell, *Shadows on the Sand*, p. 16

24 Newbold to Perham, 4 July 1938, in Henderson, *Modern Sudan*, p. 85

25 *Ibid.*

26 Only thirteen of the thirty-one talks concerned British Africa; *Oxford University Summer School*, passim

27 Hesketh Bell, 'Oxford and the colonies', *The Times* (12 July 1937), p. 15

28 'Lecture 2: Summer School July 9 1938', RHO Mss.Perham.242/1/30; 'Lecture 1: Summer School July 1938', [delivered 2 July 1938], RHO Mss.Perham.242/1/4

29 'Lecture 2: Summer School July 9 1938', RHO Mss.Perham.242/1/17–18

30 Newbold to Kennedy-Shaw, 21 April 1934, in Henderson, *Modern Sudan*, pp. 62–3. Emphasis in original

31 Lea, diary, 15 September 1932, in C. A. E. Lea, *On Trek in Kordofan: The Diaries of a British District Officer in the Sudan, 1931–1933*, ed. M. W. Daly (Oxford: Oxford University Press, 1994), p. 219

32 A. Weatherhead, diary, 6 May–14 November 1913, RHO Mss.Afr.s.1638/9; C. R. Walker, diary, 11–18 September 1916, RHO Mss.Afr.s.435/9–10; Walker, diary, 1 January–16 April 1918, RHO Mss.Afr.s.438/1–32

33 See, for example, Kirk-Greene, 'Scholastic attainment and scholarly achievement in Britain's Imperial Civil Services: the case of the African governors', *Oxford Review of Education* 7:1 (1981), 17; Kuklick, *Imperial Bureaucrat*, p. 21

34 'Blues' refers to the awards given for sporting prowess at Oxbridge; see, for instance, Spender, '"Old Blues" oust the slaves', p. 8

35 Snow, *'The Masters*, p. 22; see also Collins, 'Sudan Political Service', 296; Crowder, 'The white chiefs of Tropical Africa', in Gann and Duignan (eds), *Colonialism in Africa 1870–1960 Volume 2: The History and Politics of Colonialism 1914–1960* (Cambridge: Cambridge University Press, 1970), p. 324; Gann and Duignan, *Rulers of British Africa*, p. 230; Kirk-Greene, 'Scholastic attainment', 11

36 Collins, 'Sudan Political Service', 296

37 Such decisions were being made when the role of 'intellectuals' in public life was under relatively intense metropolitan scrutiny; Collini, *Absent Minds*, ch. 4

38 Furse, *Aucuparius*, p. 15; Furse to Milner, 18 June 1919, RHO Mss.Brit. Emp.s.415/1/2/14. Despite enlisting the help of a classics scholar, Furse was unable to track the term *Aucuparius* down, but liked the sound of it nevertheless; Furse, *Aucuparius*, pp. 4, 9

39 *Ibid.*, p. 11

40 Kirk-Greene, 'Sudan Political Service', 37; this undermines Collins, 'Sudan Political Service', 296

41 B. Hamad, '*Sudan Notes and Records* and Sudanese nationalism, 1918–1956', *History in Africa* 22 (1995), 239–70; J. A. de C. Hamilton (ed.), *The Anglo-Egyptian Sudan from Within* (London: Faber and Faber, 1935)

42 P. J. Jaggar, 'Obituary: Frederick William Parsons', *Bulletin of the School of Oriental and African Studies* 58:1 (1995), 109–12

43 F. Longland, *Field Engineering* (Dar es Salaam: Government Printers, 1935)

44 On laziness, see B. W. Savory, diary, 10 August 1934, reproduced in Heussler, *British Tanganyika*, p. 97; see also Chapter Three.

45 See, for instance, J. Griffiths, '210: snuff taking and the use of nose clips in Buha, Tanganyika Territory', *Man* 34 (1934), 185–6

46 Kuklick, *Imperial Bureaucrat*, p. 56; Johnson, 'Political intelligence', pp. 309–35

47 Johnson, 'Political intelligence', pp. 315–17
48 *Ibid.*, p. 328
49 Newbold to F. Cottrell, 29 October 1933, in Henderson, *Modern Sudan*, p. 57. Lugard was also disdainful of anthropologists, and was chastised accordingly by the Colonial Office; A. Fiddian and C. Strachey notes, 13 November 1913, NA CO 96/538
50 D. Johnson, 'Evans-Pritchard, the Nuer, and the Sudan Political Service', *African Affairs* 81 (1982), 231–46
51 J. W. Robertson to mother, 7 December 1931, SAD 531/3/16
52 Bradley to Furse, 12 February 1936, RHO Mss Brit.Emp.s.415/6/1/10
53 Daniell, diary, 18 October 1937, SAD 777/13/9
54 Regarding a lack of knowledge of specific details concerning Africa, see Davies, *Camel's Back*, p. 7; Dundas, *African Crossroads*, p. 11
55 L. Portman, *Station Studies* (London: Longmans, 1902), p. 56
56 Kirk-Greene, 'Sudan Political Service', 36
57 Of the twenty lectures, eight were with the Structural Functionalist Alfred Radcliffe Brown, five were with Evans-Pritchard, and seven were with Margery Perham; Daniell, diary, 11 October–3 December 1937, SAD 777/13/10–17
58 'Colonial Service Probationers Examination, Lent Term 1930: Social Anthropology', in RHO Mss.Brit.Emp.s.364(1)/3; 'Colonial Service Probationers Examination, Monday, December 2, 9½–12½: Primitive Thought and Religion', in RHO Mss.Brit. Emp.s.364(1)/6
59 There is an ongoing debate as to the degree to which anthropologists did or did not underpin imperial power; the following section is concerned only with anthropologists' public pronouncements; for a brief outline of this debate, see Bush, *Imperialism and Postcolonialism* (Harlow: Pearson, 2006), p. 129
60 A. W. Cardinall, *The Natives of the Northern Territories of the Gold Coast: Their Customs, Religion and Folklore* (London: Routledge, 1920), p. xi
61 *Ibid.*, p. 115
62 Such as M. J. Field, government anthropologist in the Gold Coast from 1937 to 1944; Kuklick, *Imperial Bureaucrat*, p. 50; see also J. R. Wilson-Haffenden, *The Red Men of Nigeria* (London: Seeley, Service & Co., 1930)
63 Westermann, *The African To-day* (London: Oxford University Press, 1934), pp. 30, 331
64 Westermann, 'A visit to the Gold Coast', *Africa* 1 (1928), 107–11; see also 'Common script for Gold Coast languages: report by Professor D. Westermann', [1927], CO 96/675/11; S. Newell, *Literary Culture in Colonial Ghana: How to Play the Game of Life* (Manchester: Manchester University Press, 2002), p. 64
65 M. Fortes, 'Culture contact as a dynamic process: an investigation in the Northern Territories of the Gold Coast', *Africa* 9:1 (1936), 42
66 Westermann to Lugard, 20 March 1928, RHO Mss.Afr.s.1150/6/30; W. Gowers to Amery, 26 September 1927, RHO Mss.Afr.s.1150/6/19; 'Babel in Africa: the barriers of language, a way through', *The Times* (18 December 1928), p. 15; Westermann, *African To-day*, pp. 7, 165
67 Wallace, *Again Sanders*, pp. 84–5. This is not to suggest that anthropologists all argued that Africans would not face difficulties in adjusting to cultural contact. However, those who noted such difficulties invariably did so in tones redolent of Elspeth Huxley's novel *Red Strangers*. In spite of a lengthy period of adaptation, Africans would ultimately be reconciled with Western ways; Thurnwald, 'The social problems of Africa', *Africa* 2 (1929), 130–4; Thurnwald, 'Social systems of Africa', *Africa* 2 (1929), 238–42; J. E. T. Philipps, 'The tide of colour: II. – Pan-Africa, anti-white or not? The economic remedy', *Journal of the African Society* 21 (1922), 312; E. Huxley, *Red Strangers* (1939; London: Penguin, 1999), pp. 198–204, 405–6
68 For example, see C. Lucas, *The Partition and Colonization of Africa* (Oxford: Oxford University Press, 1922), p. 173
69 'Cambridge University Tropical African Services Course', [1929], in RHO Mss.Brit. Emp.s.364(1)/50
70 'Cambridge University Tropical African Services Course: Syllabus of Lectures – History', [1929], in RHO Mss.Brit.Emp.s.364(1)/27

71 Cameron, 'Native Administration in Tanganyika and Nigeria', *Journal of the Royal African Society* 36 (1937), 9; see also 'Colonial governor: Sir Donald Cameron's memoirs', *The Times* (24 February 1939), p. 22

72 'Cambridge University Tropical African Services Course: Syllabus of Lectures – History', [1929], in RHO Mss.Brit.Emp.s.364(1)/27

73 Publisher's statements in RHO Mss.Lugard 29/3/1–34

74 See Lugard, *Representative Forms of Government and "Indirect Rule" in British Africa; Being an Extract from the Text-Book Edition of the 'Dual Mandate'* (Edinburgh: Blackwood and Sons, 1928)

75 'Colonial services probationers exam Thursday, December 5', [1929], in RHO Mss. Brit.Emp.s.364(1)/1

76 In addition to the works noted in the Introduction, see, for example, Hyam, *Britain's Imperial Century, 1815–1914: A Study of Empire and Expansion* (1976; Basingstoke: Macmillan, 1993), p. 269

77 F. Lugard, *The Dual Mandate in British Tropical Africa* (Edinburgh: Blackwood and Sons, 1922), p. 220

78 *Ibid.*

79 *Ibid.*, pp. 236–7, 242–3, 250

80 *Ibid.*, pp. 200–1

81 *Ibid.*, p. 536

82 *Ibid.*, p. 252

83 Quoted in M. Bull, 'Indirect rule in Northern Nigeria', in K. Robinson and F. Madden (eds), *Essays in Imperial Government* (Oxford: Blackwell, 1963), p. 51

84 S. Berry, 'Hegemony on a shoestring: indirect rule and access to agricultural land', *Africa* 62:3 (1992), p. 329; Daly, *Darfur's Sorrow: A History of Destruction and Genocide* (Cambridge: Cambridge University Press, 2009), p. 123; L. S. Amery and Ormsby-Gore, 'Problems and development in Africa', *Journal of the African Society* 28 (1929), 335–6; M. Perham, 'A re-statement of indirect rule', *Africa* 7 (1934), 334; see also Cameron, 'Governor's tour through Mwanza Province: Report', [1928], NA CO 691/100/20/10

85 Cameron to Lugard, 22 October 1925, RHO Mss.Lugard.9/1/10

86 Cameron was Governor of Tanganyika (1925–31) and Nigeria (1931–35); Clifford was Governor of the Gold Coast (1912–19), and Nigeria (1919–25); Gowers was lieutenant-governor of Northern Nigeria and Governor of Uganda (1925–32); Temple was Resident in Bauchi, Kano and Sokoto, and lieutenant-governor of Northern Nigeria (1914–17)

87 A. J. Harding minute, 9 January 1920, NA CO 583/78; see also S. J. S. Cookey, 'Sir Hugh Clifford as Governor of Nigeria: an evaluation', *African Affairs* 79 (1980), 532, 537–8; M. Crowder, *West Africa under Colonial Rule* (London: Hutchinson, 1968), p. 169; Gailey, *Clifford: Imperial Proconsul* (London: Collings, 1982), p. 105

88 Cameron to C. Bottomley, 28 September 1933, NA CO 583/191/3/23; Perham, *East African Journey* (London: Faber & Faber, 1976) pp. 209–10

89 Cameron to Lugard, 20 April 1930, RHO Mss.Lugard.9/1/52; Cameron, *My Tanganyika Service and Some Nigeria* (London: Allen and Unwin, 1939), p. 34

90 See, for instance, Lugard, 'Northern Nigeria', *Geographical Journal* 1:23 (1904), 5–6, which disproves Gann and Duignan, *Rulers of British Africa*, p. 27

91 Hesketh Bell, diary, 21 July 1909, BL Add Mss 78721/50; Hesketh Bell to home, 26 December 1909, BL Add Mss 78721/92; Hesketh Bell to home, 14 February 1910, BL Add Mss 78721/106; Hesketh Bell, 'Recent progress in Northern Nigeria', *Journal of the African Society* 10:10 (1911), 377

92 Cameron, 'Native Administration', 10

93 *Ibid.*, 15–16

94 Darwin, 'Imperialism in decline?', 679

95 H. MacMichael, *The Anglo-Egyptian Sudan* (London: Faber & Faber, 1934), p. 240

96 Temple, 'Northern Nigeria', *Geographical Journal* 40:2 (1912), 160

97 Lugard, *Dual Mandate*, pp. 197–8; see also W. Hailey, 'Nationalism in Africa', *Journal of the Royal African Society* 36 (1937), 146

 98 Jeffries, *Colonial Empire*, p. 224
 99 M. Havinden and D. Meredith, *Colonialism and Development: Britain and its Tropical Colonies, 1850–1960* (London: Routledge, 1993), p. 167; A. O. Nwauwa, *Imperialism, Academe and Nationalism: Britain and University Education for Africans 1860–1960* (London: Frank Cass, 1997), pp. 35–100; Roberts, 'The imperial mind', pp. 63, 66, 76
100 Hailey, *An African Survey: A Study of Problems Arising in Africa South of the Sahara* (London: Oxford University Press, 1938), pp. 537–8
101 *Ibid.*, p. 247; see also *ibid.*, pp. 1207, 1280, 1290
102 *Ibid.*, p. 542
103 Regarding 'dogma', see Hailey, 'Some problems dealt with in the "African Survey"', *International Affairs* 18:2 (1939), 202
104 Bush, *Imperialism, Race and Resistance*, p. 263
105 'Africa surveyed', *The Times* (8 November 1938), p. 15
106 Bush, *Imperialism, Race and Resistance*, p. 34
107 J. D. Graham, 'Indirect rule: the establishment of "chiefs" and "tribes" in Cameron's Tanganyika', *Tanzania Notes and Records* 77 (1976), 3; see also, Crowder, *West Africa*, p. 171
108 Lugard, 'The colour problem', *Edinburgh Review* 233 (1921), 283; see also Lugard, *Dual Mandate*, p. 87
109 *Ibid.*, pp. 193–4; see also Lugard, 'Studying our primitive races', *Daily Telegraph* (30 July 1934), p. 8
110 Cameron, *The Principles of Native Administration and their Application* (Lagos: Government Printer, 1934), pp. 5, 8
111 Cameron, 'Native Administration', 15
112 Clifford, 'United Nigeria', *Journal of the African Society* 21 (1921), 4–14; see also R. Slater, 'The Gold Coast of to-day', *Journal of the African Society* 27 (1928), 321–8; MacMichael, *Anglo-Egyptian Sudan*, p. 101
113 Lugard, 'The colour problem', 269; Lugard, *Dual Mandate*, pp. 79–80
114 F. M. Mannsaker, 'The dog that didn't bark: the subject races in imperial fiction at the turn of the century', in D. Dabydeen (ed.), *The Black Presence in English Literature* (Manchester: Manchester University Press, 1985), pp. 118–19; L. Chatteris, *The Holy Terror* (1932; London: Hodder and Stoughton, 1940), pp. 121, 145, 151
115 Bhabha, *Location*, pp. 66–88, quote at p. 66
116 Lugard, 'The colour problem', 283; see also A. S. Rush, 'Imperial identity in colonial minds: Harold Moody and the League of Coloured Peoples, 1931–50', *Twentieth Century British History* 13:4 (2002), 383
117 'An experiment in African education in Kenya', *Round Table* 79 (1930), 570, 572
118 *Sierra Leone Weekly News* (1 December 1934), cited in Briggs, *History of Broadcasting*, Volume Two, p. 393
119 *Ibid.*, Volume Two, p. 372
120 Newbold to mother, 28 July 1933, in Henderson, *Modern Sudan*, p. 52
121 Quote from Briggs, *History of Broadcasting*, Volume Two, p. 409; Duncan-Johnstone, diary, 24 June 1933, RHO Mss.Afr.s.593/2/7/23
122 'The superficial aspect', *Tanganyika Times* (30 March 1928), p. 7; 'Educating the native', *Tanganyika Times* (9 March 1928), p. 7; 'Native policy', *Tanganyika Times* (30 March 1928), p. 20; 'Administrative officers again', *Tanganyika Times* (7 October 1927), p. 4; 'S. O. S.: settlers or slaves', *Tanganyika Times* (24 December 1927), p. 4
123 Quote from 'Halfa notes', *Sudan Herald* (26 February 1921), p. 3; 'Labour situation', *Sudan Herald* (7 May 1921), p. 2; 'Cost of labour', *Sudan Herald* (25 June 1921), p. 2
124 For instance, see the response to Francis Brett Young's *My Brother Jonathan* in B. McDonnell Dee, diary, 1 March 1930, SAD 890/3/56
125 One recently retired official deemed the desire for mail 'a significant pathological phenomenon'; W. Crocker, *Nigeria: A Critique of British Colonial Administration* (London: George Allen & Unwin, 1936), p. 196
126 Field, '*Verb Sap.*', p. 81

127 H. Childs, diary, 9 July 1933, RHO Mss.Afr.s.1861(1)/I
128 Percival to mother, 7 August 1930, RHO Mss.Brit.Emp.s.364(5)/15
129 Portman, *Station Studies*, p. 47; emphasis in original.
130 Percival, diary, 6 September 1930, RHO Mss.Brit.Emp.s.364(2)/27; Percival to mother, 4 September 1930, RHO Mss.Brit.Emp.s.364(5)/28; F. Dowsett to mother, 30 August 1931, RHO Mss.Afr.s.1276/6; Bell to parents, 16 November 1936, SAD 698/1/48; J. V. Shaw, diary, RHO Mss.Afr.s.357/*passim*; R. A. Roberts to D. Roberts, 15 July 1917, RHO Mss.Afr.s.1348/16
131 Dowsett to mother, 5 November 1931, RHO Mss.Afr.s.1276/23; W. H. Beeton, diary, 4 October 1935, RHO Mss.Afr.s.1608(9); Beeton, diary, 19 November 1935, RHO Mss.Afr.s.1608(9)
132 Dowsett to parents, 19 August 1931, RHO Mss.Afr.s.1276/4
133 Thompson, *The Empire Strikes Back?*, *passim*
134 S. Dark, 'The pick of the bookstall', *Daily Express* (24 December 1906), p. 4
135 'The administrative problem in Equatorial Africa', *The Times* (1 October 1901), p. 11
136 P. J. Yearwood and C. Hazlehurst, '"The affairs of a distant dependency": the Nigeria debate and the Premiership, 1916', *Twentieth Century British History* 12:4 (2001), 397–431
137 J. F. E. Bloss, 'The experiences of a medical inspector', 15 November 1948, SAD 704/1/5
138 See, for instance, Bush, *Imperialism, Race and Resistance*, ch. 3
139 'Egypt: the background of negotiation', *Round Table* 102 (1936), 267, 269; A. C. McBarnet, 'Egypt and judicial reform', *Quarterly Review* 509 (1931), 46–62
140 E. Barkan, *The Retreat of Scientific Racism: Changing Concepts of Race in Britain and the United States Between the World Wars* (Cambridge: Cambridge University Press, 1992), pp. 23–34, 138–40; D. Stone, *Breeding Superman: Nietzsche, Race and Eugenics in Edwardian and Interwar Britain* (Liverpool: Liverpool University Press, 2002), p. 93
141 R. H. Macdonald, 'Reproducing the middle-class boy: from purity to patriotism in the Boys' Magazines, 1892–1914', *Journal of Contemporary History* 24 (1989) 519–39
142 P. Crook, 'Historical monkey business: the myth of a Darwinized British imperial discourse', *History* 84:276 (1999), 633–57
143 Editorial, *Morning Post* (8 October 1904), p. 6; 'Japan's ambition', *The Globe* (29 November 1904), p. 1; C. Holmes and A. H. Ion, 'Bushido and the Samurai: images in British public opinion, 1894–1914', *Modern Asian Studies* 14:2 (1980), 309–29
144 Bush, *Imperialism, Race and Resistance*, ch. 1
145 Westermann, *African To-day*, pp. 18–19, 39, 324; L. W. LaChard, 'The correlation of finger impressions and racial characteristics', *Journal of the African Society* 19 (1919), 61–2; J. Huxley, 'Racial chess', *Cornhill Magazine* 69 (1930), 541, 546–8; R. A. C. Oliver, 'Mental tests in the study of the African', *Africa* 7 (1934), 46
146 M. Wiener, *English Culture and the Decline of the Industrial Spirit 1850–1980* (1981; Harmondsworth: Penguin; 1985), *passim*, quote at p. 154; see also C. Barnett, *The Audit of War: The Illusion & Reality of Britain as a Great Nation* (London: Macmillan, 1986), *passim*, especially pp. 11–18
147 For opposition to Inge, see 'Dean Inge on progress', *The Times* (28 May 1920), p. 13; '"All stark mad together." The blindness of Dean Inge', *The Times* (31 July 1922), p. 6; A. Fox, *Dean Inge* (London: J. Murray, 1960), pp. 139–49
148 'Rural planning', *The Times* (10 April 1926), p. 11; J. Stobart, 'Building an urban identity: cultural space and civic boosterism in a "new" industrial town: Burslem, 1761–1911', *Social History* 29:4 (2004), 493, 495; see also J. Lawrence, 'The transformation of British public politics after the First World War', *Past and Present* 190 (2006), 185–216
149 G. Gould, 'Arnold Bennett: his rank in fiction', *The Observer* (29 March 1931), p. 14; G. Lafourcade, *Arnold Bennett: A Study* (London: Frederick Muller, 1939), pp. 51, 63; see also 'Plato's slave: mechanical man', *The Observer* (16 October

1927), p. 16; Lord Gorell, 'Tradition and change', *Quarterly Review* 537 (1938), 16–26; A. Bingham, *Gender, Modernity, and the Popular Press in Inter-war Britain* (Oxford: Clarendon Press, 2004); P. Readman, 'The place of the past in English culture c.1890–1914', *Past and Present* 186 (2005), 147–99

150 G. Mosse, *Fallen Soldiers: Reshaping the Memory of the World Wars* (1990; Oxford: Oxford University Press, 1991), pp. 66, 101; see also Bienhard Rieger's excellent '"Modern wonders": technological innovation and public ambivalence in Britain and Germany, 1890s to 1933', *History Workshop Journal* 55 (2003), 153–71

151 Any number of sources could have been selected to demonstrate this; H. Samuel, 'Sir Herbert Samuel on the Empire Conference', *News Chronicle* (2 October 1930), p. 6; M. L. Dawes, 'The late German colonies in Africa', *Quarterly Review* 459 (1919), 476–7; A. P. Newton and J. Ewing, *The British Empire since 1783: Its Political and Economic Development* (London: Methuen, 1929)

152 C. F. Strickland, 'Co-operation for Africa' *Africa* 6:1 (1933), 15–26

153 Strickland, 'Cooperation and the rural problem of India', *Quarterly Journal of Economics* 43 (1929), 500–31

154 Lord Curzon, quoted in A. M. Windholz, 'An emigrant and a gentleman: imperial masculinity, British magazines, and the colony that got away', *Victorian Studies* 42:4 (1999), 631

155 For Disraeli's 'apes and angels' speech, see 'Mr. Disraeli on the Church of England', *Caledonian Mercury* (29 November 1864), p. 3

156 W. Bagehot, *The English Constitution* (Oxford: Oxford University Press, 2001), p. 6; 'So far, so good', *The Times* (28 March 1919), p. 13; 'Students of socialism', *The Times* (31 August 1923), p. 9; W. Frewen Lord, *The Lost Empires of the Modern World* (London, Richard Bentley and Son, 1897), pp. 10, 25–6

157 *Rules and Bye-laws of the Western Ridge Sports Club, Accra* (Accra: Government Press, 1918), in PRAAD CSO 25/1/7; J. A. Mangan, 'Grammar schools and the games ethic in the Victorian and Edwardian eras', *Albion* 15:4 (1983), 313–35

158 B. Darwin, *The English Public School* (London: Longmans, 1929), p. 27; see also Heussler, *Yesterday's Rulers*, p. 78

159 Johnson, 'The death of Gordon'; K. Surridge, 'More than a great poster: Lord Kitchener and the image of the military hero', *Historical Research* 74:185 (2001), 298–313

160 P. Williamson, *Stanley Baldwin: Conservative Leadership and National Values* (Cambridge: Cambridge University Press, 1999), ch. 7

161 S. Baldwin, 'Our freedom is our own' (1934), in *This Torch of Freedom: Speeches and Addresses* (London: Hodder and Stoughton, 1935), p. 20; Williamson, *Stanley Baldwin*, p. 205

162 Williamson, *Stanley Baldwin*, p. 218

163 J. Stapleton, 'Political thought and national identity, 1850–1959', in S. Collini, R. Whatmore and B. Young (eds), *History, Religion and Culture: British Intellectual History, 1750–1950* (Cambridge: Cambridge University Press, 2000), p. 265

164 Baldwin, 'Piety and freedom' (1931), in *This Torch of Freedom*, p. 304

CHAPTER THREE

Individualism, intrigue
and *esprit de corps*

In order to get a better sense of their mental landscapes, this chapter will consider the ways officials engaged with one another. Officials' memoirs stress a unity of purpose, sometimes as a precursor to collective self-aggrandisement. 'Generally speaking', wrote one retired Nigerian official,

> the type of men recruited into the colonial administration after the First World War were strong, courageous leaders of men with a gift for organisation and 'man management', the type, in short, who were required for the pacification of turbulent tribes, the administration of primitive peoples and the gradual building up of a strongly-based government on modern lines.[1]

The claim goes that particularly following the standardisation of their backgrounds under Furse, officials developed *esprit de corps*. Seeing themselves pitched against anti-imperialism and postcolonial ignorance of empire, retired officials' memoirs often unite all from across a colony, or even British Africa as a whole, in brotherly altruistic duty. Kirk-Greene has accepted such claims.[2] Drawing upon other sources created retrospectively, Heussler and Gann and Duignan concur with Collins that 'ultimate devotion to their mission embodied in themselves transcended whiskey gossip'.[3] Collins agrees with the well-established notion that it was an all-pervasive public school ethos of service that created the '*esprit de corps* which bolstered the provincial polo team' that proved 'equally applicable in organizing an African road gang or supervising the construction of a bridge'.[4] Furthermore, because the men got on with one another, they were better able to face Africa, more confident in the knowledge that no one was going to let the side down administratively (with esoteric ideas) or racially ('going native').

This chapter will suggest otherwise. Instead, the official corps was fragmented along a number of axes. Fault lines were created by differences in age, place of work and personal interests. Driven by the belief that they each knew best, officials' criticisms of one another were frequently generated by concerns about the efficacy of the colonial state. However, because of the highly personalised nature of colonial rule, criticism of other officials as professionals easily slipped into criticism of other officials as individuals. This was underpinned by the manner in which officials interacted (or did not interact) with each other. Living insular lives governed by immersive work, officials were often simultaneously ignorant of, and hostile to, those outside their own districts. In addition, officials were torn between a need for a certain amount of socialising with other Europeans as a means of maintaining their well-being on the one hand, and a desire to live as pioneers on the other. Officials with the strongest pioneer impulse resented the presence of others as an impediment to the realisation of this vision. Amongst those more at ease with frequent socialising as a respite from work, limited social horizons and endless gossip nevertheless created feelings of constraint. This is not to say that officials were incapable of forming genuine bonds of friendship with others. It does, however, demonstrate that the vision of life as a pioneer ultimately proved more powerful than a public school emphasis upon team spirit and white solidarity.

We will start with the relationships between officials from different colonies. Feeling it would lead to improvements within their own administrations, elites provided officials with the opportunity to learn about other areas of Africa. Government offices across the colonies groaned with works concerning imperial administration, anthropology and language. In 1932, the central office in Kaduna in Northern Nigeria had over 300 books for officials to consult, as well as periodicals and gazetteers.[5] Whilst the majority of these works concerned Nigeria, besides general books on Africa as a whole, the library contained fourteen on North Africa, two on Sudan and eight on East Africa.[6] Not a high proportion, but they were at least available.[7] Nevertheless, when officials read about Africa, they inevitably chose works concerned with their own backyards. When officials read travel works, Nigerian officials turned to Mungo Park and Hugh Clapperton, whilst SPS men turned to Sir Samuel Baker, Bertram Thomas and Charles Doughty.[8] Officials in West Africa read works by Mary Kingsley.[9] When it came to anthropology, those in the Gold Coast read official-turned-ethnographer R. S. Rattray, whilst those in Sudan read studies by elite SPS man and amateur ethnographer Harold MacMichael.[10]

Such intellectual localism is entirely understandable, particularly in light of the arguments to be made in Chapter Four about officials' search for information about their own working environments. It did, however, help foster insularity. Occasional (relatively) strong-selling works such as Julian Huxley's *An African View* could puncture this tendency by dealing with more than one colony.[11] In contrast to their reflections upon works dealing with their own territories, officials' responses to studies of other regions nevertheless suggest these were not given a great deal of thought.[12] At any rate, officials preferred to spend their evenings reading fiction, letters or newspapers, or writing home, rather than learning about a different colony, or even a different part of their own colony. It was frustration with such parochialism that led Arthur Creech Jones and Andrew Cohen to devise *Corona* in 1948 as a platform for sharing ideas between administrators, something that the earlier, albeit more general, *Crown Colonist* evidently failed to do.[13]

Ignorance about what occurred elsewhere largely prevailed. Colonial officials' attitudes were shaped by two forms of insularity: *operational* insularity (the scope and content of their work) and *social* insularity. Firstly, we have to consider the demands of the job in hand. Overseeing a region's political, economic and social life was an all-consuming and exhausting business.[14] One official serving in Tanganyika would later recount that, when on leave, he was reminded of 'how detribalised one became when one is completely wrapt up in district, in a job, in the personalities with whom one is in everyday contact'.[15] This occurred quickly. After only two weeks in his job, one official wrote from Bauchi that, 'It does not take long to become entirely accustomed to this life and immersed in the ordinary day to day routine'.[16] Although officials would not have welcomed the comparison, there are evident parallels here with other European communities in Africa, such as the Kenyan settlers.[17]

There were enormous disparities between the ways elites and officials interacted with their peers elsewhere in Africa. Elites were frequently transferred between colonies.[18] They were directly tied into wider personal networks across the empire as both an administrative necessity and a means of career advancement. In addition, it was the administrative tier immediately below the very highest elites, rather than officials, that invariably undertook the fact-finding missions to other parts of Africa. From Edwardian Northern Nigeria, it was a Resident who toured the West African coast, Egypt and Sudan collecting information on education.[19] It was Sudan's Assistant Director of Intelligence who visited northern Nigeria in the 1920s to study indirect rule *in situ*.[20] Those of similar rank jointly investigated Mahdism in Nigeria and Sudan, and shared ideas on courts between Uganda, Tanganyika and Sudan.[21] Those working in non-administrative departments often undertook a good deal of research in other colonies.

For instance, medical services staff engaged in extensive tours across Africa to determine best practice on disease control.[22] In contrast, whilst elites wanted officials to learn of other places, they limited officials' physical movement between colonies because they chose to prioritise having men on the spot versed in a single colony's idiosyncrasies. Even after the unification of the administrative services in 1932 had made it much easier for elites to transfer new officials from colony to colony if necessary, most DCs spent their professional lives operating within a single administrative system.[23]

If officials came into contact with their counterparts from other colonies in their working lives, it was for brief periods of time, such as at boundary commission meetings or when rectifying subsequent border disputes.[24] Some temporary re-posting occurred during the wars of 'pacification' when officials were loaned to neighbouring British colonies to bolster numbers, whilst during and immediately after the Great War some switched to staff the new administrations in ex-German territories.[25] The figures involved in both actions were nevertheless relatively small. In the case of Tanganyika, the earliest officials instead tended to be military men who had seen combat in German East Africa, and who had decided to stay in the area. It was fresh recruits, rather than existing officials from elsewhere, who gradually augmented their numbers.[26] This is not to suggest that officials were totally ignorant of other parts of Africa. After all, as Chapter One argued, a rudimentary understanding of the continent helped influence where young men applied. It is, however, important to stress the limits of their knowledge even after officials had commenced service in Africa. Officials' relative state of insularity was in part a result of the spheres within which they worked.

We turn next to social insularity. Elites attempted to foster a 'healthy' amount of inter-colonial rivalry and a 'healthy' intra-colonial camaraderie simultaneously. By moving officials around within a colony, elites rejected the overwhelming significance Lugard attached to continuity of administration.[27] Instead, elites tried to ensure that officials prioritised the bigger colonial picture over local particularism or regionalism, although staffing shortages meant regular relocation was not always possible.[28] Large amounts of money were spent on clubs to bind Europeans together. In 1925, Accra gave the Chief Commissioner of Asante £1,600 for a 'European Club' to be built in an unused part of Kumasi Fort.[29] Additionally, in introducing recreational facilities such as clubs and sports grounds, colonial elites were concerned with more than simply officials' physical health. Following the lead of their superiors in London, they used team games to try and encourage intra-colonial camaraderie via managed interactions with other services, such as inter-colonial tennis tournaments, and the annual inter-service cricket matches between Nigeria and the Gold Coast that began in 1926.[30] This was a common colonial feature.[31]

In spite of their attempts at social engineering, elites were nevertheless unable to control how officials regarded each other. Hostility often took the place of friendly rivalry. Having reached the rank of Lieutenant-Governor of the Northern Provinces of Nigeria, Herbert Goldsmith retired from the service in 1921, but remained heavily involved in imperial organisations. In 1931, Goldsmith wrote to the Governor of the Gold Coast, Alexander Ransford Slater, wanting his blessing for the establishment of a West African Association. The plan was to promote greater camaraderie by replacing colony-specific dinners with functions open to all who served in West Africa.[32] Although personally amenable to the idea, Slater replied that he doubted whether the 'rank and file' would agree to such a plan.[33] The Director of the Gold Coast's Medical Services, Dr W. J. D. Inness, provided the reason, stating that 'those officers who have served in one Colony only do not care a hoot in hell about the other ... in fact they generally have an active dislike for people coming from another Colony'.[34] Another senior Gold Coast official warned Slater that a similar association that existed in East Africa was full of infighting, which supports Perham's claim of 1930 that 'officials [in that region] in general are almost all bitter about the administration beyond their own frontiers'.[35] In spite of support from prominent figures such as Cameron, the scheme for a West African Association did not get off the ground.[36]

Elites hoped that the introduction of a unified appointments system in 1932 would see such antagonism falling away over time, but it was enduring.[37] Officials looked down on those from services they felt inferior to their own, and disliked those who in turn looked down on them. In the place of firsthand experience of other officials' working environments, these sentiments were instead shaped by the pecking order discussed in Chapter One. As officials learnt more about Africa from their journey out onwards, a fuller hierarchy became apparent to them. In West Africa, Northern Nigeria was followed in order by Southern Nigeria, the Gold Coast, Sierra Leone and The Gambia.[38] In East Africa, the pecking order was more flexible, but Sudan tended to trump Uganda, whilst officials from both looked down on the Tanganyikan upstart.[39] This hierarchy was based on an awareness of the relative size of the services, the seniority of each colony's governor and the proportion of what little domestic press attention each colony received. When officials from different services met at occasional boundary meetings, the ensuing brief glimpse into the lives of others seemingly confirmed these hierarchies.[40]

Whilst a state of insularity may have in part been a by-product of officials' working environments, for those officials who travelled out to Africa from Britain, self-segregation and animosity often commenced before arrival. Ships undertaking the voyage to Africa were divided places. Bored and fuelled by a large amount of alcohol, officials complained not only about the quality of their accommodation, but also about other passengers.[41] There were social divisions between missionaries, traders and officials. Seeking a quiet journey, some railed against the 'idiots with an unhealthy longing after sports and other turbulent forms of amusement'.[42] It can also be assumed that Gold Coast official Angus Duncan-Johnstone's propensity for playing the bagpipes every day he was at sea did little to endear him to fellow passengers travelling out to service in West Africa.[43]

More importantly, new recruits had relatively little opportunity to bond with their counterparts from other colonies, being encouraged by old-timers to stick to their 'own kind' from the first voyage out onwards.[44] These colony-specific groups were then maintained on subsequent journeys, as photographs of officials taken in April 1919 onboard the RMS *Elmina* between Liverpool and West Africa demonstrate.[45] This was consolidated by visible expressions of affiliation to a particular colony, such as the different coloured cummerbunds worn to dinner.[46] Observing these cliques, a doctor heading out on the SS *Mendi* to join the West African Medical Service in 1913 noted how officials 'from the Gold Coast condescended towards those from Sierra Leone, Nigerians were grave and dignified as befitted the largest colony ... Officials from the other colonies thought Nigerians gave themselves airs more befitting an Indian pro-consul'.[47] Judging that they looked upon one another with 'equal contempt', the ship's purser knew never to put officials from different colonies at the same table.[48] Surviving signed menu cards testify to this division.[49] On East African journeys, officials were less segregated from each other, but they nevertheless tended to associate by territory.[50]

Whilst officials associated themselves with a colony, they did not necessarily associate themselves with the other officials working within that colony. We now turn to five potential causes of intra-colonial conflict. These are regional and governmental diversity, age, nationality, officials' different working priorities, and the conflict between individualism and the need for a social life.

We will first examine regional and governmental diversity. However much an annual cricket match may have briefly united a small portion of a service in pursuit of collective victory over another service, it was unable to bond officials who had long operated in different ways and environments. One example is of officials who served in the north and south of Nigeria after the unification of 1914. Those serving in the north felt sorry for, or hostile towards, those working in the south. Charles Walker was an official in the north with very limited experience of the south and its officials. In 1918, he wrote in his diary that

'You live in mud-houses in an atmosphere of dirt and dignity, you tie a horse to a tree and draw two and six a day – that is Northern Nigeria.' I do not know who was responsible for the above but give me the 'dirt and dignity' every time after what I have heard from Dew Hughes and Dodds about some of the persons and places in the Southern Provinces.[51]

This was reciprocated in kind. Neil Weir had identified with southern Nigeria from the very start of his time in the colonial service in 1925. He thoroughly enjoyed the work.[52] In 1928, Weir went on local leave to Zaria, where he 'had the opportunity to see the running of a big Northern Province Native Administration Emirate'.[53] He was unimpressed. 'One noticed', he commented,

how out of touch the administrative officer was with the native. He always seemed to be hob-nobbing with the 'big man'. I had the impression that an A.D.O. was quite satisfied with himself when he had satisfied the louder noises in the Hausa world. Naturally, the dignity, good manner and picturesque life is bound to inspire one and lead one into the happy opinion that everything is alright. I wonder if it is. The Admin[istrative] Officer seemed rather aloof from the details of Native Administration.[54]

This animosity was such that elites new to the region were quick to pick up on it, whilst even civil servants back in London occasionally got involved and took sides.[55]

There were real grounds for such differences.[56] Broadly speaking, officials in the two regions were used to different systems of governance. Officials in the south were more accustomed to working with councils of African elites or groups of policymakers, than with a single emir or paramount chief, as was the norm in the north.[57] In addition, unified Nigeria had three secretariats, helping to perpetuate a pre-unification feeling of administrative distinctiveness.[58] As I. F. Nicolson has suggested, 'Easily the most remarkable thing about Lugard's "amalgamation" of Nigeria is that it never really took place'.[59] The Charles Walker complaint about 'dirt and dignity' also suggests that a clash between northern and southern Nigeria was a product of localised pockets of gossip.

However, it seems that this conflict was fundamentally rooted in a battle over what constituted 'authentic' Africa. Officials wished that they themselves experienced whatever this was, and feared that others in Africa were having a more 'authentic' experience. This explains why those in the north chose to frame the south, with its urban cinemas, neat avenues and governor's luncheons, as over-civilised, even though many southern officials' experiences were just as rural as those of their northern counterparts. Conversely, feeling that they too were living in an 'authentic' African environment, southern officials chose to question the political authenticity of their northern contemporaries' experiences, marred as these were by a supposed disinclination to engage with all levels of African society.

Conflict also had its roots in colonial and London elites' belief that different types of men were needed in different parts of Africa. Men were not allocated to districts at random. If a provincial governor knew a newly appointed official coming out, he might see to it that they were appointed to his province, as was the case in Moshi in Tanganyika in the 1920s.[60] More frequently, those in charge of recruitment asked governors for details on the type of officials they were looking for to fill each post.[61] Men could therefore be posted to areas in which it was felt they would be of particular use. One example is southern Sudan, where a distinct and well-known group of officials called the 'bog barons' emerged. Khartoum was generally more worried about the potential for peoples of the south to rise against the British than those of the north. Long wars of 'pacification' in the south were punctuated by anti-European violence of sufficient ferocity to disturb post-1918 visions of a smooth, inexorable move towards the routine of law and order. Particularly disturbing was the murder of the much-admired Captain Vere Fergusson ('Fergie Bey') near Lake Jorr in December 1927.[62] The Nyuong were blamed, and subjected to punitive strikes from both ground patrols and the Royal Air Force.[63] Such violence meant that, even as it was posting increasing numbers of graduates elsewhere, Khartoum maintained its policy of filling southern posts with those military men who remained in Sudan.

Unsurprisingly, a distinct military ethos disdainful of the 'soft' ways of the north developed.[64] The 'bog barons' viewed themselves as akin to paramount chiefs of their regions, and were more hostile to their superiors than any other group of officials in British Africa.[65] This was especially the case since, unlike their northern counterparts, the 'bog barons' were not required to do a period of service in Khartoum.[66] Elite figures' belief that there was a pressing need for military men in the south receded towards the end of the 1920s, but any attempts by Khartoum to dismantle the 'bog baron' ethos were subsequently hampered by civilian SPS officials' self-interest.[67] Once acquainted with the Condominium, civilians sometimes became unwilling to serve in the south because to gain a good knowledge of the region's customs and languages would have involved extended tours. Officials would have had to abandon the yearly leave they were able to enjoy in the north.[68] The self-interest of both the imperial state as a collective entity, and of individuals, had a part to play in shaping division.

In the 1920s, southern Sudan was unique amongst the regions covered in this study in terms of imperial violence. Nevertheless, an elite propensity for recruiting people to places they were felt suited was the norm across British Africa both before and after the First World War. For example, those deemed best able to cope when not surrounded by other Europeans were naturally more likely to be chosen to go out to the most rural areas.[69] Even the most self-absorbed of elites, such as Hesketh Bell in Uganda and later Northern Nigeria, were alert to the problems likely to emerge if men were sent to places to which they did not feel temperamentally suited.[70] This was entirely reasonable from the point of view of maintaining officials' psychological health, but it nevertheless proved a further barrier to the unification of officials through social contact. For instance, giving 'bush' DCs time away from African urbanity seems to have merely reinforced their disinclination to return to the socialising whirl of the city.[71]

A second source of tension was the changes in recruitment discussed in Chapter One. The change to civilian recruitment angered many, the speed at which it occurred amplifying the feeling of differentiation. Believing in the virtues of the 'old Sudan school and the old Sudan generation', James Currie, the first Director of Education in Sudan, wrote to Furse in 1935 that the SPS had 'deteriorated woefully ... thanks to the selectors concentrating on a peculiarly conventional type of school prefect'.[72] He said much the same, albeit a little more politely, in public speeches.[73] Currie's distaste for younger administrators was shared by many of an older generation whose service spanned both Edwardian and post-Edwardian eras, such as William Gowers.[74] The Governor-General of Sudan, Reginald Wingate, had tried to delay the Edwardian demilitarisation of Sudan's government. Furthermore, he preferred to promote military officials over the heads of civilian officials.[75] That the majority of elites in both East and West Africa acted this way is perhaps unsurprising, given that so many of them had previously served in the Royal Engineers or Royal Artillery.[76] There were exceptions to this, although there were specific reasons for these. For example, as Governor of the Gold Coast, Hugh Clifford was not opposed to this change in recruitment, but this can be explained in part by an unusual personal conflict with the Chief Commissioner of the Northern Territories, Captain Cecil Armitage, which prompted Clifford's 1917 complaint against 'colourless and old' officials.[77]

Nevertheless, because so many of the military officials were older than civilian officials, differences in age played their part in stoking this tension. Imperial elders bristled when younger officials aired their convictions and clashed on matters of policy.[78] They felt graduates lacked both experience of the 'real' world and the deferential demeanour thought a natural product of military training.[79] The difference between the old and the new was brought into sharper relief by the presence of a younger generation of military men in the colonies, such as members of the West African Frontier Force (WAFF). Such military types were a visible reminder to elites of what the African official corps might have comprised, had London not altered its recruitment policies.[80]

Some elite military and administrative figures did at least try to smooth over such differences.[81] Nevertheless, younger military men disliked civilian officials, and were disliked in return. The problem was such that the ability of graduates to command the respect of military men loomed large in Edwardian London's recruitment decisions.[82] This division was part of a broader tendency. For instance, for one official talking of the WAFF men, it came 'as a shock to see one with a newspaper in his hand: it somehow never occurs to you that they can read'.[83] Nevertheless, the idea of two monolithic generations – one military, the other civilian – needs qualifying. Evidence suggests that some who commenced service at the start of the 1920s felt it hard to relate to those who commenced service at the end of the 1920s.[84] Furthermore, with most of the post-1918 entry having fought in the Great War, some older military officials' portrayals of younger civilian officials as weaklings became more muted, but generational differences continued.[85] This was for three principal reasons. Firstly, in order to emphasise their experiences as imperial trailblazers, older officials – military and civilian alike – regaled younger men with doubtlessly exaggerated stories of earlier colonial life. This helped make new recruits feel they were of a different era. In 1932, R. E. H. Baily, the Provincial Governor of Kassala, informed new SPS recruits that, upon arrival in Sudan in 1909, he and the rest of his cohort had been informed that they 'couldn't hope to get in touch with the people or earn their respect unless they took an Arab wife'. This, and stories like this, led new recruits to marvel at how quickly times changed.[86] The 'old coasters', whose grim stories had so delighted Mary Kingsley on her first journey to West Africa in 1893, show this tendency was not a new phenomenon.[87]

Secondly, that those pre-1914 officials who remained in Africa after 1918 were now elites meant they were set apart socially and institutionally from new recruits. Officials did not socialise with a provincial governor or resident in the same way as they socialised with a fellow DC. Lastly, young men were changing. New recruits were of a generation increasingly inclined to mock a particular type of empire-building and a particular type of empire-builder. At one end of the spectrum, Zoltan Korda's film version of *The Four Feathers* gently mocked late-Victorian imperialists as boorish buffoons.[88] This was part of a broader trend, embodied by David Low's Colonel Blimp character, which first appeared in the *Evening Standard* in 1934. At the other, Lytton Strachey's *Eminent Victorians* frustrated polite society with its less-than-flattering portrait of General Gordon.[89] Criticism of figures such as Cecil Rhodes also became more vigorous, particularly in the 1930s.[90] Younger officials, delighting in figures such as Strachey, criticised those previously only assailed from the left-wing margins. During his time at university, John Daniell read an unflattering biography of Gordon. Daniell consequently went out to Sudan already armed with the idea that Gordon had been unsuited to the task of imperial governance.[91] This notion remained anathema to an older generation of both officials and metropolitan commentators.[92]

Some newcomers criticised their superiors in a similar manner to Korda or Low. The 'stupidity' of older officials was highlighted, and they were sarcastically labelled 'gallant'.[93] When looked at collectively, older officials were sometimes disparaged as 'mostly retired military gentlemen' inferior to their juniors in the manner they executed their duties.[94] Such conflicts were, it seems, not limited to Africa.[95]

We now turn to officials' national identities as a potential source of division. Imperial service in Africa did not effect a hybridisation of identities to the same extent as in India. Officials went out to Africa for the most part knowing that it would never become their home. They invariably became emotionally connected to Africa, but as a result of their hostility to white settlers, officials had little interest in living in the Highland regions deemed acceptable for long-term European inhabitation. Officials accepted the metropolitan argument that they would not be bound to the continent *en masse* as 'Anglo-Africans'.[96] More pre-1914 officials remained in Africa upon retirement than post-1918 officials, but this was a minority activity across both periods.[97]

Service in Africa washed away feelings of national affiliation in some and replaced it with something pan-imperial, however vaguely this was defined. For SPS official Basil Duke, 'I cannot but realise that I am more of a citizen of the Empire than of England'.[98] However, whilst service in Africa led officials to feel some disconnection from Britain, most did not stop identifying with their place of origin. Andrew Dewar Gibb's 1937 work *Scottish Empire* considers the IBEAC, which boasted Sir William Mackinnon, Sir John Kirk, Sir Donald Stewart, A. L. Bruce and Sir George Mackenzie amongst its directors. Dewar Gibb recounted the anecdote that, when in Kenya with a party of officials, Mackenzie declared 'Thank God we are all Scotsmen here'.[99] As a Scottish nationalist, Dewar Gibb used imperial servants to further his agenda of demonstrating Scotland's national distinctiveness and ability. However, absence from Scotland certainly sharpened an identi-fication with it.[100] Coming during a period of what John Mackenzie has called a 'Scots cultural awakening', this identification sometimes led to the institution of Caledonian Societies, such as in Uganda in 1907, the Gold Coast in 1920 and Tanganyika in 1923.[101] Scottish elites actively participated in these societies' events. At a Caledonian Society dinner in Uganda at the start of the 1930s, William Gowers gave a speech in which he suggested the protectorate was the 'Scotland of Africa' because it was a small country 'inhabited by tribes of great intelligence and enterprise'.[102]

Nevertheless, officials' national identities do not appear to have been a major source of conflict. Tensions seem to have been caused more by a dislike of an individual than by a dislike of the nation from which the individual hailed. This conclusion is a tentative one, demonstrated more by an absence of evidence to the contrary than by its existence. William Gowers was a Scotsman disliked by some. Known to Britons in Uganda as 'Wicked Willy', Gowers could disturb polite social relations by being 'very rude and very unpleasant to us poor mutts ... he was frightfully rude'.[103] Additionally, whilst some merely labelled his attitude 'dry', there were ongoing questions about what his enemy Cameron referred to as Gowers' 'moral laxity (in more directions than one)',[104] principally regarding unmarried women. Others noted he was 'remarkably able, though lazy'.[105]

Much the same can be said of an Irish example. Maurice de Courcy Dodd served as a clerk with the Royal Niger Company at the end of the nineteenth century. Hailing from Kerry, he spoke Gaelic and had links with members of the Gaelic League. In other words, on paper he was precisely the sort elites would have rather wished to avoid recruiting.[106] He looked out for and identified with the other Roman Catholics in his region, and had a wry, detached take on imperial affairs. Talking about an attack on a military official in Northern Nigeria, for instance, he noted that 'the chief of the village apologized and as we had killed 10 of his men without any loss to ourselves we accepted the apology'.[107] De Courcy Dodd nevertheless held the same racial and pro-imperial attitudes as his English peers, but still regis-tered a sense of separateness from his colleagues.[108] Friction appears to have been generated more by de Courcy Dodd's being a teetotaller, and consequently missing out on an important aspect of colonial life, than by his nationality.[109]

In making this conclusion, we are reliant on the letters de Courcy Dodd unfailingly wrote to his mother every week. It is possible that de Courcy Dodd drank, but hid this, highlighting differences between himself and his English peers as a means of reassuring his mother of his impeccably abstemious credentials. The limitations of what the source material can tell us are evident. However, even if we are once again reliant on their own testimonies, it appears as if those who came from Australia and New Zealand did not register any hostility on account of not being from the mother country.[110]

There were other types of social and cultural difference that do not appear to have generated significant hostility. The present author could find no examples of religious division causing animosity between officials. Indeed, in contrast to discussions about missionaries and African religiosity, private religious reflections appear remarkably rarely in officials' letter and diaries.[111] In addition, the fine social gradations created by officials' *almae matres* do not appear to have generated division.[112] The colonial services were not absent of snobbishness. Hesketh Bell was obsessed with proper 'breeding', and looked down on Northern Nigerian Resident William Wallace for being a 'self-made

Figure 2 Scottish connections: St Andrew's Dinner, Khartoum, 30 November 1933

man'.[113] Nevertheless, such attitudes were not present in the papers of the DCs examined for this study. Given officials' relative homogeneity in terms of social background, this is understandable.

It is therefore important to note that the aforementioned ruptures between small groups of men do not in themselves mean *esprit de corps* could not have existed. After all, even if one was a younger official opposed to the ways and attitudes of an older generation, or one was serving in the south of Nigeria and did not take to one's counterparts in the north, there were others with whom one could get on. Some ties of friendship or, at least, temporary conviviality, were indeed formed.[114] Officials may also have felt an affiliation with a broader community of men whom they had never met. At this stage in proceedings, then, it is still possible to argue that, in spite of a perhaps surprising level of conflict, camaraderie won the day.

In considering this, we turn next to the everyday working environment as a source of tension. Friction with those in one's immediate vicinity generated tension of greater everyday significance than the regional differentiation discussed above. The Great War was felt to have handed a career advantage to those who remained 'safely' in Africa instead of serving on the Western Front. There was, according to one Nigerian official,

> a feeling that was extant when I came out [in 1928] ... between those officers who had been in their [Imperial Institute] training when the war started, but who nevertheless were sent out in 1915 – and between those who served through the war and came out as ex-soldiers afterwards ... it soon became apparent that to us the [sic] – very much juniors then – that there was a good deal of feeling. After all, the war-joiners had something like four, five, six years seniority over those of their same age who had come out after the war, having done war service. And there is no doubt, I think, that there was a great deal of ill-feeling as a result.[115]

Veterans of the First World War, such as James Elliot in Entebbe, also registered ill-feeling.[116] This was part of a broader dislike of officials felt to have been promoted over the heads of others without 'paying their dues'. Amongst elites, resentment was aimed at those drafted in from outside the colony and given the most important jobs in the secretariat.[117] Amongst officials, resentment was aimed at those who became provincial governors through supposedly suspect means. In spite of his remarkably diverse and energetic career, DCs gossiped that the bagpipe-playing Duncan-Johnstone had married Gold Coast Governor Gordon Guggisberg's niece in order to get ahead.[118]

The way officials went about their work, and their responses to how others went about theirs, created friction. As is well known, officials frequently came to see themselves as the 'father' of their people, benevolent yet firm when the African 'child' was unruly.[119] Some clearly anticipated that those outside of Africa would be surprised by the extent of this identification. For one Edwardian official writing home from Northern Nigeria, 'I dare say you find it hard to understand how much one gets attached to these absurd black people'.[120] Officials nevertheless attached a good deal of importance to what they thought was a reciprocal recognition of a father/son bond. For instance, officials took the indigenous names given to them by Africans as confirmation of their status as governor or overseer of a region.[121] Officials' memoirs invariably mention the bonds of friendship maintained with African elites into retirement. As officials saw it, that African leaders gained no political advantages from remaining friends with a retired Briton was testament to the genuine nature of such bonds.[122] Officials knew the development of such relationships was an important element of governance, but felt the resultant ties were nevertheless real.[123] Officials consequently came to verbal blows over the impact of neighbouring officials' actions upon their own regions, as external observers such as Perham observed in Tanganyika.[124]

At the same time, officials were fiercely defensive of their own actions. This was a natural consequence of the diversity of officials' preoccupations. What interested officials, and how they chose to interact with Africa, was varied. Some enjoyed overseeing road building, some were concerned with bringing in revenue, whilst others were primarily interested in anthropological study.[125] For some of the time, this variety was not problematic and, once again, officials later attempted to minimise the importance of such divergences. For one retired Nigerian official,

> Many used to say that the great thing was to have a succession of people posted through a small Division. You would have your keen P.W.D. type and you would get magnificent roads and chaotic Treasuries. Then to follow him before the auditor arrived you would have a chap who would be keen on Treasury work who would satisfy the auditor, who perhaps by then might not be able to get there because the roads were worn out … if you could switch them around sufficiently and things didn't fall to bits in the meantime, you had quite a good division.[126]

However, differing priorities did cause problems. When tinkering with Native Administrations, one Nigerian DC noted 'most of the difficulties are caused by too frequent changes of staff, for everyone approaches the problem in a different way and from a different angle'.[127] The combination of officials' paternalism and such differences in interests led them to resent others working with 'their' Africans after having left a posting for pastures new. Officials felt discrepancies undid their own efforts. On returning to Africa after leave, an official in southeast Nigeria was appalled to find that the DC who had taken his place 'paid more atten-tion to the development of roads and buildings than to the ruthless suppression of disorders'.[128] Conversely, DCs complained about the state in which their predecessors had left districts.[129] As a consequence, being posted to a newly created station frequently pleased officials because they were 'not bound by any predecessors' ideas'.[130]

Another fault line was how far officials applied themselves to their work. Public discussions of empire emphasised the dynamism and hard-working nature of Britons abroad. *The Times'* correspondent who accompanied Kitchener's men to Sudan commented that 'the presence of energetic British officers here [Wadi Halfa], as in many other waste places of the earth where we have the outposts of our Empire, has introduced civilization and prosperity', which was in contrast to the 'slovenliness of the East'.[131] This image was later updated, with one DC's wife painting a favourable picture of her husband's generation of civilians in Tanganyika by emphasising that they had more 'drive' than the older military officials.[132] Besides boosting the image of officials back home, laying emphasis upon hard work in the colonies could also have rewards, such as an increased chance of promotion. Nevertheless, castigating what one ADC referred to as 'those energetic blokes', some officials displayed laziness as a visible badge of pride.[133] One official in Tanganyika in the 1920s reported 'with a smile that he never had less than a hundred [Treasury queries regarding accounts] a month and that he already had six months' supply in his drawer which he had not attempted to answer'.[134] Overt or not, such 'wasters' who 'didn't care tuppence' for their work naturally secured the immediate disap-proval of those who were more energetic.[135] Similarly, those felt too lax or too firm with Africans risked being labelled 'a public danger' by their peers.[136] Each official's belief that their attitudes to governance in Africa were right helped create an imperial system made up of a series of unilateral relationships between officials and Africans, rather than a collective European experience of governance.

Although officials felt superior to each other in terms of their ability, they were quick to covet others' living conditions.[137] Clifford toured Nigeria soon after becoming Governor there in 1919. Clifford's report of the tour noted that, whilst officials in the north were

> for the most part fairly contented, in spite of the fact that they are infamously housed, and regard this as a serious grievance, the majority of the officers in the Southern Provinces, who have watched the ameni-ties of their lives steadily deteriorating, and rightly or wrongly believe themselves to have received less consideration than has been shown to their brother officers in the Northern Province, are a very disgruntled set of men.[138]

At other points in time, officials in the north were under the impression that living conditions were better in the south.[139]

Most significant in causing tension, however, was the clash between officials' need to socialise with other Europeans and their wish to be individualistic. Most sought after some form of social life for their psychological well-being, and complained when personal differences prevented them forming social bonds. In 1906, one official in Northern Nigeria felt he was at times surrounded 'by nothing but natives, at others by a few Europeans with not one of whom one has the slightest taste or sentiment in common'.[140] Some interwar officials felt likewise.[141] The frequency with which officials sought company nevertheless differed. Crudely, officials belonged to one of two camps. There were those who rejected a continual stream of social functions, resenting time spent in the city when they could be living as a pioneer. Then there were those who embraced socialising, feeling the act of reproducing metropolitan social norms was a routine means of surmounting and temporarily escaping everyday African life. Some officials alternated between the two, but in different ways both attitudes created pressure that chafed with officials' ultimate pursuit of individualistic experiences.

'Bush' DCs invariably rejected the pomp and pageantry of the secretariat wallah. They were nevertheless happy to have a certain degree of interaction with other Europeans out in the bush, particularly at the start of a tour when advice was most eagerly sought after.[142] However, this changed once affairs settled into a routine. 'Bush' DCs required 'just enough and not too much society and entertainment', but a visiting official could quickly turn into a guest who had overstayed his welcome.[143] Europeans were welcomed to a bush station for only as long as it took them to administer an invigorating reconnection with home by proxy, at which point they were rejected for breaking the 'rhythm of existence' of life as a pioneer.[144] By providing an inconvenient reminder of those likewise engaged, the very presence of others detracted from an official's ability to act as an imperial frontiersman. Similarly, whilst officials may have resented visits from their superiors because this detracted from their ability to get on with their jobs, they also resented the temporary diminution of their individuality.[145] It was usually felt that maintaining a certain bearing in front of Africans was a part of the job, but stiff formality and continual scrutiny from superiors was an unwelcome additional process of performance. In comparison, when travelling to Kassala in 1910, an SPS official noted, 'Absence of company delicious. Delightful being amongst men uncivilised enough to be natural'.[146] This type felt it necessary to be away from other Europeans in order to live up to their ideal of what it meant to be an official. Individualism was all-important.

Figure 3 The joy of the safari: SPS official C. A. Lyall on a successful hippopotamus hunt, 23 March 1910

This desire to act as pioneer was particularly prevalent amongst those selected for service in Tanganyika. Some of these men had wanted to go to the mandate because its status as a recent addition to the empire led them to believe it would be 'wilder' than elsewhere in Africa.[147] John Griffiths was selected as the sort of man able to survive in the remote Buha region. Griffiths revelled in the work and immersed himself in detailed anthropological study of the Ha cultural group.[148] He liked occasional company, but was more vociferous in claims such as that talking to other DCs caused a 'nervous strain', and that after having travelled for '3 days without so much as seeing a white man', he was 'not very thrilled' to finally do so.[149] Another official in Dodoma in 1924 argued 'it is time I went on Safari ... There is nothing like it for cultivating brotherly love. One is apt to get stale living on the station for a long time'.[150]

Those who were more comfortable with socialising, and indeed increasingly viewed it as a necessity, naturally conceptualised their relationship with Africa differently. These were the officials for whom 'living in solitude or in small communities for too long certainly warps one's mentality'.[151] From the very start of our period, new recruits knew they would be expected to do a certain amount of socialising with Europeans. They took formal dress with them to Africa accordingly.[152] The opportunities to interact both increased as the number of officials rose, and became more varied as more clubs and sports grounds were built.[153] In urban areas, officials could increasingly expect a full social calendar. A Nigerian DC recalled that interwar Kano – which contained around 140 Europeans – played host to

> dinner-parties at the Residency and private houses, or invitations to the mess and drink parties at various places. At the club there was tennis and golf, and polo also was played three days a week – probably the cheapest polo in the world, and of quite a good standard. Race meetings were also held periodically.[154]

Sokoto, also in northern Nigeria, contained approximately thirty Europeans, who had access to tennis and fives courts, a golf course, a polo ground, and a football pitch.[155] One official critical of such efforts suggested the bigger northern Nigerian stations were trying to recreate the atmosphere of Bexhill-on-Sea.[156] Even in stations that contained a handful of officials, tennis was often played nearly every afternoon after work.[157]

It could be that references to tennis or polo were inserted into letters home purely as a means of reassuring family and friends that officials were maintaining as 'civilised' an existence as possible. However, these social occasions were of genuine importance to our second category of official. The careful preservation of dinner menus attests to their importance as proof of officials' interactions with their peers. Dances remembered (or misremembered) years after the music had ended were also important, as was sport. Illness or disability sometimes created resentment when officials were unable to interact with their surrounding European community.[158] There were important reasons for this. As Betty Joseph has observed, 'colonial power repeatedly broke down distinctions between public and private'.[159] Though there were opportunities for safari or taking horses out in the evening, it was hard to 'get away from the atmosphere of "shop"'.[160] One Nigerian DC later wrote that the 'plain truth is that a Political Officer's job is his life in whatever country it may be his good fortune to be placed, and his life is his work. He is never away from it; there are no set hours; he is never free from it'.[161] As an indicator to both oneself and others that one was not like the poor pen-pushers of home, this could be worn as a badge of pride, but it was not without problems. Nevertheless, activities such as social drinking were seized on with gusto because this was the closest officials could get to a retreat from Africa.

Many officials consequently resented their social spaces being altered in ways they could not control. One important change was the increasing number of wives who accompanied officials to Africa. After the First World War, London was prepared to pay half of the cost of officials' wives' passage to Africa provided they were certified physically fit enough to stand the African climate.[162] Enough wives travelled to Africa for publishers to feel it worth their while to begin commissioning books about what to expect from life married to a colonial official.[163] London nevertheless preferred single men as recruits, and stipulated that married officials' wives could not live in a colony without the governor's permission.[164] In 1930, the Sudan Government introduced a regulation whereby an SPS official could not bring his wife out with him until he had served five years or reached the age of twenty-eight.[165] Whilst they consequently remained relatively few in number even after the First World War, the wives who did go out attained a high visibility because they were living in what was invariably judged to be 'a man's country'.[166]

Unsurprisingly, those whose wives came to Africa tended to believe the move was beneficial. They reinforced their emotional justification for their spouses' presence with a rational one, namely that this ensured men took better care of themselves.[167] Without wishing to address the 'memsahibs debate' regarding the real impact of wives on the running of empire, it is clear that the officials whose wives went out to Africa were often the men keenest to work in colonial centres.[168] This was possibly to ensure their wives could more readily socialise with other women.[169] Married officials underestimated (or played down) the amount of opposition they faced from those who did not bring spouses to Africa.[170] Behind the need for polite social relations that presumably impelled some single men to hold their tongue on the issue in public, there was frequent hostility to the presence of women. For one southern Nigerian DC in the 1920s, 'At the bottom of my heart I think that other people's wives are rather a bother in the bush'.[171] Although it is impossible to quantify, there is the possibility that affairs drove officials apart from one another. After all, it was often suggested that Edwardian West Africa was defined by the '3 Ds' of drink, debt and divorce.[172]

At any rate, there was the notion that female company would prove a distraction. Unmarried colonial officials often advanced the Kiplingesque notion that women 'dull the edge of their husband's visions'.[173] According to unmarried officials, the presence of wives merely encouraged more women to go out, with the resultant 'domestication' of colonial social lives reducing officials' contact with, and consequently their regard for, indigenous populations. The rise in the number of wives in Africa therefore generated a concurrent increase in animosity against their husbands. One SPS man noted bitterly that the newly domesticated officials of the 1920s 'went home to their charming houses on the river with their well irrigated gardens and trees while their [African] subordinates were relegated to dismal rows of houses in the dusty back parts'.[174]

More important than this, however, was the impact of social interactions upon officials' sense of self. As we have already seen, officials went about their everyday work individualistically. There are therefore clear limits to how far peer pressure standardised officials' actions. Increased socialising nevertheless generated feelings of constraint. With the growing routinisation of social life came the gradual accretion of the 'proper' ways of doing things. Helen Callaway has demonstrated that in its 'elaborate rules and formal rituals, the Colonial Service articulated its symbolic order into every aspect of daily life for those within its ranks'.[175] Upon arrival in a new place, cards had to be left and books had to be signed, starting at the residence of the most senior official in the station, followed by all other Europeans' homes in diminishing order of superiority. This practice declined in importance as time went on, but other conventions, such as seating arrangements and what one wore at dinner, continued to be upheld.[176] Norms of acceptable white behaviour were adhered to in part because they helped maintain the barrier between ruler and ruled, as well as officials' mental well-being.[177] As one official's wife in Nigeria recounted, 'material discipline represents – and aids – a moral discipline'.[178]

The prevalence of gossip meant officials knew such social norms were policed rigorously through informal means. Although often neglected by scholars, gossip was a crucial part of colonial life that defined officials' relationships with their peers. Some commentators attempted to discourage it. According to a guide for those new to West Africa, gossip was 'the cause of as much trouble as fever' and therefore to be avoided.[179] Officials did indeed seek to steer clear of regions that had a particularly bad reputation for intrigue and infighting. Edward Lumley tried to avoid being posted to Mbulu District in northern Tanganyika in the 1930s because 'a lot of backbiting goes on there'.[180] However, once on a station with limited outlets for social interaction, it was very hard to avoid getting drawn into the gossip.[181] This was often powered by drinking, another practice that elites and metropolitan commentators tried, and failed, to control.[182] Edwardian West Africa had a particularly strong reputation for heavy drinking, but the practice was common amongst officials across the period throughout the continent.[183] With officials' social lives invariably revolving around 'sundowners' with a small group of people, insularity and a taste for enlivening scandals naturally led to prejudice.[184] The aforementioned guide noted that the 'honeysuckle English village has its scandal, Anglo-India has its "gup," but the Coast has an ear-burning talk of its own'.[185] '"Everybody else" seems to be the engrossing topic of conversation out here', wrote one Northern Nigerian official in 1911.[186]

Officials consequently felt they were living in the midst of a society given over to an extreme form of self-surveillance. DCs were well aware that they would be the subjects of gossip were they to transgress accepted norms, which would only serve to make their lives uncomfortable. Those felt to have 'gone native' attracted the most opprobrium.[187] Whilst respected as a scholar, Rattray was one such example.[188] However, most watched their behaviour very carefully. Some doubtless used their memoirs to exaggerate how far they openly displayed friendship with Africans as a means of retrospectively demonstrating impeccably modern credentials.[189] Testimonies from the time nevertheless attest to the problems such interactions could cause. On going out to Sudan in 1931, Gawain Bell felt there was a need to maintain a certain distance between himself and those whom he governed. His belief that voluntarily choosing to associate with Sudanese peoples was not 'normal' diminished the longer he remained in the Condominium.[190] However, Bell's residual aversion to doing so in the presence of other Europeans was due less to fears about a diminution of his prestige in the eyes of Africans than to worries about how such actions would be perceived by his peers.[191] In addition, even if they did not want to, officials had to turn out for colonial social occasions for fear of being ostracised. As one DO complained of life in Zungeru, 'you have to keep up a great deal of appearances'.[192] Such complaints signified both officials' frustration with their environs and a feeling of impotence in their inability to change this. Officials needed the company of other officials, but resented the constraints that this company placed upon them.

Officials nevertheless derived pleasure from regaling their relatives back home when they met someone with whom they had a metropolitan link. For example, Old Marlburians were delighted to meet each other, as this provided them with a very personal means of reconnecting with home.[193] Because changes in recruitment meant that officials enjoyed increasingly homogenised social experiences prior to leaving for Africa, these searches for common metropolitan bonds bore ever more fruit. Officials had mutual friends, knew each other's relations, and so on.[194] Whilst providing pleasure, these links were a double-edged sword. Officials now not only needed to be seen to be doing the right thing in order to remain accepted members of colonial society. They also had to behave in order to remain accepted members of metropolitan society. This is reminiscent of William Reader's point that recruitment to the higher professions in Victorian England meant 'admitting educated gentlemen to small, self-governing groups of their social equals to whom they would be personally known and by whom their fitness would be judged'.[195] Behaviour felt different now no longer merely had the capacity to ruin an official's career in Africa.

Conclusion

Officials resented the constraints central control placed upon them. It is pushing matters too far to suggest, as Kuklick has done, that officials were *inherently* opposed to their superiors, because there were many elites for whom officials had a good deal of respect.[196] Opposition was often directed against the impersonal 'red tape' of the secretariat, rather than a governor.[197] From Southern Nigeria, Christopher Wordsworth wrote:

> Oh! Commissioners may prose
> Of their districts and their woes
> But the duties are but trifling and allowances are fat
> But the culminating pleasure
> That we treasure beyond measure
> Is to answer little minutes from the Secretariat.[198]

The central government in Dar es Salaam even felt it necessary to establish a European Civil Servants Association in 1920 with a view to the 'promotion of sympathy and understanding between the Government and its servants'.[199] Officials also criticised those who worked for other sections of government, such as the forestry, veterinary and public works departments, for supposedly encroaching upon their own spheres of influence.[200] Elites were aware of this, and called for officials to cooperate more fully with such specialists.[201]

This is well known. In contrast, the prevailing historiographical tendency has been to stress the essential unity of the official corps across Africa. Any rivalries were 'harmless', 'foolish snobbery' at worst, caused by what Kirk-Greene obliquely refers to as the 'occasional nuanced post-prandial incident'.[202] This chapter has demonstrated that there are a number of difficulties with this argument. Firstly, officials developed a more myopic vision of empire than their superiors. Officials took little sustained interest in their supposed 'brother' officials beyond their district. If they did, it was in a competitive manner where the significance of a region or colony, or the capacity of its officials to experience 'authentic' Africa, came under scrutiny. The relatively limited operational and social horizons of everyday life, fed in part by the imperative needs of the colonial state, facilitated intra-colonial tensions, which were reinforced by conflicting visions of imperial rule and officials' self-interest. The continual pressures of work, combined with social lives steeped in alcohol and gossip, created hothouses of discord. In conjunction with the points made in Chapter Two, this demonstrates the importance of informal over formal knowledge networks in shaping officials' attitudes.

In response to this argument, objections might naturally be raised. In particular, one point and one counterclaim need to be borne in mind. The point is that officials' views were not static. During the early stages of an official's safari away from a station, we are often presented with a man at peace with the world. As time passed, and the vicissitudes of an active solitary lifestyle became more of a burden, the same official increasingly pined for nothing more than a 'perfectly sedentary job where one walks daily from a *habūb*-proof house equipped with electric light and an ice-chest to a solid *habūb*-proof office also equipped with electric light and an ice-chest'.[203] It could be argued that this had a direct impact on men's relationships with other officials.

After all, Charles Wordsworth wrote to a friend in 1905 about how he intended to avoid Degema 'as far as possible in the future' because of its incoming DC, 'whom I do not love'.[204] Wordsworth was only four months from the end of his tour, and was writing on Christmas Day, the communication going on to note that, 'If you find the tone of this letter at all depressed, please bear in mind that, to keep up the idea of Christmas, I have made and eaten a mince pie'.[205] Although never the most cheery of souls, Wordsworth was in a more positive frame of mind at the start of his tours.[206] Alternatively, one might turn to broader events to explain changing moods. For instance, J. P. Ross, a senior official in the Colonial Secretary's Office in Accra, felt that conflicts between personnel were heightened when Clifford and Guggisberg attempted to significantly reshape the direction in which the Gold Coast was headed.[207]

The counterclaim to be considered concerns the types of source material this study has used. Some retired officials admitted that when writing memoirs there was a 'general tendency among all of us to pinpoint congenial recollections and to overlook the rest'.[208] Furthermore, memoirs' emphasis upon collective nouns is at variance with sources created at the time, which more frequently constructed colonial governance as an individual act. 'I' only became 'we' later. The natural response to this would be that whilst historians who have used sources created upon retirement have found harmony, a heavier reliance on sources created at the time may have led the present author to exaggerate the importance of conflicts that were, in actuality, only fleeting concerns. After all, some officials did indeed form long-lasting friendships. Perhaps, then, letter- or diary-writing was the very act of exorcism that allowed a basic underlying *esprit de corps* to be restored?

In response to both point and counterclaim, however, it needs to be borne in mind just how trapped officials felt. Respected biologist Julian Huxley noted that even the European who visited Africa only briefly found it difficult to escape a certain intellectual climate which 'enfolds him, and because almost everyone he meets tacitly makes the same general assumptions, he very often falls into the current way of thinking'.[209] This was how officials felt they had to act on the surface. Behind this, however, lay simmering resentment. The very existence of a normative order impinged upon the idea that imperial endeavour was an act of independence, of making one's mark on the continent.

Discord between officials therefore owed something to the metropole. Attempts to instil future officials with the belief that imperial governance was a collective experience were up against the visions of the idiosyncratic imperial heroes to which young men had been exposed their whole lives. Ultimately, in spite of the pragmatic concerns that frequently drove young men to work in Africa, these visions created tensions that could not be resolved. Officials' need for at least some social contact with other Europeans was granted in an environment governed by conventions that hampered their pursuit of the romanticised individualism indelibly associated with life on Britain's imperial frontiers. Officials pursued that which they could never have.

Notes

1   J. Allen, 'Nigerian panorama – 1926–1966', [undated], RHO Mss.Afr.s.1551/10
2   A retired Nigerian official himself, Kirk-Greene has been keen to emphasise the camaraderie of his predecessors; Kirk-Greene, *Symbol of Authority*, pp. xx, 236
3   Heussler, *Yesterday's Rulers*, p. 83; Gann and Duignan, *Rulers of British Africa*, p. 203; Collins, *Shadows in the Grass: Britain in the Southern Sudan, 1918–1956* (London: Yale University Press, 1983), p. 75
4   Collins, *Shadows in the Grass*, p. 297; Hesketh Bell, *A Witch's Legacy* (London: Sampson Low, Marston & Company, 1893), Volume One, p. 153; see also Porter, *Absent-minded Imperialists*, p. 41
5   *Kaduna Secretariat Library: Catalogue of Books* (Kaduna: Government Printers, 1932), in RHO Mss.Brit.Emp.s.364
6   These works were mainly concerned with particular peoples, such as Roscoe's *The Baganda* and *The Banyankole*, and Driberg's *The Lango*; *Kaduna Secretariat Library*, in RHO Mss.Brit.Emp.s.364
7   Similarly, *Memorandum on Native Policy in East Africa* (London: HMSO, 1930) was circulated to Provincial Commissioners in the Gold Coast by the Secretariat in Accra, although there is no evidence that the text was passed any further down the administrative hierarchy; PRAAD CSO 21/1/122

8 Bell to parents, 26 January 1932, SAD 697/5/47; Bell to parents, 17 June 1932, SAD 697/7/10; Bell, diary, [n.d.], SAD 698/8/3; Bloss, memoirs, [1948], SAD 704/1/72; T. R. H. Owen to mother, 18 July 1928, SAD 414/2/7; C. Orr, *The Making of Northern Nigeria* (1911; London: Frank Cass, 1965), pp. 5–11; C. Walker, diary, 19 September 1916, RHO Mss.Afr.s.435/10

9 Crocker, *Nigeria*, pp. 146–7

10 H. Amherst, diary, 26 August 1930, RHO Mss.Afr.s.1207/32; Lea, diary, 21 January 1932, in Lea, *On Trek*, p. 201

11 Dowsett to parents, 22 May 1932, RHO Mss.Afr.s.1276/63; Lea, diary, 25 December 1931, in Lea, *On Trek*, p. 174

12 Lea, diary, 24 November 1931, in Lea, *On Trek*, p. 151; Robertson to father, 20 May 1923, SAD 531/2/90

13 Kirk-Greene, 'Introduction', in Kirk-Greene (ed.), *Glimpses of Empire*, p. xi. *Crown Colonist* nevertheless contained a good deal of information on administrative affairs; see, for instance, R. Oakley, 'Native Administration in Nigeria', *Crown Colonist* 11:2 (1932), 172–5

14 See, for example, S. Ormsby to mother, 18 August 1908, RHO Mss.Afr.r.105/23

15 Sillery, 'Working backwards', [c.1975], RHO Mss.Afr.r.207/115

16 A. J. Phillips, diary, 22 August 1931, RHO Mss.Afr.s.803/18

17 C. J. D. Duder and C. P. Youé, 'Paice's place: race and politics in Nanyuki district, Kenya, in the 1920s', *African Affairs* 93 (1994), 254

18 This was an established tendency; Wiener, *An Empire on Trial: Race, Murder, and Justice under British Rule, 1870–1935* (Cambridge: Cambridge University Press, 2009), pp. 12–13

19 Bull, 'Indirect rule in Northern Nigeria', p. 73

20 R. Davies to C. E. Lyall, Khartoum, 22 January 1925, NA Foreign Office papers (hereafter FO) 141/632/17679

21 Regarding the former, the joint report concluded that there were no grounds for fearing the rise of Mahdism in Nigeria; Gailey, *Clifford*, p. 151; C. Griffin to Cameron, 15 April 1929, NA CO 536/157/4; Collins, *Shadows in the Grass*, p. 164

22 Tilley, 'Ecologies of complexity: tropical environments, African trypanosomiasis, and the science of disease control in British colonial Africa, 1900–1940', *Osiris* 19 (2004), 31

23 On this unification, see Kirk-Greene, *Britain's Imperial Administrators*, pp. 148–9

24 W. A. Walker, 'Report of a visit to the French Ivory Coast', [August 1933], RHO Mss.Afr.s.1064/1–9; regarding pre-1914 boundary fixing with German Cameroon, see C. Boyle, diary, 27 February 1909, RHO Mss.Afr.s.2324/95

25 Chamberlain to Low, 29 June 1900, PRAAD ADM 1/1/755/336; Low to W. MacGregor, 30 June 1900, PRAAD ADM 1/1/755/343; MacGregor to Low, 1 July 1900, PRAAD ADM 1/1/755/344; M. de Courcy Dodd to mother, 3 July 1898, RHO Mss.Afr.s.1995/41; J. K. Flynn, 'Ghana-Asante (Ashanti)', in Crowder (ed.), *West African Resistance: The Military Response to Colonial Occupation* (London: Hutchinson, 1971), p. 48

26 Furse, Miscellaneous notes, [1935], RHO Mss.Brit.Emp.s.415/6/1; Iliffe, *Tanganyika*, pp. 262–3, 325

27 Lugard, *Dual Mandate*, p. 136

28 Kirk-Greene, *Symbol of Authority*, p. 98

29 J. C. Maxwell to J. A. Ballantyne, 21 February 1925, PRAAD CSO 25/1/62

30 Kirk-Greene, 'Badge of office: sport and His Excellency in the British empire', in Mangan (ed.), *The Cultural Bond: Sport, Empire, Society* (London: Frank Cass, 1992), p. 187; E. O'Halpin, *Head of the Civil Service: A Study of Sir Warren Fisher* (London: Routledge, 1989), p. 156; C. Owen Butler to Duncan-Johnstone, 26 March 1934, RHO Mss.Afr.s.593/5/4/33A

31 A. Saunders, Weekly Force Order, 3 March 1937, RHO Mss.Afr.s.1827(1)/190–1; Robertson to mother, 2 July 1931, SAD 531/3/14

32 H. S. Goldsmith to Slater, 8 September 1931, PRAAD CSO 25/3/61

33 Slater to Goldsmith, 24 December 1931, PRAAD CSO 25/3/61

34   W. J. Inness to J. P. Ross, [October 1931], PRAAD CSO 25/3/61
35   Slater to Goldsmith, 23 September 1931, PRAAD CSO 25/3/61; Perham, *East African Journey*, p. 46
36   Goldsmith to Slater, 17 November 1931, PRAAD CSO 25/3/61
37   Ross, untitled note, 23 October 1931, PRAAD CSO 25/3/61
38   Bell, *Shadows on the Sand*, p. 16; E. J. Scott to father, 19 February 1903, RHO Mss.Afr.s.1564/3; A. Milverton, interview with Kirk-Greene, 22 February 1969, RHO Mss.Brit.Emp.s.368/13–16; see also Churchill to H. Campbell-Bannerman, 15 October 1907, BL Add Mss 52516; 'Aide-memoire', 22 August 1908, NA FO 881/10505
39   J. N. Richardson, 'Comparative note on the S.P.S. and the Colonial Civil Service in Uganda', 28 March 1931, NA CO 323/1162/5; C. W. M. Cox, diary, 27 June 1939, SAD 673/4; Daniell, diary, c.31 December 1937, SAD 777/13/19; A. Haarer, 'Memories concerning twenty-two years of Kenya, Uganda and Tanganyika Territory', [undated], RHO Mss.Afr.s.1144/15–16; Perham, *East African Journey*, pp. 45–6; Iliffe, *Tanganyika*, p. 302
40   Richardson, 'Comparative note', NA CO 323/1162/5
41   *Hansard*, 5th series, vol. 200, cols 1940–2; D. A. Macalister to family, 12 November 1901, BL Add Mss 49357/2; see also Hesketh Bell, *A Witch's Legacy*, Volume One, pp. 191–3. This undermines Kirk-Greene, *Symbol of Authority*, p. 61. In 1913, wine expenditure of approximately 30 shillings per week whilst on the journey to and from Africa was felt usual. With wine costing approximately 18 shillings per imperial gallon in Britain, 30 shillings would have purchased over 7.5 litres of wine at home. Even allowing for an onboard mark-up, considerable amounts of alcohol must therefore have been consumed; Field, *'Verb Sap.'*, p. 50; 'National drink bill', *The Times* (22 March 1913), p. 4
42   Tomlinson to mother, 8 October 1904, RHO Mss.Afr.s.372/31
43   Duncan-Johnstone, *With the British Red Cross in Turkey 1912–1913* (London: James Nisbet & Co., 1913), pp. 12, 84
44   C. Woodhouse, diary, 13 June 1909, RHO Mss.Afr.s.236; Callaway, *Gender, Culture and Empire*, p. 68
45   C. Walker, diary, [April 1919], RHO Mss.Afr.s.438/34
46   Bush, *Imperialism, Race and Resistance*, p. 56
47   Clearkin, 'Ramblings', RHO Mss.Brit.r.4/1/27
48   Interview with S. Leith-Ross, quoted in Allen, *Plain Tales*, p. 307; however, see G. Ormsby to mother, 30 October 1910, RHO Brit.Emp.s.287/119
49   C. Walker, diary, [April 1919], RHO Mss.Afr.s.438/33
50   Officials travelling to East Africa spent less time onboard a ship with each other than those travelling to West Africa. For instance, prior to 1922, many travelling to Sudan did not take a boat through the Suez Canal, unlike their Tanganyikan and Ugandan counterparts. Instead, some SPS men disembarked at Egypt, taking a steamer up the Nile to Wadi Halfa, and then on to their Sudanese destination by train; Davies, *Camel's Back*, pp. 17–18
51   C. Walker, diary, 13 July 1918, RHO Mss.Afr.s.437/36–7; see also Kirk-Greene, 'Forging a relationship', p. 69
52   N. Weir, diary, [1926], RHO Mss.Afr.s.1151(1)/33
53   Weir, diary, [1928], RHO Mss.Afr.s.1151(1)/47
54   *Ibid.*
55   Hesketh Bell to parents, 26 December 1909, BL Add Mss 78721/86; Strachey note, 14 November 1913, NA CO 96/538
56   See also Maxwell, diary, 27 August 1917, in Williamson and Kirk-Greene (eds), *Gold Coast Diaries*, p. 116
57   Crowder, 'The white chiefs of Tropical Africa', pp. 339–40
58   For one implication of this, see C. Newbury, 'Accounting for power in Northern Nigeria', *Journal of African History* 45:2 (2004), 269
59   Nicolson, *The Administration of Nigeria*, p. 180
60   Surridge, 'Salad days', p. 283

61 Heussler, *Yesterday's Rulers*, p. 73
62 Wingate later wrote a glowing preface to a book published on Fergusson; V. H. Fergusson *et al.*, *The Story of Fergie Bey* (London: Macmillan, 1930)
63 W. A. Porter, diary, January–February 1928, SAD 700/11/7–15; D. E. Omissi, *Air Power and Colonial Control: The Royal Air Force, 1919–1939* (Manchester: Manchester University Press, 1990), pp. 86–8
64 Collins, *Shadows in the Grass*, p. 15
65 Daly, *Empire on the Nile*, p. 415
66 Kirk-Greene, *Britain's Imperial Administrators*, p. 191
67 There were nevertheless limits to Khartoum's desire for change; Collins, *Shadows in the Grass*, p. 123
68 Daly, *Empire on the Nile*, p. 272
69 See, for instance, Lea, 'Explanatory note', in Lea, *On Trek*, p. 12
70 E. Scott, interview with W. Beaver, 19 May 1980, RHO Mss.Afr.s.1765; G. Ormsby to mother, 11 December 1910, RHO Mss.Brit.Emp.s.287/124
71 Childs, diary, 24 September 1933, RHO Mss.Afr.s.1861(2); Childs, diary, 29 December 1933, RHO Mss.Afr.s.1861(2)
72 Currie served between 1899 and 1914; J. Currie to Furse, 7 August 1935, RHO Mss. Brit.Emp.s.415/6/7/9
73 Currie, 'Oxford Luncheon Club paper', 3 May 1935, RHO Mss.Brit.Emp.s.415/6/7/11–12; see also Currie, 'Present-day difficulties of a young officer in the Tropics', *Journal of the African Society* 32:126 (1933), 31–6
74 W. Gowers diary, 25 April 1931, RHO Mss.Afr.1150/4/23; see also Clearkin, 'Ramblings', RHO Mss.Brit.r.4/1/54
75 Daly, *The Sirdar: Sir Reginald Wingate and the British Empire in the Middle East* (Philadelphia, PA: American Philosophical Society, 1997), p. 148
76 Kirk-Greene, 'Sudan Political Service', p. 26; Kirk-Greene, 'Canada in Africa: Sir Percy Girouard, neglected colonial governor', *African Affairs* 83 (1984), 212–13
77 Gailey, *Clifford*, pp. 98–106, quote at p. 106
78 R. Hill, *Slatin Pasha* (London: Oxford University Press, 1965), p. 76
79 Heussler, *British Tanganyika*, p. 19
80 Colonial Office desk diary, 19 August 1907, RHO Mss.Brit.Emp.r.21; Wordsworth to R. Wordsworth, 6 February 1902, RHO Mss.Afr.s.1373/20; F. P. Crozier, *Five Years Hard* (London: Jonathan Cape, 1932), pp. 28–32, 57; C. H. Stigand, *Administration in Tropical Africa* (London: Constable & Co., 1914), pp. 4–5
81 W. Wright, 'Soldier notes', in Field, *'Verb Sap.'*, p. 163; Lugard, *Dual Mandate*, pp. 582–3
82 P. Gifford, 'Indirect rule: touchstone or tombstone for colonial policy?', in Gifford and Louis (eds), *Britain and Germany in Africa: Imperial Rivalry and Colonial Rule* (New Haven, CT: Yale University Press, 1967), p. 357
83 Crocker, *Nigeria*, p. 117
84 H. Pollock to mother, 19 November 1930, RHO Mss.Afr.s.419/226
85 Surridge, 'Salad days', p. 284; Kirk-Greene, 'Sudan Political Service', 26 n. 9
86 Bell to parents, 3 June 1932, SAD 697/7/2. As a new recruit, Baily had himself been fed horror stories by his superiors about the difficulties of life in Sudan; Baily, 'Early recollections of the Sudan', SAD 533/4/23
87 M. Kingsley, *Travels in West Africa* (Teddington: Echo Library, 2008), p. 44; K. Frank, *A Voyager Out: The Life of Mary Kingsley* (1986; London: I. B. Tauris, 2005), pp. 64–5; see also Wilson-Haffenden, *Red Men*, pp. 22–3; Hastings, *Nigerian Days*, p. 2
88 Z. Korda (dir.), *The Four Feathers* (1939)
89 Scholars have nevertheless subsequently exaggerated how far the account of General Gordon was hostile; L. Strachey, *Eminent Victorians* (1918; Harmondsworth: Penguin, 1971), pp. 189–267
90 Bell to parents, 25 August 1933, SAD 697/10/31; W. Plomer, *Cecil Rhodes* (London: Peter Davies, 1933); P. Maylam, *The Cult of Rhodes: Remembering an Imperialist in Africa* (Claremont, South Africa: David Philip, 2005), p. 122

91 Daniell, diary, 1 October 1937, SAD 777/13/7; see also Bell to parents, 29 July 1934, SAD 697/12/13

92 S. Low and L. C. Sanders, *The History of England during the Reign of Victoria (1837–1901)* (London: Longmans, 1907), pp. 357–8; 'Cecil Rhodes: two new biographies', *The Times* (3 February 1933), p. 15; Johnson, 'The death of Gordon', 285–310

93 Bell to parents, 8 February 1933, SAD 697/9/23

94 R. E. H. Baily, 'Early recollections of the Sudan', [c.1971], SAD 533/4/21

95 W. Somerset Maugham made this generational divide the focal point of his short story 'The Outstation', set in the Malay Peninsula; W. S. Maugham, 'The Outstation', in *The Casuarina Tree* (New York: George H. Doran, 1926), pp. 103–48

96 C. Christy, 'White settlement in tropical Africa', *Journal of the African Society* 27 (1928), 338–41; Hesketh Bell, 'Recent progress', 380; L. S. Suggate, *Africa* (London: George Harrap & Co., 1929), p. 58; C. Gillman, 'White colonisation in East Africa, with special regard to Tanganyika Territory', [1938], RHO Mss.Afr.s.999(2)/138–40

97 See Bell and Kirk-Greene, *The Sudan Political Service 1902–1952: A Preliminary Register of Second Careers* (Oxford: no publisher, 1989); G. Adams, private papers, RHO Mss.Afr.s.375

98 Quoted in R. Bickers, 'Introduction', in Bickers (ed.), *Settlers and Expatriates: Britons over the Seas* (Oxford: Oxford University Press, 2010), p. 4

99 A. D. Gibb, *Scottish Empire* (London: Alexander Maclehose & Co., 1937), p. 142

100 J. Hyslop, 'Cape Town Highlanders, Transvaal Scottish: military "Scottishness" and social power in nineteenth and twentieth century South Africa', *South African Historical Journal* 47 (2002), 98

101 Mackenzie, 'Essay and reflection: on Scotland and the empire', *International History Review* 14:4 (1993), 737; Duncan-Johnstone, diary, 27–28 August 1929, RHO Mss. Afr.s.593/1/34; Sayers (ed.), *Handbook of Tanganyika*, p. 487. Other nationalities did organise societies in Africa, although not to the same degree as the Scottish; Sayers (ed.), *Handbook of Tanganyika*, p. 488; Mackenzie and N. R. Dalziel, *The Scots in South Africa: Ethnicity, Identity, Gender and Race, 1772–1914* (Manchester: Manchester University Press, 2007), ch. 8

102 Gowers, 'Speech to Caledonian Society c.1931–2', RHO Mss.Afr.s.1150/258

103 E. Scott, interview with W. Beaver, 19 May 1980, RHO Mss.Afr.s.1765

104 Cameron to Lugard, 20 April 1930, RHO Mss.Lugard.9/1/52; see also Hastings, *Nigerian Days*, p. 125

105 Lugard to Cameron, 31 May 1930, RHO Mss.Lugard.9/1/54

106 Regarding the Colonial Office's attitudes towards the Irish, see Heussler, *Yesterday's Rulers*, p. 76

107 de Courcy Dodd to brother, 19 October 1898, RHO Mss.Afr.s.1995/81

108 de Courcy Dodd to mother, 25 July 1898, RHO Mss.Afr.s.1995/51; de Courcy Dodd to mother, 3 July 1898, RHO Mss.Afr.s.1995/43

109 See, for example, de Courcy Dodd to mother, 22 February 1898, RHO Mss. Afr.s.1995/1

110 W. Tripe to parents, 29 March 1929, RHO Mss.Afr.s.868/1/30; Tripe, 'Anger in Africa', [undated], RHO Mss.Afr.s.868/4; however, see K. C. P. Struvé, 'Handing over notes', 11 August 1926, SAD 212/9/9

111 However, see Orr to Leviseur, 30 October 1904, BL Add Mss 56100/22

112 G. Ormsby to mother, 3 March 1908, RHO Mss.Brit.Emp.s.287/15

113 Hesketh Bell, diary, 9 July 1911, BL Add Mss 78721/236; Hesketh Bell to home, 26 December 1909, BL Add Mss 78721/91

114 G. Ormsby to mother, 8 October 1909, RHO Mss.Brit.Emp.s.287/95

115 Letchworth, interview, RHO Mss.Afr.s.2112/33

116 J. R. Elliot, 'Notes and memoirs', [19 February 1969], RHO Mss.Afr.s.1384/1; see also Crocker, *Nigeria*, p. 200

117 L. M. Thomas, 'Reminiscences', [n.d.], RHO Mss.Brit.Emp.s.492/14

118 Duncan-Johnstone's wife was Guggisberg's niece by marriage; D. Daltry to mother, 6 May 1927, RHO Mss.Afr.s.2222/28; see also Daltry to mother, 3 June 1927, RHO Mss.Afr.s.2222/34

119 H. B. Arber, Memoirs, [c.1982], SAD 736/2/6, 10; Tomlinson to mother, 22 August 1908, RHO Mss.Afr.s.372/81; K. Curtis, 'Smaller is better: a consensus of peasants and bureaucrats in Colonial Tanganyika', in W. G. Clarence-Smith and S. Topik (eds), *The Global Coffee Economy in Africa, Asia, and Latin America, 1500–1989* (Cambridge: Cambridge University Press, 2006), p. 324

120 Tomlinson to mother, 22 August 1908, RHO Mss.Afr.s.372/81

121 Collins, *Shadows in the Grass*, p. 93

122 P. B. E. Acland, memoirs, [1982], SAD 707/15/9, 20

123 F. Addison, diary, 20 April 1926, SAD 294/19/20–1

124 Perham, *East African Journey*, p. 211

125 Weir, diaries, undated [1925], RHO Mss.Afr.s.1151(1)/1–2, 47; Weir, 'Ogoja Province, Abakaliki Division annual report, 1931', 7 January 1932, RHO Mss. Afr.s.1151(4)/48–63; E. H. Macintosh, 'Note on the Dago tribe', *Sudan Notes and Records* 14 (1931), 171–7

126 Letchworth, interview, RHO Mss.Afr.s.2112/22

127 Childs, diary, 27 January 1936, RHO Mss.Afr.s.1861/3

128 Allen, 'Nigerian panorama', RHO Mss.Afr.s.1551/69

129 E. A. Balfour to mother, 28 November 1934, SAD 606/5/4

130 Wordsworth to G. Young, 14 May 1905, RHO Mss.Afr.s.1373/30. New stations were created more frequently before 1914 than after it

131 E. F. Knight, *Letters from the Sudan: Reprinted from* The Times *of April to October, 1896* (London: Macmillan, 1897), p. 17

132 Lady Surridge, interview with J. Tawney, 3 February 1972, RHO Mss.Afr.s.1480/276

133 Dowsett to parents, 29 July 1932, RHO Mss.Afr.s.1276/77

134 The quotes are at Surridge, 'Salad days', p. 283 and Heussler, *British Tanganyika*, p. 15 n. 9 respectively; R. Alford, 'Travelling hopefully', in Kirk-Greene (ed.), *Glimpses of Empire*, p. 292

135 See Furse's annotations on his 'Quarterly list of the Sudan Government: 1st January 1936', RHO Mss.Brit.s.415/6/7/3

136 Owen to mother, 6 March 1930, SAD 414/2/40; Owen to mother, 10 November 1930, SAD 414/2/48; Alford, 'Travelling hopefully', p. 291

137 S. Ormsby to father, 15 May 1903, RHO Mss.Afr.r.105/9b

138 Clifford to Milner, 28 October 1919, NA CO 583/78

139 Crocker, *Nigeria*, p. 194

140 Orr to E. Leviseur, 27 May 1906, BL Add Mss 56100/34

141 Crocker, *Nigeria*, p. 195

142 Childs, diary, 12 August 1933, RHO Mss.Afr.s.1861(1); Childs, diary, 1 January 1934, RHO Mss.Afr.s.1861(2); see also Childs, diary, 18 February 1934, RHO Mss. Afr.s.1861(2)

143 Lea, diary, 9 February 1932, in Lea, *On Trek*, p. 217; E. Lumley, *Forgotten Mandate* (London: C. Hurst & Co., 1976), p. 46

144 Lumley, *Forgotten Mandate*, p. 46

145 Miller-Stirling to mother, 30 June 1910, RHO Mss.Afr.s.2051/41

146 Baily to parents, 6 January 1910, SAD 533/4/48

147 Popplewell, 'Random recollections', RHO Mss.Afr.s.2156/1; Tanganyika was better known than other ex-German territories such as Togoland or German Kamerun and, being larger, was felt to offer greater opportunities for officials to act independently

148 Griffiths, '210: snuff taking and the use of nose clips in Buha, Tanganyika Territory', 185–6; see also M. Wagner, 'Environment, community & history: "Nature in the mind" in nineteenth- & early twentieth-century Buha, Tanzania', in G. Maddox, J. Giblin, and I. Kimambo (eds), *Custodians of the Land: Ecology & Culture in the History of Tanzania* (Oxford: James Currey, 1996), pp. 177–8

149 Griffiths, diary, 23 August 1931, RHO Mss.Afr.r.180/30; Griffiths, diary, 19 January 1932, RHO Mss.Afr.r.179/5; Griffiths, diary, 25 January 1932, RHO Mss.Afr.r.179/13

150 Pollock to mother, 18 October 1924, RHO Mss.Afr.s.419/77

151 Duncan-Johnstone, diary, 9 September 1928, RHO Mss.Afr.s.593/1/8

152 For inventories of the clothing, including formal dress, one was expected to take to

Africa, see *West African Pocket Book*, pp. 42–4; Field, '*Verb Sap.*', p. 22
153 See the list of clubs in Sayers (ed.), *Handbook of Tanganyika*, pp. 474–6
154 Oakley, *Treks & Palavers*, p. 243
155 A. Sheffield to mother, 31 December 1930, RHO Mss.Brit.Emp.s.310/85
156 Crocker, *Nigeria*, p. 99
157 Oakley, *Treks & Palavers*, p. 43; G. Ormsby to mother, 22 August 1909, RHO Mss. Brit.Emp.s.287/88
158 Balfour to mother, 12 December 1934, SAD 606/5/10; Balfour to mother, 28 December 1934, SAD 606/5/13
159 B. Joseph, *Reading the East India Company, 1720–1840: Colonial Currencies of Gender* (Chicago, IL: Chicago University Press, 2004), p. 92
160 Jeffries, *Colonial Empire*, p. 125; see also Hastings, *Nigerian Days*, p. 91
161 Oakley, *Treks & Palavers*, p. 8
162 Jeffries, *Colonial Empire*, p. 33
163 'Irish blood', *Everyday Sudan Life* (London, 1937)
164 Jeffries, Annotated comments on 'Vacancy Form', 22 November 1927, NA CO 536/145/14; Sayers (ed.), *Handbook of Tanganyika*, p. 153
165 Bell, *Shadows on the Sand*, p. 14
166 Callaway, *Gender, Culture and Empire*, pp. 4–8; see also Wilson-Haffenden, *Red Men*, pp. 23–4; Tripe, diary, 14 September 1929, RHO Mss.Afr.s.868/1/125
167 Hastings, *Nigerian Days*, p. 127
168 K. Ballhatchet, *Race, Sex, and Class under the Raj: Imperial Attitudes and Policies and their Critics, 1793–1905* (London: Weidenfeld and Nicolson, 1980), p. 153; C. Knapman, *White Women in Fiji 1835–1930: The Ruin of Empire?* (Sydney: Allen & Unwin, 1986); M. Strobel, *European Women and the Second British Empire* (Bloomington, IN: Indiana University Press, 1991), p. 2
169 Surridge, 'Salad days', p. 284; Lady Surridge, interview, RHO Mss.Afr.s.1480/286; W. T. C. Berry to unknown, 9 November 1938, RHO Mss.Afr.t.12/38
170 Surridge, 'Salad days', p. 284
171 Tomlinson to mother, 28 November 1923, RHO Mss.Afr.s.372/188; see also Miller-Stirling to father, 21 November 1911, RHO Mss.Afr.s.2051/73
172 Quoted in Field, '*Verb Sap*', p. 56
173 Newbold to Moore, 25 May 1939, in Henderson, *Modern Sudan*, p. 111; see also Bell, *Shadows on the Sand*, p. 12
174 Baily, 'Early recollections of the Sudan', SAD 533/4/28
175 Callaway, *Gender, Culture and Empire*, p. 56
176 *Ibid.*, pp. 69–72
177 C. Cockey to J. L. Stewart, 4 October 1936, RHO Mss.Afr.s.1138/17–18; Stewart to Cockey, 9 October 1936, RHO Mss.Afr.s.1138/19
178 S. Leith-Ross, in M. Crowder (ed.), *Stepping-Stones: Memoirs of Colonial Nigeria, 1907–60* (London: Peter Owen, 1983), p. 69, quoted in Callaway, *Gender, Culture and Empire*, p. 72
179 Field, '*Verb Sap.*', p. 82; see also Lugard, 'Northern Nigeria: discussion', *Geographical Journal* 40:2 (1912), 164
180 E. Lumley, *Forgotten Mandate*, ch. 7; Lumley, diary, 9 April 1935, RHO Mss. Afr.s.785/61
181 R. K. Rice to mother, 5 December 1914, RHO Mss.Afr.s.1511/3
182 See, for example, the temperance propaganda of R. M. Ballantyne, *Blue Lights: Or Hot Work in the Soudan* (London: J. Nisbet & Son, 1888)
183 Clearkin, 'Ramblings', RHO Mss.Brit.r.4/1/16; Sheffield to mother, 11 December 1930, RHO Mss.Brit.Emp.s.310/79; C. Walker, diary, 15 September 1915, RHO Mss. Afr.s.433/103–4; Weir, diary, [c.1929–30], RHO Mss.Afr.s.1151(1)/57; Woodhouse, diary, 3 January 1909, RHO Mss.Afr.s.236; Kisch to home, 8 November 1908, in Kisch, *Letters & Sketches*, p. 50; M. Macoun, *Wrong Place, Right Time: Policing the End of Empire* (London: Radcliffe, 1996), p. 15; Oakley, *Treks & Palavers*, p. 206
184 Hastings, *Nigerian Days*, p. 38. Of course, not all sundowners were taken with company; Lumley, *Forgotten Mandate*, p. 12

185 Field, 'Verb Sap.', p. 43
186 Mathews to parents, 6 June 1911, RHO Mss.Afr.s.783/1/1/26
187 Kenrick to parents, 16 June 1937, SAD 647/5/60
188 A. F. Robertson, 'Anthropologists and government in Ghana', *African Affairs* 74:294 (1975), 54; see also J. W. Kenrick to parents, 16 June 1937, SAD 647/5/60; Hill, *Slatin*, p. 73
189 H. A. Nicholson, Memoirs, [n.d.], SAD 777/11/passim; T. H. B. Mynors, memoirs, [March 1982], SAD 777/8/8
190 Bell to parents, 17 October 1931, SAD 697/4/35
191 Bell to parents, 27 January 1933, SAD 697/9/16
192 Miller-Stirling to mother, 17 June 1910, RHO Mss.Afr.s.2051/29; see also Cameron to Oldham, 26 July 1925, RHO Mss.Lugard.9/1/1
193 Heussler, *The British in Northern Nigeria* (London: Oxford University Press, 1960), p. 43
194 For one of many examples, see Walker, diary, 17 April 1915, RHO Mss.Afr.s.433/56; Walker, diary, 23 November 1919, RHO Mss.Afr.s.438/104
195 W. J. Reader, *Professional Men: The Rise of the Professional Classes in Nineteenth-century England* (London: Weidenfeld and Nicolson, 1966), p. 47
196 Kuklick, *Imperial Bureaucrat*, pp. 4, 8–10; see also S. Butler to parents, 2 April 1912, SAD 304/6/23; Daltry to mother, 6 May 1927, RHO Mss.Afr.s.2222/28; F. Pedler, interview with D. Fieldhouse, 24 August 1970, RHO Mss.Afr.s.1718/7; Sillery, 'Working backwards', [c.1975], RHO Mss.Afr.r.207/57
197 However, see Tomlinson to mother, 28 June 1904, RHO Mss.Afr.s.372/27
198 Wordsworth, 'The day's work', RHO Mss.Afr.s.1373/4; see also Henderson, *Modern Sudan*, pp. 21–2; W. Ward, 'My Africa', [undated], RHO Mss.Afr.r.127/10
199 Sayers (eds), *Handbook of Tanganyika*, p. 487
200 Kuklick, *Imperial Bureaucrat*, p. 106; Duncan-Johnstone, diary, 27 March 1928, RHO Mss.Afr.s.593/1/32; Dowsett to parents, 26 December 1931, RHO Mss. Afr.s.1276/34
201 Jeffries, *Colonial Empire*, pp. 132–3; Furse, untitled and undated memorandum, [probably 1936], RHO Mss.Brit.s.415/6/7/81; du Boulay, circular, 8 May 1935, in RHO Mss.Afr.s.593(5)/4/53–4
202 Heussler, *Yesterday's Rulers*, p. 39; Kirk-Greene, *Symbol of Authority*, p. 236
203 Newbold to Kennedy-Shaw, 11 September 1928, in Henderson, *Modern Sudan*, p. 30; compare this to Newbold to Kennedy-Shaw, 3 August 1930, in *ibid.*, p. 31, and Newbold to G. Moore, 25 May 1939, in *ibid.*, p. 111. A *habūb* is a dust storm.
204 Wordsworth to Young, 25 December 1905, RHO Mss.Afr.s.1373/36
205 Wordsworth to Young, 25 December 1905, RHO Mss.Afr.s.1373/36; see also Childs, diary, 18 November 1932, RHO Mss.Afr.s.1861(1); Orr to Leviseur, 27 May 1906, BL Add Mss 56100/34
206 Wordsworth to Young, 6 February 1904, RHO Mss.Afr.s.1373/23
207 Ross, untitled note, 23 October 1931, PRAAD CSO 25/3/61
208 L. M. Buchanan, memoirs, 10 April 1979, SAD 797/8/6
209 Huxley, 'Racial chess', 538

CHAPTER FOUR

Envisioning imperial authority: power, ritual and knowledge

During a 1910 speech in Liverpool, Lord Milner declared the 'era of expansion is over ... the era of organisation is just beginning'.[1] In Africa, Milner's emphasis upon administrative discontinuity was taken up in earnest in the years immediately following the First World War. Colonial elites became more ambitious about the role of British administrations in Africa. According to a rather wordy 1920 circular issued from central headquarters to Residents in northern Nigeria, the

> administration of a province to-day no longer mainly consists of the maintenance of law and order, of a fair standard of justice, of good political relations with the Emirs and with the Native Administrations, and the efficient supervision of assessment for and collection of revenue, but, on the contrary, necessitates even now, and in the years to come will necessitate in an ever increasing degree, strenuous efforts being actively made to aid and stimulate development.[2]

After 1918, the British were better able to invest more resources into altering Africa. Nigerian revenues increased as exports of cotton, cocoa, palm oil, hides and skins and tin grew rapidly, even if other industries such as gold and diamonds proved more erratic.[3] The Gold Coast was affected by the contraction of the cocoa trade in 1914–16, but recovered relatively quickly afterwards.[4] The Sudanese gum trade followed a similar pattern.[5] Other changes occurred. At the start of the interwar period, transport links were still patchy across large sections of British Africa. For example, in 1922, there were few motorcars in Sudan, whilst the journey from Khartoum to Geneina, capital of Dar Masalit Province, could only be partly taken by rail, after which a thirty-three-day camel ride was necessary. This meant access to information was also often slow.[6] The importation of more cars, the development of African road networks – John Iliffe has called the 1920s the 'great period' of road building – and other innovations such as air communications, reduced officials' fear of being vulnerable and isolated were conflict to break out.[7] Increased governmental ambition was also facilitated by expanding secretariats. For example, the number of central secretariat staff in Nigeria grew from seven in 1919 to twenty-four in 1924.[8]

Differences between the pre- and post-Great War periods can nevertheless be exaggerated. Edwardian officials certainly felt an 'uncomfortable awareness' that governmental power 'really was quite limited, and that only occasionally could administrators deploy sufficient coercive resources to impose their will'.[9] However, such limits did not necessarily lead to fears that a 'native' enemy awaited them around every corner. In 1908, Wingate and his close associate Slatin Pasha suggested that Mahdism had not been quelled since Sudan's conquest, but was once again 'becoming a very real and present danger to the peace and security' of the Condominium.[10] In the face of this, younger Edwardian SPS men felt fears of a 'Mahdist revival' were 'unjustified', perhaps brought about by a paranoia stemming from Slatin's 'black fits of depression'.[11]

Furthermore, British Africa continued to be a site of uprisings and instability after 1918, albeit not as frequently as before. Rebellions were varied in nature. They included the Abeokuta riots of 1918, which the British quelled with 2,600 WAFF troops; the Igbo Women's War of 1929 in south-east Nigeria; and those that more closely resembled post-1939 nationalist activity, such as the 1924 White Flag League mutiny in Sudan.[12] Regardless of whether they acted in what officials deemed the public interest or not, interwar Native Administration police forces were frequently understaffed, and failed to halt localised instances of violence.[13] Officials serving in Africa during the First World War did not believe that the colonies would fall due to indigenous rebellions.[14] However, the reduced number of men on the ground in Africa during the conflict served as a reminder that, for reasons beyond officials' control, the colonial state could still be prone to extended periods of weakness.[15]

Therefore, whilst officials serving in the interwar period would later wax nostalgic about the tough circumstances in which they worked as a means of distinguishing themselves from their successors, in many areas of Africa this was justified.[16] In the wake of severe population declines across East Africa from the 1880s onwards, certain medical improvements were made, particularly with regards to African trypanosomiasis. Africans and officials nevertheless had to contend with the influenza outbreak of the immediate postwar years, alongside other illnesses such as smallpox and meningitis, localised instances of famine, high indigenous mortality rates in Bunyoro and the decimation of cattle herds through rinderpest, such as occurred in Tanganyika into the 1930s.[17] Despite improvements in transport infrastructure and an increase in the number of officials working in Africa, most still had to cover large regions of Africa, and could invariably only do so gradually. As late as 1925, there were remote villages in the Western Province in the Gold Coast that had not yet been visited by a Briton.[18] The same remained true of parts of Tanganyika into the 1930s.[19] One consequently needs to take care to avoid the impression that the ability of the British to counteract insurrection suddenly rocketed after the First World War.

Consequently, even if becoming an official was decreasingly viewed as working for a state defined by economic weakness in a continent defined by internecine conflict, the role still required a good deal of confidence after 1918. Going beyond the frequent assertion that public school imparted the quality of being able to 'tackle a lonely job in a strange country amongst strange people', this chapter will examine changes to the bedrock upon which confidence rested.[20] This is especially important considering that the official corps was marked by tensions, which meant that DCs were perhaps less likely to draw strength from the presence of other Europeans around them. Particularly in light of Bernard Cohn's discussion of the various 'investigative modalities' within British 'officializing' procedures, it is well known that knowledge gathering – recording and classifying indigenous societies – played an important part in increasing officials' sense that they possessed imperial power.[21] What has not been interrogated, however, is the possibility that there were variations in attitudes towards knowledge gathering amongst officials. An ardent desire for knowledge was not an inherent product of the colonial encounter, but the result of a particular metropolitan mentality. Military officials were both more inclined to rely upon force and the use of prestige, and more at ease with their not knowing everything about those they governed, than civilian officials. Changes in the type of official recruited injected a new sense of urgency into the knowledge-gathering enterprise. Whilst such enquiries were underway, ritual, grand spectacle and the creation of a false omnipotence were judged crucial to the maintenance of imperial authority in the short term. As far as civilian officials were concerned, the process of collecting information about Africa meant that imperial authority increasingly rested on *real* power, rather than *symbolic* power. This underpinned the confidence that meant civilian officials accepted the expansion of the imperial remit more readily.

However, this transition to 'knowledge' of Africa was never felt complete. Africa still remained partially 'unknowable'. Here, the unique relationship each official developed with Africans came into its own. As the 'father' of his district, the longer an official stayed in

Africa, the more he believed he could manage Africans without necessarily fully understanding them. An emotional bond with Africans
filled the knowledge gap. Nevertheless, there were distinct limits as
to how far experiences of the continent were able to reshape officials'
attitudes towards imperial confidence. This is demonstrated by a
minority of officials whose formative, pre-African experiences generated an ambiguity as to the benefits of imperial governance that then
stayed with them in Africa.

In the early years of the twentieth century, a lack of knowledge
shook some elites' confidence. Surrounded by what he termed 'unsettled districts' such as Tivland, and assisted by only nine officials, in
his early years as High Commissioner of Northern Nigeria, Lugard
also felt hampered by the relative lack of information available to him
about the regions in which he worked.[22] Consequently, in spite of his
ambition and drive, Lugard felt his schemes for colonial governance
had to be reined in temporarily. Shortly after the conquest of Northern
Nigeria, he wrote that there was 'obvious folly' in 'attempting any
drastic reform which would cause a dislocation of methods which,
however faulty, have the sanction of traditional usage and are acqui-
esced in by the people, until we had an increased knowledge both of
Moslem methods of rule and of Native law and custom'.[23] Similarly,
for 'the new governors [in 1900] the Sudan was virgin land; they knew
so little about it. There were no administrative handbooks to guide
them, no tax rolls, no gazetteers of place-names, no comprehensive
tribal Who's Who'.[24]

Anxiety about being surrounded by Africans who might resist at
any moment was therefore bound up with the belief that little was
known about them. Besides the stretched nature of British resources in
Uganda, it was a lack of knowledge about Ankole that led to the paranoid
(and incorrect) belief that official Harry Galt's murder in 1905 was the
result of a conspiracy by local pastoralists.[25] A lack of knowledge also
diluted officials' authority in relation to other Europeans. The unusual
reliance of Bunyoro's Edwardian officials on Church Missionary Society
missionaries was partly because Nyoro resistance led them to look for
powerful local allies, and partly because a high turnover of officials
provided little opportunity for detailed opinions of the Banyoro to be
formed.[26] British elites in Africa consequently felt themselves living
through a 'transition period' insofar as imperial rule was concerned.[27]

Some Edwardian officials nevertheless had a problematic relationship with knowledge collection. In 1903, Allen Upward, a recently
retired official in Northern Nigeria, gave a talk to the African Society
(renamed the Royal African Society in 1935), that august institution
of scholars and others keen for news from Africa. The talk was low on

specific details about the places in which Upward worked. He partly excused himself by saying that the 'very great pressure of official work left me no time for independent study'.[28] Besides this, Upward suggested that,

> Although anxious to acquire as much information as possible, I was necessarily obliged to approach the natives in the character of a judge and ruler, rather than in that of a scientific enquirer; and I take this opportunity of saying that in dealing with African natives I consider it is not always wise nor practicable to play both parts at once. Scientific curiosity is likely to be misunderstood by savages, and to provoke either contempt or resentment.[29]

This explains why Upward's talk principally contained details of what had been immediately visible to him in Nigeria, such as living conditions, trading activity and the region's geography. Upward was happier collecting information in a courtroom than in other scenarios, because the provision of information was an inherent part of court proceedings.[30] Upward felt this would disguise his true intentions because the Africans present would think he sought to understand the specificities of a particular court case, rather than to study the case in order to understand how their society functioned.

However, even by the eclectic standards of the day, Upward's work as a novelist and avant-garde poet admired by Ezra Pound meant he was atypical of officials.[31] In contrast, military officials felt they should rely on prestige and bluff, rather than surreptitious anthropological observations, to get what they wanted. Captain Bertie Taylor came to the Gold Coast after nine years as a Cape Mounted Rifleman in South Africa. In 1906, he was working in Ulu in the North Western District. There he addressed a crowd of 300 on who they might select as their next chief. On the one hand there was

> Kombiri the fool, who did not believe in the power of the white man until he was caught, the fool who told them to cultivate only enough for their own needs and could not see that trade meant money, the fool who would not obey the king and had made a big people into a lot of leaderless compounds, the man who lived like a dog in a broken kennel.

On the other, there was Seidu, 'their rightful king, son of a big king who had fought and died for them, a man who the villages would follow, who would make them again into a big people'. After instructing them that they had a free say in their choice, Taylor felt there was 'rather a critical moment, as I was not at all sure what effect my invective had had on them, but they plumped for Seidu to my relief'. Concluding the palaver, Taylor made a declaration borne of a need to reassert the image of omnipotence: 'I then told the people that having shown that

Figure 4 Ali el Tom, 1911

they were sensible I would tell them how to improve their country. Had they chosen Kombiri I would not have wasted my time on them'.[32]

In spite of their awareness of the limits of colonial authority, military officials were generally more doubtful than civilian officials that systematic enquiry into a region would reveal much. Taylor clearly felt that his bluff was of genuine benefit in improving his district and, in line with the points made in Chapter Two, he was less imbued with the idea that anthropological investigation was a routine governmental process than those who had been to university.[33] In 1906, Taylor gave consideration to the 'backward state of things' in the North Western District. In rectifying this, he mooted two potential schemes. Firstly, Taylor suggested breaking up the peoples in the region and placing them under imported chiefs. Secondly, he suggested compulsory education for chiefs' sons. Whilst he plumped for the latter option, both plans were marked by a notable lack of detail. In distinct contrast to his civilian successors, Taylor did not suggest any study be made into the roots of the 'appalling state of savagery in Dagarti', or consider the likely implications of his recommended scheme.[34] Instead, his secret to governance was that 'Truly the rule by force seems to be appreciated'.[35] This is unsurprising given that, although invariably not as violent as King's African Rifles staff officer Richard Meinertzhagen, military officials were more at ease than civilians with any violence that went beyond the striking of a servant.[36] Where violence and a show of force obtained results, knowledge collection was felt too much work for too little apparent benefit for anyone except academics. This would explain why one of Taylor's military official contemporaries in the North Western District quickly gave up when asked to research Dagara origins.[37] Consequently, such officials experienced Africa as a continent defined primarily by homogeneity rather than by heterogeneity, the only real source of differentiation being whether an African society was hostile or not.

Changes in the type of officials recruited brought other attitudes to prominence. Reginald Davies embodied this change. A Cambridge mathematics graduate, Davies came into contact with the Kababish, a confederation of Arab nomads in Kordofan in Sudan, when stationed at Bara between 1912 and 1915. One learned SPS official had recently published an introductory work on the complicated history of the Kababish, as had the noted ethnographers Charles and Brenda Seligman.[38] Davies nevertheless felt an absence of detailed knowledge had allowed the *nazir* of the Kababish, Ali el Tom, to enhance his own position considerably. El Tom was 'in a better position than Government to gauge the taxpaying capabilities of his tribe', possessing 'ample power to enforce his views on the subject'. Consequently, since the conquest of 1899, el Tom had apparently 'been collecting the tribute three- or four-fold, pocketing or disbursing to his sheikhs and agents everything over and above the small sum demanded by Government'.[39]

This state of affairs had prevailed undisturbed until September 1912, when Davies' superior at Bara, E. N. Corbyn, produced a report on the Kababish, which was then supplemented by Davies' own research on the matter.[40] Davies felt that, had the British known more about the Kababish earlier, the problem would have been avoided because it would have been possible to have switched the system of taxation from an 'arbitrary' tribute to a carefully assessed herd tax. As it stood, it was problematic that the British were only starting to address this issue in 1915. The matter was particularly pressing because, whilst Davies did not think el Tom should become too powerful, it was felt the Kababish were nevertheless in need of a strong leader to check their worst abuses. One historian has suggested that the Kababish were the '*beau idéal* of British imaginings of traditional nomad Arab rule', but before the First World War in particular, SPS officials thought them troublesome.[41] Worried by 'petty raids' launched by the Kababish into areas recognised as 'Darfurian', Khartoum launched an operation in 1912 (which met with some success) to prevent Arab gun runners loaded with rifles making their way from Abyssinia to Kordofan.[42] Negative beliefs about the Kababish proved surprisingly enduring given their reputation as a source of wonderment.[43]

In dealing with the situation, Davies was convinced of 'the necessity of totally abolishing his [el Tom's] present system of collecting an arbitrary tribute from the tribe ... it does not originate in any customary dues and therefore cannot be regulated; and its present amount added to an accurate herd tax, would be an intolerable burden on the people'.[44] Davies' solution was that 'The Nazir's remuneration from the tribe, if any, must be fixed by government and paid to him through the merkaz [government office]'. However, Davies felt any change could only come about very gradually in order to avoid social disturbances.[45] Davies believed that the *nazir* would eventually decline in importance, but this did not come to pass, and the regulation of el Tom's activities was subsequently very light. What is important, however, is Davies' conviction that abuses lain unchecked due to a prior lack of knowledge limited his room for manoeuvre.[46] The idea that 'the justest intentions are often frustrated by lack of insight, knowledge of local conditions or misunderstanding of a case' increasingly became the norm.[47]

A point of contention might reasonably be raised against the argument that the type of officials recruited was the key determinant of the rate at which information was collected and, consequently, also of how much knowledge the colonial state collectively felt it had. After all, the British had variable amounts of experience of the different parts of Africa. The British had a lengthier history of interaction with West Africa than East Africa, thanks in part to the slave trade.[48] Then there were variations in terms of the length of time each region had been under British control. Within Nigeria for instance, Lagos on the coast had been annexed as a British colony in 1861, whilst Kano in the north was not taken until 1903.

Civilian officials nevertheless felt themselves to be the first real generation to take a sustained interest in anthropological work as an essential part of their administrative routine. This universalised a belief that they had to more or less start from scratch in their endeavours. Indeed, that officials such as Davies felt themselves so different from their predecessors created conflict. There were certain regions, particularly away from the principal imperial administrative loci, where the process of gathering information took place slowly. Civilian officials blamed this on their predecessors. Kurmuk lies in the east of Sudan, close to the border with Ethiopia. For Anthony Disney:

> Up till about 1926, the administration of Kurmuk District seems to have consisted in a predominantly military regime and little was known – and still less recorded – about the tribes inhabiting it ... [However, Disney's predecessor] spent some time in trekking round the District and started studying the tribes with a view to getting to know the people better and so gradually winning their confidence ... The primitive tribes had previously been lumped together ... although speaking distinct languages having separate customs and living in well-defined areas – their tribes have been sorted out; a start has been made with the recording and study of their languages.[49]

Disney laid special emphasis upon being in possession of a file that contained a page of information for each village in his district. The change in attitude is stark. In contrast with Allen Upward, Disney did not feel that appearing as an 'enquirer' would dispel illusions of omnipotence.[50] Indeed, for Disney, the very act of such gathering showed an interest in the people of Kurmuk, which meant their confidence could be gained.[51] In contrast with military officials, Disney believed that a focus on Africa's heterogeneity was the key to effective governance.

Civilian officials were willing to accept the expansion of their administrative remit. As one Gold Coast DC wrote in the early 1920s, 'The British Empire is only now beginning to realise itself'.[52] Confidence was derived from the conviction that Africa was starting to be understood more clearly. However, there were other motives behind knowledge collection besides a desire for better governance. Whilst they were sometimes looked upon with disdain for doing so, some civilian officials took secretariats' calls for anthropological studies to be undertaken as opportunities to show off their ability to their superiors.[53] Nevertheless, the fact that, for civilian officials, an absence of information was a source of anxiety, demonstrates that their need for knowledge was genuine. Gawain Bell, who started working in Sudan in

1931, needed written accounts of new places to which he was headed. After two years working amongst a predominantly Arab population in Kassala, Bell's second posting was to Dilling in Kordofan, a region containing Nuba, a people of whom he knew little.[54] Bell consequently read all that he was able to get his hands on about the Nuba.[55] As a result, he felt he knew how to engage with them before he arrived in Kordofan. The reassurance the information provided is palpable.[56]

However, whilst knowledge gathering was being carried out, prestige had to fill any gaps. Prestige was tantamount to an obsession prior to the First World War. For elites such as Henry McCallum and Lugard, 'Prestige is everything with the Africans'.[57] The psychological need for the projection of strength through performance was naturally most marked when and where British control was felt lightest. That the Commissioner in charge of investigating Harry Galt's murder in 1905 chose to organise his camp along martial lines, with 'ostentatious displays by the army and police becoming a part of daily routine', demonstrates the significance of such displays to those who felt isolated.[58] Hubert Mathews, Assistant Resident in Okene in Northern Nigeria, attached a great deal of importance to tax collection, not so much for generating revenue to fund infrastructural development as for making officials' lives easier. 'It will do these people [living in and around Okene] good to pay a small regular tax', he wrote to his parents in 1911, 'as it will make them perforce a little more industrious and they may possible [sic] realise better what British occupation means and settle down to a more law-abiding life'.[59] So, after facing difficulties collecting taxes from the Mada in 1913, a military patrol accompanied a more rigorous inspection the following year. This elicited a response from Mathews that says much about the psychological need for the projection of permanence. He felt that the

> great virtue of the patrol was the impression it created of ponderous inevitability, like a steam-roller tidying up every bit of one patch before moving on to the next, rather than the motor flying by at high speed and dodging the holes and lumps of the road. I think *this* year's tribute will be much easier to get in from them.[60]

Nevertheless, it was not merely the more isolated parts of the empire where such concerns were present. Meticulous ceremonies and rituals increasingly supplanted the 'shock and awe' of displays of force as a means of maintaining and developing imperial authority. Whilst the 'theatre of empire' was conducted for the duration of British rule in Africa, the idea that this was the best means of maintaining, or even extending, imperial power reached its peak in the years immediately prior to the Great War.[61] The preference was for durbars much like those perceived to have been so successful in India. Lugard's visit to Kano in 1913 occasioned a procession that included 15,000 horsemen, an uncounted number of footmen, 800 WAFF troops and 300 mounted infantry with lances.[62] The apogee of such imperial display was nevertheless a royal visit. On 17 January 1912, King George V and Queen Mary visited Port Sudan for twelve hours whilst on their return home from the Indian durbar of the previous year. They were met at Port Sudan by Governor-General Reginald Wingate, and prominent sheikhs, and were treated to a series of martial displays and dances by southern Sudanese populations. A man with a firm belief in the value of PR in enhancing his own status, Wingate felt it crucial to infuse imperial rule with ritual and spectacle, being highly attuned to the potential for an impressive show of grandeur to bind Sudanese elites to the British. The general population, it was hoped, would follow.[63] As one subordinate official correctly noted, 'The Sirdar was awfully pleased' with the 1912 visit.[64] Wingate felt it 'has had an enormous effect throughout the whole of the Sudan and nothing has occurred since our re-occupation to equal it'.[65]

Officials thought much the same. Stephen Butler was a junior

Figure 5 Sudanese elites view HMS *Medina*, Port Sudan harbour, 17 January 1912

official who helped organise the visit, ensuring that sheikhs success-fully arrived in Port Sudan. Writing home two weeks after the event, he noted that King George's presentation of a silver medal on a chain to each sheikh and the sight of 'the "Medina" gliding into the docks ... has made a most enormous impression on them ... [if] the whole show ... had cost the country £50,000, [it] would still have been worth it for the general effect it will have on the country when these sheikhs get back to their tribes. They are at present quite flattened out and can hardly talk at all about it'.[66]

By demonstrating the serious and far-reaching nature of Britain's intentions as a governing power – and by making African elites aware of Britain's capacity to provide them with a wider economic reach in particular – it was felt such proactivism would rub off on the broader indigenous populace. Butler believed that those sheikhs who passed through Khartoum on the way home from meeting the King at Port Sudan were also struck by the buildings that the British had constructed, and by the receptions that SPS men held for them. By making the sheikhs realise they could profit from working with the British, Butler felt the visit to Khartoum was likely to 'prove a stimulus to trade in many respects, particularly the cattle trade with Egypt, as several big cattle owning sheikhs expressed a desire to start trading'.[67]

Although they remerged on a much diminished scale after 1918, such imperial displays were halted by the Great War.[68] At the time, there were British fears that the conflict would damage Africans' supposed belief in white benevolence and omnipotence. Indeed, some went as far as to propose a local armistice between Britain and Germany 'so as not to present the "native" with the undignified sight of white men killing one another'.[69] Most nevertheless felt the war had to be endured irrespective of the fallout. For R. E. H. Baily, who started working in Sudan in 1909, 'Up to say half way through the first war we British ... had an exaggerated reputation'. However, as a result of stretched resources during the war, some soldiers were brought in to help run wartime administrative affairs. The army 'jumped at this opportunity of getting rid of "duds" ... Two sorry specimens had been sent to help me at Singa. They thought all black people swine and their main occupation and one in which they showed considerable flair, was to try and prove their servants to be robbers'. According to Baily, their actions turned some Sudanese against the British.[70] It was not just elderly ex-officials, looking back and complaining about the turn for the worse that colonial governance had supposedly taken after the First World War, who believed prestige was diminishing. In 1914, one graduate newcomer wrote to his parents that, 'from the point of view of prestige and dignity, it seems to be regretted generally that native troops have been put at each other to settle *our* quarrels however just'.[71]

It is now well known that the Great War did indeed increase Africans' public criticism of British actions.[72] A declining ability to rely on prestige was therefore something officials felt was forced upon them. After 1918, elites still demanded that officials maintain African respect by leading 'incorruptible private lives out of office', and DCs certainly sought to maintain what prestige they felt they had left.[73] One Ugandan DC wrote in 1920 that 'Legislation which is not, or cannot, be enforced is more harmful than no legislation at all, since it merely weakens a Government's position and authority'.[74] All were concerned with Africans watching cinematic depictions of the travails and 'morally dubious' elements of Western life.[75] The incipient nature of imperial control in certain regions meant efforts were even made to enhance prestige. In southern Sudan, officials attempted to harness an indigenous belief in magic to suggest God endorsed the SPS as his designated rulers.[76] In comparison with earlier years of British rule in Africa, this use of prestige was nevertheless much diminished. Officials new to Africa after 1918 naturally had less of a yardstick against which to measure any decline in prestige ushered in by the Great War, but they still felt that prestige had been replaced with respect and influence.[77]

Nevertheless, particularly because they increasingly believed that knowledge was such an important means of enhancing imperial power, officials were increasingly reconciled to this. Even before his arrival in Sudan, Gawain Bell had written that empire would be at its most successful when there was no animosity between European and African. He suggested that the 'old days of dominion over native peoples based on the "prestige" of the white have gone never to return', and that what was needed instead was 'a spirit of co-operation, the outcome of mutual liking and respect for our statesmanship and political morality'.[78] Attitudes such as that of one Gold Coast DC suggest that this would not be a problem; 'Do not let it be thought that one considers oneself of a race set apart', the official wrote in 1922, 'It is perfectly possible to avoid this without losing respect'.[79] An increasing acceptance of this revised mandate was a direct result of the change in the type of official recruited. It might even be that anthropological study had an impact on officials in this regard. After all, Bell would have concurred with the anthropologist Meyer Fortes, who following time spent amongst the Tallensi in the Gold Coast, suggested that

> The District Commissioner's power as a sanction of political conduct does not depend upon some mysterious awe of the white man. There are, indeed, elements of fear in the attitude of the native towards him due to recollections of the military pacification of the country less than a generation ago ... What keeps this sanction alive and effective

is the direct intercourse between the District Commissioner and the native community ... by the fact that he is known to be an all-powerful dispenser of impartial justice whose vigilance never abates'.[80]

In their search for information about Africans living in their regions, this new generation of officials did not get all it wanted.[81] Certain elements of African life remained shrouded in mystery. As late as 1930, officials were still trying to work out the system of succession amongst the Gonja in the Gold Coast's Northern Territories.[82] In the same region, Britons were prevented from attending certain rituals, such as the fire festival in Chama, and the discovery and prevention of witchcraft proved an elusive task that led both officials and anthropologists to frequently admit defeat.[83] Of course, officials did not need to know everything about African societies for the imperial state to function. These gaps did not prevent officials from collecting taxes and from feeling that they understood most of the motivating factors behind court cases. Furthermore, it was felt that some of the institutions and customs that perpetuated such gaps would gradually cease to exist.[84] Secret societies were investigated across the continent, and it was believed their influence would recede as Africa became 'civilised'.[85] Officials were frustrated that they remained unaware of everything that went on in the Yoruba *ogboni* council meetings of south-west Nigeria. However, because it was believed that the typical African was resentful of 'any interference in his family affairs', but happy to accede to governmental authorities on matters more broadly concerned with the 'country's good', the British felt they could work round this issue.[86]

Nevertheless, there were other, more sizeable, obstacles in officials' paths. The most obvious of these was the language barrier. Explanations circulated amongst elites regarding officials' frequent failure to learn local languages included officials' not seeing the use in doing so, the variety of languages and dialects spoken, and the 'inherent difficulty of the language and the lack of adequate facilities for tuition'.[87] Complaints amongst officials about whichever 'infernal' or 'appalling' language they faced were common, and in colonies with a plethora of regional languages and dialects, difficulties with learning were compounded by officials' frequent relocation.[88] However, regardless of the precise blend of factors in each instance, in 1934 the Gold Coast's Secretary of State for Native Affairs reported he was

> dismayed by the low standard of proficiency shown by candidates who have presented themselves at recent examinations ... The lack of fluency, the poor accent and the inadequate intelligibility and power of understanding exhibited by candidates during the examinations [suggested that] ... officers regard the examinations as no more than an obstacle to

be surmounted by a course of intensive cramming and not as an incentive to acquiring a proper grip on the language they are required to learn.[89]

This was in spite of threats from elites that a lack of linguistic ability restricted a move up the salary scale.[90] It was also in spite of the importance officials themselves attached to speaking another language. Some agreed with Gowers' assertion that 'nothing is so important for an African administrator as to learn thoroughly some African language', but chose to rely on interpreters nevertheless.[91] This created other problems. One official in southern Nigeria believed the difficulty of learning Igbo played into the hands of elders and chiefs, 'who often conspired with the interpreters to maintain their oppressive rule over the people who were thus deliberately prevented from discovering the enlightenment and progress which the new regime was anxious to introduce'.[92] There were also suspicions amongst officials that interpreters provided distorted translations of Africans' conversations with officials because of the interpreters' political or social bias, or because they said what they felt officials wanted to hear.[93]

Of course, some officials argued it was 'absolutely impossible to get on, to really understand and get on with native tribesmen unless you speak their language' as an entry into a discussion of their own linguistic ability.[94] Other issues nevertheless remained. From Sudan's Fung Province, Elliott Balfour wrote, 'The natives here are mostly Arabs and consequently the intrigue and double dealing that goes on is inconceivable'.[95] Another SPS official felt that, 'Nothing is sure in the east, not even justice, but life gains a speculative interest unknown to the west except from the Dublin sweepstake'.[96] Africa was never felt mastered, even if declarations such as, 'The more you see of the niggers [sic] mind the less comprehensible it becomes' became less frequent after the First World War.[97] The very logistics of the colonial state imposed further constraints on officials' ability to know. In spite of the improvements in transport noted at the start of the chapter, officials could not be in all places at once. Furthermore, excellent studies have demonstrated how, despite their best efforts at creating precisely defined and ordered societies – the neat lines demarcating different 'racial' zones of inhabitation in Dar es Salaam and Mombasa, for instance – officials were aware of the limits of their knowledge about the 'faceless' urban masses.[98]

However, the confidence gained from the formal acquisition of knowledge was both partially superseded and supplemented by a confidence that arose from the belief that Britons and Africans were connected in other ways. As noted in Chapter Three, officials primarily imagined their relationship with Africans as a unilateral bond rather than as a part of a multilateral network. Their gradually becoming 'father' of their people led officials to speak of developing an 'inner knowledge' or 'instinct' of how to work with Africans that could not be learnt from books.[99] It might be that officials made such claims publically to justify their ongoing struggle against others, such as missionaries, who supposedly diluted officials' authority. The belief in this bond was nevertheless genuine.[100]

Officials felt that the development of a 'fatherly' status amongst Africans would have its own rewards. By establishing a bond with, and winning the trust of, 'their' Africans, officials believed information would increasingly be offered up to them voluntarily. Officials complained of the number of disputes with which they had to deal, but these complaints nevertheless convinced them that their brand of justice was trusted. Instead of remaining hidden away, Africans with issues most in need of resolution would come to them. Hubert Mathews became an official in 1910 after graduating from Jesus College, Oxford. From the very start of his career Mathews invested a good deal of effort in anthropological study and, unusually for an official, returned to Oxford to study cultural anthropology at Exeter College whilst on leave in 1912.[101] For all his concern with the pursuit of knowledge (reflected in his very complete personal archive of circulars and reports, later bequeathed to the Colonial Records Project at Rhodes House), Mathews nevertheless felt that this knowledge needed to be applied in a particular manner. He believed it had a role in developing an empathetic connection with Africans that surmounted some of the logistical limitations of the colonial state. The 'one encouraging thing about the number of complaints', he wrote from Kabba in 1911, 'is that it is increasing mainly on account of a growing confidence in the white man's justice and not due to any increase in lawlessness'.[102] Officials' actions, rather than simply their knowledge, were overcoming African recalcitrance. Mathews even suggested that a new station had been created at Iddo just to keep up with Africans' growing belief in the impartiality of the imperial state.[103] The good relations officials cultivated with local elites would supposedly encourage the latter to act responsibly, and establish responsible courts that perpetuated the 'white man's justice' even in his absence. However, thanks to the relationship between the two, chiefs would still choose to consult officials over important matters.[104]

Whilst experiences of Africa resulted in a shift in attitudes, we nevertheless have to be mindful of the limits to which the experience of being an official entirely reoriented officials' attitudes. The very process of being an official freshly graduated from university did not inherently lead to their developing a confidence underpinned by both real and emotional knowledge, and an enthusiasm for an expansion of the imperial remit. Whilst the majority of officials felt their job was worth doing in the first place, we turn next to the minority of officials who were uncertain about empire.

Leonard Heaney and Robert Greig commenced service in Tanganyika in 1929 and 1932 respectively. When in Tanganyika, the two became friends, Greig believing that Heaney had a 'charming personality' and a 'very balanced outlook'.[105] There are good reasons for this. They both had ever-fluctuating relationships with modernity and empire. They sometimes took great delight in emphatically endorsing Western, and more specifically English, ideals and customs. Heaney complained that Africa impaired his ability to act as he had done back home, suggesting that life in Tanganyika was

> merely an unending struggle to reap a sufficiency of food in the face of floods, drought and the depredations of elephants, baboons and locusts. The constant struggle leaves little time for the pursuit of intellectual excellence or anything which does not give immediate satisfaction to material needs.[106]

At other times, Heaney would declare himself a 'wide open spacer', rejecting modernity and eulogising Africa's 'primitive' nature.[107] Greig alternated in a similar fashion, although his criticisms of modernity were in a more spiritualist vein.[108] Heaney fluctuated between saying he cared deeply for the Africans in his district, and claiming that he would have no objection to leaving Africans to their perceived idleness-induced fate 'were I not under some pressure to see that tax comes in, and no one dies of starvation'.[109] His stance towards Western-educated Africans also moved between extreme admiration, and extreme resentment for their not being like 'more primitive natives'.[110]

Greig voraciously devoured difficult-to-obtain highbrow works.[111] These included Kagawa Toyohiko's Christian Socialist work *A Grain of Wheat*, which advocates a workers' democracy in which vertically structured industrial unions under the 'wardship' of national guilds would create 'a proletarian paradise within which each individual would be freed from the bonds of wage-slavery to realize his own innermost creative potential'.[112] The work led Greig to wonder 'how much opportunity for real service there is in our job here'.[113] 'Life as an Administrative Officer', he confided to his diary

> is bound if not counteracted to cause the feeling of all the powerful-ness of the state of and intrinsic superiority of its will to predominate over the individual. No state, God, or person has any right intrinsically over the individual ... At best it must be a compromise of social necessity of combined conclusions of the many exercising a right within

certain limits. To secure a ready delight in feeling for the individual as a humanity [sic] rather than a cog in the state's machine, exercise of the will must be made for the spontaneous love of mankind. This I feel is pre-eminently necessary if one would free onself [sic] from the slavery of the God of Government.[114]

This stance led to arguments with those of his peers who were 'so very confident in the superiority of the Administrative Officer and the Administration above all departments and non-officials'.[115]

Heaney thought highly of the Germans for having 'opened up' Tanganyika to development in the face of 'suspicious and hostile' Africans.[116] However, he felt that the African, if left alone by the British, would sit in the shade and start

gossiping with his neighbours ... Probably, if we are to believe D. H. Lawrence he 'looks into the heart of the cosmos' and has 'the oldest kind of wisdom' ... But we government officials must not suspect this. He must call on him to fill up holes in the road inconvenient for motor cars ... he will tell him to carry his tent over twelve miles a day for fifty miles, so that [t]he bwana can quickly reach another office and start his occupation of signing his name on many pieces of paper.[117]

The 'heart of the cosmos' refers to D. H. Lawrence's *The Plumed Serpent* (1926), in which a sentimental primitivism is a constant.[118] The reference to the 'oldest wisdom' – that there are truths in the 'primitive' world that have been ignored by modern man – is central to Lawrence's *Psychoanalysis and the Unconscious* (1921) and *Fantasia of the Unconscious* (1922), which tackle alienation and frustration with modernity and is echoed by Birkin's statement in *Women in Love*: 'I abhor humanity, I wish it was swept away'.[119] In reading Lawrence, who was relatively neglected at the time, Heaney was unusual amongst his peers.[120] Heaney's response to Lawrence was nevertheless noncommittal and detached, perfectly typifying his ambivalence about the modernity he felt the colonial state represented.

There are good reasons why officials in Tanganyika may have displayed such uncertainty. As a new addition to the empire, the mandate was the greatest cause for concern. On the positive side, Germans left behind detailed administrative records in their *bomas*, whilst some DOs took comfort from a belief that German colonies were more stable and better organised (though also more oppressed) than those belonging to France.[121] Nevertheless, in comparison with the older colonies in British Africa, there was less conviction that the government had attained legitimacy. The presence of white settlers there caused officials headaches. There were concerns that large number of German settlers still living in Tanganyika might turn hostile to British rule and, towards the end of the 1930s, there were persistent rumours that Tanganyika was to be returned to Germany as part of some form of appeasement package.[122] Furthermore, some officials were worried that they did not know the mandate. As one Tanganyikan DO wrote in 1926, 'I don't believe there are twenty people in the country who understand the native, and they are mostly German and Scandinavian missionaries who keep their knowledge to themselves'.[123] This stands in contrast to what officials felt elsewhere in Africa. Of all of British Africa, it was Tanganyika that was most likely to disabuse anyone of their confidence, particularly those who placed their faith in knowledge collection.

There were nevertheless officials elsewhere who were also uncertain about whether or not what Britain was doing in Africa was right. David Bayley arrived in Nigeria in 1932. In 1936, Bayley read Trotsky's *History of the Russian Revolution* (1930), which rejects the Stalinist belief of 'socialism in one country' in favour of international revolution.[124] Upon finishing the work, Bayley began to believe that it was the Trotskyists, rather than 'Constitutional Socialists' such as himself, who might be in the right.[125] In spite of this, he sometimes advocated imperialism as a means of pushing civilisation forward, railing against those who opposed British rule in India, for example, and sometimes went against it.[126]

In all three cases, it would appear as if uncertainty about the civilising mission were a product of pre-African experiences, rather than something that emerged in the midst of colonial service. As an Oxford undergraduate, Heaney drank in Oriel College's irreverent undercurrent at a time when it was home to the famously oppositional A. J. P. Taylor and an infamous aesthete group that used to frequent the nearby St George's restaurant.[127] Heaney was a well-read student, dwelt on matters with a constant view to the 'bigger picture', and was certainly intelligent enough to know how to appear the unashamed empire enthusiast for whom Furse was looking.[128] Heaney was also an outsider, and cut a marginal figure amongst his cadet contemporaries. He was picked on and taunted by his peers who accompanied him on the voyage out to Tanganyika, which was only compounded by his 'childlike' appearance and supposed naivety in the ways of romancing women.[129] It was consequently as a precocious and marginalised twenty-three-year-old aesthete, armed with much-loved jazz records and the *Oxford Book of English Verse*, and signing off letters home with flourishes such as 'Yours the Mephistophelean', that Heaney, a man already ambivalent about empire, arrived in Tanganyika.[130]

Greig and Bayley's undergraduate experiences at Cambridge were different from that of Heaney, but both emerged ambivalent about empire nevertheless. Whilst at university Bayley described himself as 'Conservative in imperial affairs Liberal [*sic*] in economic and Socialist in foreign' – an eclectic mix if ever there was one – and stated that he could not see 'why Communism should not work, and raise up an entirely new civilization'.[131] A sceptic who railed against big business, the mass media and 'polite society', he seems to have actively courted antagonism; at a public lecture in Cambridge he suggested that the United Kingdom return Gibraltar to Spain, which unsurprisingly aroused hostility.[132] Bayley was simultaneously worried about imminent global conflict and ambiguous as to whether he should be. Before leaving for Africa, he wrote that,

> Whether civilisation could stand another war I don't know. perhaps [*sic*] it would be as well if it couldn't. After all, the human race is only a lot of little maggots crawling about on a decaying planet.[133]

Though not the closest of friends, Greig and Bayley met on several occasions prior to their setting out for Africa.[134] Following one of their meetings, Bayley sympathised with Greig's idea that the economic collapse of the West was due any time soon, and that 'politically there seems to be every chance of us returning to a Dark Age'.[135]

An extended study of these three officials demonstrates two things. Firstly, towards the end of the interwar period, a minority of young men who became officials started to mix mainstream ideas about empire with radical ones emerging from either the political left or that section of the 'Bright Young Things' that professed a profound ambiguity about the value of modernity. These officials consequently departed for Africa uncertain as to what their purpose on the continent should be and, indeed, whether what they were doing there was right. Secondly, we must resist the temptation to suggest that there was a uniform process by which graduates went out to Africa, learnt of African societies, and became more confident about, and comfortable with, the expansion of the boundaries of imperial state actions as a result.

Conclusion

Modern discussions of the agency of Britons who worked in the empire frequently return to 'Shooting an elephant', George Orwell's 1936 essay in which his role as police officer in Burma is shaped largely by its performative aspect.[136] Orwell had to shoot an elephant that had been on the rampage and killed a man. Orwell did so not because he wanted to – after all, the elephant was now at rest in a field near to the village, and Orwell was naturally disinclined to shoot the animal

– but because it was expected of him by the villagers. 'And it was at this moment', he wrote,

> as I stood there with the rifle in my hands, that I first grasped the hollow-ness, the futility of the white man's dominion in the East. Here was I, the white man with his gun, standing in front of the unarmed native crowd – seemingly the leading actor of the piece; but in reality I was only an absurd puppet pushed to and fro by the will of those yellow faces behind. I perceived in this moment that when the white man turns tyrant it is his own freedom that he destroys.[137]

Orwell's essay raises interesting questions: how far did officials consider themselves involved in a performance of colonial authority that was disassociated from actions they felt necessary for the improvement of their district? And was officials' sense that they needed to wear a performative mask a constant irrespective of time and place?

This chapter has charted changes in the roots underpinning officials' ideas about why they were able to act as they did. Rather than driving all to try and study Africa with equal enthusiasm, the continent elicited varying responses from officials. In their belief that 'it will never be through the fear of physical force that good work will be accomplished but solely through his [an officials'] own moral authority', civilian officials rejected the approach of military officials.[138] Where previously anthropological nuance had been thought less mighty than the sword, with this change in personnel, information about African societies started to be collected with greater enthusiasm.

Civilian officials never completely abandoned the notion that perfor-mance had a part to play in imperial governance. However, over time, a greater proportion of officials believed that British prestige needed to be replaced by an African respect that was earned more carefully by the completion of good works. Officials increasingly considered the use of prestige a means to an end that enabled them to get a job done whilst the process of acquiring information about African socie-ties was underway. For all officials' railing against the bureaucratic tendencies of the colonial state, the growing paper trail did more than simply demonstrate the ongoing professionalisation of the adminis-trative services in Africa. It generated confidence, hence the tangible pride officials felt at having a file that contained a page of information for each village in their districts.[139]

It was nevertheless felt that constraints placed upon the colonial state, as well as Africans' supposedly irrational and secretive nature, limited the extent that routine processes of anthropological enquiry would uncover everything about African societies. Officials' belief that they were the 'father of the people', and that Africans would voluntarily confide in officials, partially ameliorated such concerns. Complicating this image of young graduates confident in the imperial mission was a group of officials that stood apart from its peers. It should be quite apparent that men such as Bayley, Greig and Heaney were in a distinct minority. Officials did not, on the whole, reflect on theosophist plans for attaining a higher state of consciousness or the virtues of a Trotskyist world revolution. The consumption of modernist ideas did not inherently lead to tension, because other officials kept up with the latest modern works but nevertheless remained conventional in outlook.[140] However, the uncertainty demonstrated by a small number of officials was not a direct result of African experiences. This minority instead became unsure about empire because traditional ideas about imperial service were already being overlaid with radical ones by their time at university. The experience of being an official was insufficient to instil normative interwar pro-imperial feelings in those whose sense of moral purpose was already being assailed by new strains of thought that would blow with greater force after the Second World War.

Notes

1   E. H. H. Green, *The Crisis of Conservatism: The Politics, Economics and Ideology of the British Conservative Party, 1880–1914* (London: Routledge, 1995), p. 194. By 'organisation', Milner was primarily suggesting that Britain was moving towards tariff reform; *ibid.*, pp. 298–9, 303

2   Secretary, Northern Provinces, to Residents and Heads of Departments, 29 June 1920, RHO Mss.Afr.s.783/2/3/89

3   A. G. Adebayo, 'The production of hides and skins in colonial Northern Nigeria, 1900–1945', *Journal of African History* 33:2 (1992), 278; T. Falola and M. Heaton, *A History of Nigeria* (Cambridge: Cambridge University Press, 2008), pp. 119–20; S. Martin, 'Gender and innovation: farming, cooking and palm processing in the Ngwa Region, South-Eastern Nigeria, 1900–1939', *Journal of African History* 25:4 (1984), 421; for a partial contrast, see Roberts, 'The gold boom of the 1930s in East Africa', *African Affairs* 85:341 (1986), 545–62

4   F. M. Bourret, *The Gold Coast: A Survey of the Gold Coast and British Togoland, 1919–1946* (Stanford, CA: Stanford University Press, 1949), p. 26; D. Killingray, 'Repercussions of World War I in the Gold Coast', *Journal of African History* 19:1 (1978), 42

5   Daly, *Empire on the Nile*, pp. 430, 459

6   This was particularly the case in Tanganyika. Although he was only 50 miles from Tabora, the capital of Tanganyika's Western Province, it took the DO in Urambo a week to hear of the 1918 Armistice; Heussler, *British Tanganyika*, p. 11

7   Iliffe, *Africans: The History of a Continent* (Cambridge: Cambridge University Press, 1995), p. 212; Daly, *Darfur's Sorrow*, p. 133; R. McCormack, 'Airlines and empires: Great Britain and the "Scramble for Africa", 1919–1939', *Canadian Journal of African Studies* 10:1 (1976), 88, 104–5

8   Gailey, *Clifford*, p. 135

9   Willis, 'Violence, authority, and the state in the Nuba Mountains of Condominium Sudan', *Historical Journal* 46:1 (2003), 94

10 Wingate, 'Memorandum by Governor-General Sir R. Wingate', 9 August 1908, NA FO 407/173

11 Baily, 'Early recollections of the Sudan', SAD 533/4/23; see also Hill, *Slatin*, pp. 76, 90

12 Gailey, *Lugard and the Abeokuta Uprising: The Demise of Egba Independence* (London: Frank Cass, 1982). For the events of 1924, see Chapter Six.

13 Killingray, 'The maintenance of law and order in British Colonial Africa', *African Affairs* 85:340 (1986), 411–37

14 E. Wrangham, 'The Gold Coast and the First World War: "Carrying on" – the service under strain', in J. Smith (ed.), *Administering the Empire: The British Colonial Service in Retrospect* (London: University of London Press, 1999), pp. 167–80

15 Mathews, 'Half yearly report on Lafia Division, Nassarawa Province', 30 June 1917, RHO Mss.Afr.s.783/2/5/3

16 Clearkin, memoirs, RHO Mss.Brit.Emp.r.4/1/33; R. Niven, 'Along the road', in Kirk-Greene (ed.), *Glimpses of Empire*, pp. 288–9; see also Callaway, *Gender, Culture and Empire*, pp. 176–7

17 Slater to Milner, 14 June 1920, PRAAD ADM 1/2/132/508; *Hansard*, 5th series, vol. 200, col. 7; Daly, *Empire on the Nile*, pp. 449–50; Doyle, 'Population decline and delayed recovery in Bunyoro, 1860–1960', *Journal of African History* 41:3 (2000), 429–58; Iliffe, *Tanganyika*, pp. 270, 315; K. D. Patterson, 'The influenza epidemic of 1918–19 in the Gold Coast', *Journal of African History* 24 (1983), 485–502

18 W. Simpson, *Report to the Secretary of State for the Colonies on the Sanitary Conditions of the Mines and Mining Villages in the Gold Coast Colony and Ashanti* (London: Waterlow and Sons, 1925), p. 6

19 Heussler, *British Tanganyika*, p. 23; see also Wordsworth to Young, 27 August 1905, RHO Mss.Afr.s.1373/31

20 Darwin, *English Public School*, pp. 100–1

21 Cohn, *Colonialism and its Forms of Knowledge*, pp. 3–15

22 Quoted in Dorward, 'Development of British Colonial Administration', 317

23 As later quoted in Lugard, 'Memorandum Number 9: Native Administration', [August 1917], RHO Mss.Afr.s.783/2/5, p. 3

24 Hill, *Slatin*, p. 72

25 Willis, 'Killing Bwana: peasant revenge and political panic in early colonial Ankole', *Journal of African History* 35:3 (1994), 379–400

26 Doyle, *Crisis & Decline*, pp. 104–5

27 A. Colquhoun, *The Africander Land* (London: John Murray, 1906), p. 17; see also F. R. Cana, 'Problems in exploration: Africa', *Geographical Journal* 38:5 (1911), 547

28 A. Upward, 'The Province of Kabba, Northern Nigeria', *Journal of the African Society* 7 (1903), 237

29 *Ibid.*

30 Upward, 'In the Provincial Court: notes of cases tried in the Provincial Court of Kabba, Northern Nigeria', *Journal of the African Society* 3:12 (1904), 405–9

31 Upward, *Athelstane Ford* (London: Arthur Pearson, 1899); J. J. Wilhelm, *Ezra Pound in London and Paris, 1908–1925* (University Park, PA: Pennsylvania State University Press, 1990), pp. 120–2

32 B. H. W. Taylor, diary, 5 May 1906, in Williamson and Kirk-Greene (eds), *Gold Coast Diaries*, p. 64

33 See Taylor, diary, 9 May 1906, in *ibid.*, p. 67

34 Taylor, diary, 9 May 1906, in *ibid.*. Colonial administrators used 'Dagarti or 'Lobi' instead of 'Dagara'; C. Lentz, 'A Dagara rebellion against Dagomba rule? Contested stories of origin in North-West Ghana', *Journal of African History* 35:3 (1993), 457 n. 2

35 Taylor, diary, 9 May 1906, in Williamson and Kirk-Greene (eds), *Gold Coast Diaries*, p. 67; see also G. Austin, *Labour, Land and Capital in Ghana: From Slavery to Free Labour in Asante, 1807–1956* (Rochester, NY: University of Rochester Press, 2005), p. 212

36 R. Meinertzhagen, diary, 8 September 1902, in *Kenya Diary 1902–1906* (Edinburgh: Oliver & Boyd, 1957), p. 51; Bell to parents, 7 August 1933, SAD 697/10/22; Childs,

diary, 13 January 1933, RHO Mss.Afr.s.1861/1; F. Ruxton, 'Muri Province: Political Report No 22', [October 1903], RHO Mss.Afr.s.1037/55–6; Woodhouse, diary, 14 December 1908, RHO Mss.Afr.s.236; Wordsworth to Young, 27 August 1905, RHO Mss.Afr.s.1373/31

37 Lentz, 'A Dagara rebellion?', 468
38 H. A. MacMichael, 'The Kababish: some remarks on the ethnology of a Sudan Tribe', *Journal of the Royal Anthropological Institute of Great Britain and Ireland* 49 (1910), 215–31; MacMichael, *The Tribes of Northern and Central Kordofan* (1912: London: Frank Cass, 1967), ch. 15; Willis, 'Hukm', 44
39 R. Davies, 'Policy in Dar Kababish', 9 June 1915, SAD 627/1/3
40 Davies, 'Policy in Dar Kababish', SAD 627/1/3
41 Willis, 'Hukm', 30
42 S. Butler to parents, 24 April 1912, SAD 304/6/24; Butler to parents, 9 June 1912, SAD 304/6/28. Indeed, el Tom's earlier raids on neighbouring tribes had led one early official to admit he wished to 'beat first and then hang ... the insolent scoundrel'; quoted in Daly, *Empire on the Nile*, p. 10
43 For example, when undergoing his Oxford training in the late 1930s, John Daniell took an intense dislike to Margery Perham; of that 'awful woman', he particularly railed against 'her studied impromptu manner which wouldn't deceive a Kabbabish [*sic*]'; Daniell, diary, 25 October 1937, SAD 777/13/10; Daniell, diary, 1 November 1937, SAD 777/13/11
44 Davies, 'Policy in Dar Kababish', SAD 627/1/9
45 *Ibid.*, SAD 627/1/9
46 *Ibid.*, SAD 627/1/10
47 Owen to mother, 6 March 1930, SAD 414/2/40; see also Y. Hunter, 'A walking tour in Mongalla', [n.d.], SAD 745/4/10. Such an attitude continued on into the post-1945 period; Willis, '"A model of its kind": representation and performance in the Sudan self-government election of 1953', *Journal of Imperial and Commonwealth History* 35:3 (2007), 485–502
48 See, for example, P. Lovejoy, *Transformations in Slavery: A History of Slavery in Africa* (1983; Cambridge: Cambridge University Press, 2000), ch. 11
49 A. Disney, untitled memorandum, [c.1931], SAD 716/1/7
50 For more on this change, see Hamad, '*Sudan Notes and Records*', 249
51 Disney, untitled memorandum, [c.1931], SAD 716/1/7
52 L. G. Dixon, 'Life and duties of an administrative officer in the Gold Coast Colony', [c.1922], RHO Mss.Afr.s.356/1
53 Crocker, *Nigeria*, p. 131
54 Bell to parents, 13 January 1933, SAD 697/9/6
55 Bell to parents, 12 February 1933, SAD 697/9/26
56 Bell to parents, 27 July 1933, SAD 697/10/17
57 H. McCallum to Chamberlain, 8 December 1897, JC 9/5/1/5; see also Lugard, 'Northern Nigeria', *Geographical Journal* 23:1 (1904), 19–20; Perham, *Years of Authority*, p. 92
58 Willis, 'Killing Bwana', 383
59 Mathews to parents, 28 February 1911, RHO Mss.Afr.s.783/1(1)/15
60 Mathews to parents, 2 August 1914, RHO Mss.Afr.s.783/1(5)/64; emphasis in original; see also Mathews to parents, 16 June 1914, RHO Mss.Afr.s.783/1(5)/no number
61 Callaway, *Gender, Culture and Empire*, ch. 3
62 Nicolson, *Administration of Nigeria*, p. 199
63 A. Clarkson, 'Pomp, circumstance, and wild Arabs: the 1912 Royal visit to Sudan', *Journal of Imperial and Commonwealth History* 34:1 (2006), 71–85; Daly, 'The soldier as historian: F. R. Wingate and the Sudanese Mahdia', *Journal of Imperial and Commonwealth History* 17:1 (1988), 99–106; Daly, *The Sirdar*, pp. 163–9; see also 'Lord Kitchener Sudan Memorial', *The Times* (8 November 1916), p. 7; 'Khartum Cathedral', *The Times* (4 December 1911), p. 4
64 Butler to father, 30 January 1912, SAD 304/6/7
65 R. Wingate to Lord Stamfordham, 4 February 1912, SAD 180/2/35

66 Butler to father, 30 January 1912, SAD 304/6/7
67 *Ibid.*, SAD 304/6/9–10
68 Photographic evidence clearly demonstrates that the Royal tours of the British Empire that took place after 1918, such as that of Buganda in 1924, were decidedly less grand than those before 1914; J. Fabb, *Royal Tours of the British Empire 1860–1927* (London: B. T. Batsford, 1989), pp. 18–19
69 Reid, *History of Modern Africa*, p. 192; see also Gailey, *Clifford*, p. 82
70 Baily, 'Early recollections of the Sudan', SAD 533/4/28
71 Mathews had arrived in Africa in 1911; Mathews to parents, 5 October 1914, RHO Mss.Afr.s.783/1(5); emphasis in original
72 The classic introduction to this topic is R. Rathbone, 'World War I and Africa: introduction', *Journal of African History* 19:1 (1978), 1–9
73 Newbold to F. Cottrell, 29 October 1933, in Henderson, *Modern Sudan*, p. 53
74 Quoted in Willis, *Potent Brews: A Social History of Alcohol in East Africa 1850–1999* (Oxford: BIEA and James Currey, 2002), p. 128
75 However, younger officials followed a broader interwar metropolitan trend by being more comfortable than their elders with both the technology and the propaganda value of film; Ormsby-Gore to A. Hodson, 11 January 1938, PRAAD CSO 25/1/32; T. D. Cranston, '"The African and the cinema" – some observations', 30 April 1938, PRAAD CSO 25/1/32; see also *Hansard*, 5th series, vol. 199, col. 1518; Owen to mother, 7 February 1939, SAD 414/9/7; 'Local and personal', *Sudan Herald* (24 September 1921), p. 3; R. Nichols, 'Films and the empire', *The Observer* (7 November 1926), p. 21; more broadly, see T. J. Hollins, 'The Conservative Party and film propaganda between the wars', *English Historical Review* 96 (1981), 359–69
76 Collins, *Shadows in the Grass*, p. 29
77 Duncan-Johnstone, diary, 17 December 1929, RHO Mss.Afr.s.593/1/65; see also Haarer, 'Memories', [undated], RHO Mss.Afr.s.1144/10
78 Bell, 'Racial relations in the Sudan', [1930], SAD 700/4/18–19
79 Dixon, 'Life and duties', [c.1922], RHO Mss.Afr.s.356/5
80 Fortes, 'Culture contact', 27–8
81 A point that runs against the assumption that 'the imperialists knew exactly what they were about in Africa'; P. S. Zachernuk, 'Critical agents: colonial Nigerian intellectuals and their British counterparts', in C. Youé and T. Stapleton (eds), *Agency and Action in Colonial Africa: Essays for John E. Flint* (Basingstoke: Palgrave, 2001), p. 167
82 Amherst, diary, 26 August 1930, RHO Mss.Afr.s.1207/31
83 Amherst, diary, 5 May 1933, RHO Mss.Afr.s.1207/120; Cardinall, 'Some random notes on the customs of the Konkomba', *Journal of the African Society* 18:69 (1918), 60–1; Smith, 'Africa: what do we know of it?', *Journal of the Royal Anthropological Institute of Great Britain and Ireland* 65 (1935), 67. I am grateful to Eleanor Rooks for her discussions with me on this topic
84 Regarding witchcraft, see H. L. Ward-Price to Orde-Browne, 9 April 1934, RHO Mss.Afr.s.1117/3/3/18
85 See, for example, J. E. Phillips, 'The Nabingi: an anti-European secret society in Africa in British Ruanda and Ndorwa', 31 July 1919, RHO Mss.Afr.s.1384/477–93; Elliot, 'A note in the Nabingi movement in the Kigezi district of the Western Province of Uganda', [c.1927], RHO Mss.Afr.s.1384/474
86 R. E. Dennett, 'The Ogboni and other secret societies in Nigeria', *Journal of the African Society* 16:61 (1916), 17
87 W. Kirby to Guggisberg, 6 November 1931, PRAAD CSO 21/11/2
88 Balfour to mother, 18 July 1935, SAD 606/5/24; Orr to Leviseur, 6 February 1904, BL Add Mss 56100/12; M. P. Vidal-Hall to niece, 24 September 1937, SAD 727/1/5
89 H. W. Thomas, circular, 20 May 1937, PRAAD CSO 21/11/2
90 G. C. du Boulay, circular, 19 July 1933, RHO Mss.Afr.s.593/5/4/11–12
91 Gowers, 'Dinner of the Society', *Journal of the African Society* 26:102 (1927), 169; Bell to parents, 6 November 1931, SAD 697/4/48–9; Letchworth to mother, 7 August 1930, RHO Mss.Brit.Emp.s.364(5)/15

92 Allen, 'Nigerian panorama – 1926–1966', [undated], RHO Mss.Afr.s.1551/11; see also S. Ormsby to H. Ormsby, 30 November 1896, RHO Mss.Afr.r.105/i

93 Upward, 'The Province of Kabba', 237–8; see also Crowder, 'The white chiefs of Tropical Africa', p. 349; Hastings, *Nigerian Days*, p. 41; Lugard, *Dual Mandate*, p. 133; Stigand, *Administration in Tropical Africa*, p. 37

94 W. Forbes, interview with D. J. Johnson, 28 March 1979, SAD 863/3/16

95 Balfour to mother, 4 March 1933, SAD 606/4/4

96 I. M. Bruce-Gardyne, 'The Sudan: some native aspects', [n.d.], SAD 478/12/60

97 Quoted in Mathews to sister, 18 February 1911, RHO Mss.Afr.s.783/1(1)/14; see also Lea, diary, 31 March 1931, SAD 645/9/47; Wordsworth to Young, 15 January 1906, RHO Mss.Afr.s.1373/37

98 A. Burton, *African Underclass: Urbanisation, Crime & Colonial Order in Dar es Salaam* (London: BIEA and James Curry, 2005), pp. 12–13, 48–52; Willis, *Mombasa, the Swahili, and the Making of the Mijikenda* (Oxford: Clarendon, 1993), p. 2

99 Sillery, 'Working backwards', RHO Mss.Afr.r.207/124

100 See Chapter Three

101 Mathews, papers, RHO Mss.Afr.s.783/2/1

102 Mathews to parents, 10 February 1911, RHO Mss.Afr.s.783/1/1/12

103 Mathews to M. Mathews, 18 February 1911, RHO Mss.Afr.s.783/1/1/14

104 Hamilton, 'Devolutionary principles in Native Administration', in Hamilton (ed.), *Anglo-Egyptian Sudan from Within*, p. 185

105 R. Greig, diary, 15 January 1934, RHO Mss.Afr.s.2319/10; see also Greig, diary, 29 January 1934, RHO Mss.Afr.s.2319/18

106 L. M. Heaney to Heaney family, undated, [March 1935], RHO Mss.Afr.s.2271/79; see also Heaney to parents, 19 October 1929, RHO Mss.Afr.s.2271/4; Heaney to J. Fisher, 11 October 1930, RHO Mss.Afr.s.2271/32; Heaney to Heaney family, 25 January 1931, RHO Mss.Afr.s.2271/40; Heaney to Heaney family, 25 August 1931, RHO Mss.Afr.s.2271/48; Heaney to parents, 28 January 1934, RHO Mss.Afr.s.2271/58; Heaney to mother, 19 June 1937, RHO Mss.Afr.s.2271/97; Heaney to mother, 25 June 1937, RHO Mss.Afr.s.2271/98

107 Heaney to Fisher, 19 March 1931, RHO Mss.Afr.s.2271/41; Heaney to mother, undated, [April 1937], RHO Mss.Afr.s.2271/96; see also Heaney to Heaney family, 30 November 1930, RHO Mss.Afr.s.2271/36; Heaney to Heaney family, 5 May 1931, RHO Mss.Afr.s.2271/44

108 Greig, diary, 24 February 1934, RHO Mss.Afr.s.2319/33; Greig, diary, 12 April 1934, RHO Mss.Afr.s.2319/60; Greig, diary, 11 June 1934, RHO Mss.Afr.s.2319/94; Greig, diary, 27 October 1934, RHO Mss.Afr.s.2319/173; Greig diary, 18 November 1934, RHO Mss.Afr.s.2319/186; Greig, diary, 15 December 1934, RHO Mss.Afr.s.2319/201

109 Heaney to parents, 15 February 1935, RHO Mss.Afr.s.2271/81; Heaney to parents, 2 March 1935, RHO Mss.Afr.s.2271/83

110 Heaney to Heaney family, 5 May 1931, RHO Mss.Afr.s.2271/44; see also Heaney to parents, 8 April 1930, RHO Mss.Afr.s.2271/19; Heaney to Heaney family, 28 November 1933, RHO Mss.Afr.s.2271/53; Heaney to parents, 28 March 1934, RHO Mss.Afr.s.2271/62

111 Greig, diary, 25 January 1934, RHO Mss.Afr.s.2319/16; Greig, diary, 28 January 1934, RHO Mss.Afr.s.2319/18; Greig, diary, 3 February 1934, RHO Mss.Afr.s.2319/21; Greig, diary, 19 February 1934, RHO Mss.Afr.s.2319/30; Greig, diary, 22 April 1934, RHO Mss.Afr.s.2319/66; Greig, diary, 28 April 1934, RHO Mss.Afr.s.2319/69; Greig, diary, 14 July 1934, RHO Mss.Afr.s.2319/113

112 G. Bikle, 'Utopianism and social planning in the thought of Kagawa Toyohiko', *Monumenta Nipponica* 25 (1970), 449–50

113 Greig, diary, 5 April 1934, RHO Mss.Afr.s.2319/56

114 Greig, diary, 11 June 1934, RHO Mss.Afr.s.2319/94

115 Greig diary, 14 March 1934, RHO Mss.Afr.s.2319/43

116 Heaney to Fisher, 28 June 1931, RHO Mss.Afr.s.2271/45

117 Heaney to Fisher, 18 April 1930, RHO Mss.Afr.s.2271/20
118 B. Neilson, 'D. H. Lawrence's "Dark Page": narrative primitivism in *Women in Love* and *The Plumed Serpent'*, *Twentieth-Century Literature* 43 (1997), 310–25
119 D. H. Lawrence, *Women in Love* (1920; London: Cambridge University Press, 2002), p. 127; A. E. Fernald, '"Out of it": alienation and coercion in D. H. Lawrence', *Modern Fiction Studies* 49:2 (2003), 188
120 'June Magazines: two new reviews', *The Times* (2 June 1923), p. 10; 'New novels', *The Times* (25 May 1928), p. 9; 'Fiction: Mr. Wells's new novel', *The Times* (20 January 1933), p. 7
121 A *boma* is a government office. Boyle, diary, 27 February 1909, RHO Mss. Afr.s.2324/95; Cameron, *Tanganyika Service*, p. 276; A. Covey, diary, [September 1902], in Williamson and Kirk-Greene (eds), *Gold Coast Diaries*, p. 55; Heussler, *British Tanganyika*, p. 14; Tripe, 'Report on Tongwe', [c. May 1932], RHO Mss. Afr.s.868/2/1/6; nevertheless, see Sayers (ed.), *Handbook of Tanganyika*, p. 124
122 MacDonald to Hodson, 7 December 1938, PRAAD CSO 21/20/44; see also M. D. Callahan, 'NOMANSLAND: the British Colonial Office and the League of Nations Mandate for German East Africa, 1916–1920', *Albion* 25:3 (1993), 464. Plans for the internment of German settlers were already in place before the war; Sillery, 'Working backwards', RHO Mss.Afr.s.207/164
123 C. Whybrow to unknown recipient, 13 June 1926, RHO Mss.Afr.s.324
124 J. A. Getty, 'Trotsky in exile: the founding of the Fourth International', *Soviet Studies* 38 (1986), 24–35
125 D. Bayley, diary, 9 November 1936, RHO Mss.Afr.r.47/81–2; see also Bayley, diary, 15 May 1931, RHO Mss.Afr.r.47/42–3; Bayley, diary, 3 June 1931, RHO Mss. Afr.r.47/45; Bayley, diary, 21 November 1936, RHO Mss.Afr.r.47/83
126 Bayley, diary, 15 October 1930, RHO Mss.Afr.r.47/5; Bayley, diary, 19 December 1930, RHO Mss.Afr.r.47/23; see also Bayley, diary, 7 September 1937, RHO Mss. Afr.r.47/101
127 A. Sisman, *A. J. P. Taylor: A Biography* (London: Sinclair-Stevenson, 1994), p. 57; K. Burk, *Troublemaker: The Life and History of A. J. P. Taylor* (New Haven, CT: Yale University, 2000), pp. 49, 63
128 Tripe to parents, 7 May 1929, RHO Mss.Afr.s.868/1/50
129 Tripe to parents, 30 July 1929, RHO Mss.Afr.s.868/1/78
130 Heaney to parents, 19 October 1929, RHO Mss.Afr.s.2271/5; Heaney to parents, 27 April 1930, RHO Mss.Afr.s.2271/22
131 Bayley, diary, 21 October 1930, RHO Mss.Afr.r.47/8; Bayley, diary, 2 December 1930, RHO Mss.Afr.r.47/19; Bayley, diary, 25 January 1931, RHO Mss.Afr.r.47/30
132 Bayley, diary, 22 October 1930, RHO Mss.Afr.r.47/10; see also Bayley, diary, 25 November 1936, RHO Mss.Afr.r.47/85; L. G. Wickham-Legg to the editor, 'Gibraltar: the British title', *The Times* (15 April 1939), p. 13
133 Bayley, diary, 26 October 1930, RHO Mss.Afr.r.47/11
134 Bayley, diary, 24 January 1932, RHO Mss.Afr.r.47/63
135 Bayley, diary, 24 November 1931, RHO Mss.Afr.r.47/60; see also Bayley, diary, 10 November 1931, RHO Mss.Afr.r.47/58–9
136 See, for example, R. Guha, 'Not at home in empire', *Critical Inquiry* 23:3 (1997), 482–93
137 G. Orwell, 'Shooting an elephant' (1936), in *Collected Essays* (1961; London: Secker & Warburg, 1968), p. 19
138 Ruxton, 'Some notes on the Mushi and instructions for Political Officers', 3 March 1910, RHO Mss.Afr.s.662/1
139 See also Wingate to G. S. Symes, 14 December 1911, SAD 301/6/13; Lugard, 'Introduction', in A. R. Cook, *Uganda Memories* (Kampala: Uganda Society, 1945), pp. xi–xii; 'Conquest of tropical disease', *Observer* (3 May 1931), p. 11; 'Tropical medicine', *The Times* (29 December 1921), p. 9
140 Lea to parents, 12 December 1926, SAD 645/7/8; Lea, trek journals, 14 February 1927, SAD 645/7/40; Lea to parents, 29 December 1926, SAD 645/7/16; Lea to

parents, 7 January 1927, SAD 645/7/18; Lea to parents, 10 February 1927, SAD 645/7/37; Lea to parents, 23 February 1927, SAD 645/7/4; Lea, trek journals, 29 March 1931, SAD 645/9/44; Lea, trek journals, 4 April 1931, SAD 645/9/57

CHAPTER FIVE

Implementing colonial change: economics, infrastructure and education

Officials, it has been suggested, possessed an 'innate anti-modernism'.[1] They were what might be termed *pragmatically* hostile to all but the lightest of changes because they felt alterations threatened to destabilise, or even destroy, the imperial system. In the face of this, there were in fact a variety of reasons why officials had a vested interest in altering Africa. Alongside any sense of duty usually emphasised in officials' memoirs and by empire apologists, one set of such reasons has to date received little scholarly attention: change made officials' own lives easier or more fulfilling. For example, officials often enjoyed building roads, and revelled in the improved access to goods, information and coercive force that they provided. Of course, this does not prove officials were not simultaneously *emotionally* hostile to modernisation or change. Some scholars have suggested officials were raised and educated in a metropolitan environment where the development of trade and industry were felt inimical to all that was decent about an established socio-political system. For Cyril Ehrlich, 'it can scarcely be denied that administrative attitudes, throughout British Africa, rarely encouraged indigenous commercial initiative'. This was partly due to a 'snobbish' upper-middle-class attitude towards trade and 'getting one's hand dirty' with money that was strengthened by an 'anti-commercial and anti-industrial' public school culture.[2] This might lead one to accept certain postcolonialist claims that officials felt there was an irreconcilable tension at the heart of all that they did. Delivering changes that officials felt improved their power or standard of living may have clashed with a sentimental attachment to an unchanged Africa.

This chapter will examine officials' attitudes towards industry, trade, infrastructural development and education. It will focus more on the matter of pragmatic hostility, whilst the possible existence of emotional hostility will be considered more closely in Chapter Six.

Officials certainly complained about colonial policies imposed on them from above, and the pressures elites placed on them to act in particular ways. Officials framed these as threats to an African way of life. However, such hostility did not arise principally out of an inherent belief that it was impossible to introduce changes whilst maintaining stability. Rather, they stemmed from a conviction that these impositions were an affront to their own authority, when it was in fact officials who knew what was best for their district. Armed with a sense of their own ability, officials invariably each believed in their own capacity to manage the development of Africa, and equally that this would be knocked off course by interference from others. Rather than being an inherent feature of the imperial encounter, hostility to change was therefore a contingent product of certain colonial relationships.

To test the limits of officials' contentment with, and commitment to, change, we will firstly examine an instance where elites felt it particularly important to change a colony quickly: Northern Nigeria. The push for tax revenue in Northern Nigeria in the earliest years of the twentieth century proved a disappointment. In the years immediately prior to amalgamation, Northern Nigeria relied on approximately £300,000 annually in government grant-in-aid and subsidies from Southern Nigeria.[3] Whilst both colonial and London elites attempted to put a positive spin on the matter in public, the failure to balance the books was an embarrassment for a protectorate that prided itself on its position at the top of the West African pecking order.[4] This created a sense of urgency amongst elites that commercial revenue needed to be generated as quickly as possible.[5]

Officials became aware of such urgency during the governorship of Henry Hesketh Bell between 1909 and 1912. Privately critical of his predecessors Girouard and Lugard for knowing 'nothing about agriculture' nor taking 'any interest in trade', Hesketh Bell put himself to the task of developing tin mines and rubber and cotton plantations.[6] The desire to connect Northern Nigeria to the coast led to the expenditure of extraordinary amounts of capital, political effort and manual labour on two railway lines. The first, completed in June 1911, connected Northern Nigeria to the coast via a line from Kano to Baro on the River Niger. The second, opened in January 1912, connected the Baro–Kano line to Lagos via Zungeru.[7] Whilst it was anticipated that the lines would save money in the long term by reducing the cost of troop movements and increasing the region's access to international markets, construction of the Baro–Kano line alone cost over £1.2m in total, or approximately £3,400 per mile of track.[8] The track was laid with a speed that still impresses historians.[9]

Many parts of Africa were felt capable of rapid economic change. For example, one official newly arrived in Sudan suggested that 'They say Africa is to be the future source of raw products for Europe, but it seems that very soon Africa will be the source of manufactured goods as well'.[10] This belief that Africa would deliver what was asked of it was particularly acute in Northern Nigeria.[11] Europeans had long highlighted the vitality of Kano as an entrepot noted particularly for its cloth and leather industries, and so it was felt natural when trade continued to expand under British rule.[12] One 1911 report referred to the 'remarkable development of trade' between Sokoto and Southern Nigeria occasioned by the Zungeru road. Rice was flowing out of Sokoto, and salt was flowing in. 'This traffic', the report noted,

> has grown up almost entirely within the last two or three years, quite spontaneously and without any pressure or inducement on the part of the Government other than the clearing of the road. It shows the readiness of the Sokoto peasantry to make the most of their spare time ... and to take advantage of present conditions of settled security and improved facility of communications.[13]

Officials were faced with a rival consideration. However much most became protective of 'their' Africans, Northern Nigeria was the region in which officials were happiest with, and most admired, what they found. The region's literate culture garnered a level of respect that was in all likelihood unparalleled across the areas covered by the present study.[14] 'The people up here are intelligent and cultured and a very dignified race', wrote one newcomer to Minna in 1910.[15] Most importantly, the area was considered to be stable. Both during and following Britain's conquest of the region, officials believed its inhabitants required relatively little coercion to accept British rule. For instance, the Sokoto Caliphate's leaders had been 'wise' to recognise it was in their interests to offer little resistance during the campaigns of 'pacification' and place their lands under the 'protection' of the British.[16] Northern Nigerians were felt to possess a natural predisposition towards an authoritarian brand of stability, as demonstrated by the standard of Islamic law and the 'firm but fair' execution of justice, the quality of the Mallams, and pre-colonial taxation systems.[17] Even the appearance of Kano Province, with its hedged and fenced roads, evinced a squirearchical system, giving 'an impression of civilisation and ordered industry which is unexampled in tropical Africa'.[18]

Northern Nigerian elites were careful to stress that railways left the African 'in no way de-nationalised, or taken permanently from his familiar avocations or environment'.[19] In January 1911, however, Assistant Resident Harry Miller-Stirling wrote home about the railway line connecting Northern Nigeria to the coast via Baro. By that stage, it had made its way as far as Zaria, with its endpoint of Kano approximately 150 miles away from where Miller-Stirling was working in Kayauri. 'This country will lose all its attraction when we have the Railway up [here]', he wrote, 'and we shall get that beastly product the Coast clerk and the semi "civilized" native ... When the country becomes like Lagos it will be time to look for something else'.[20] The following year, he wrote that the railway would facilitate the development of the tin mines in Kano and Bauchi, but that 'both are probably unfortunate politically ... the advent of commercialism into this country will be unfortunate'.[21]

Such comments will be familiar to anyone who has read officials' papers, and would appear to support the claims noted above that officials were conservative to the point of feeling that any change would unravel everything.[22] However, we need to delve deeper in order to avoid making sweeping claims based on initial impressions. In particular, two points need to be considered. Firstly, Miller-Stirling opposed the appearance of tin mines in the region because they were invariably run by Europeans 'other than Government officials'. 'I am afraid', Miller-Stirling wrote, 'the closer acquaintance of the people with the white man of a new type whose word is possibly not his bond and who is trying to make money out of them will not tend to increase his respect for us'.[23] However, if there were men in charge who knew the 'correct' way to treat Africans, problems could be avoided. Miller-Stirling used the mine at Keffi as an example of this. The mine was supposedly run correctly because of ex-officials' involvement in its operations.[24] Tin mines were therefore not *inherently* problematic. Miller-Stirling's statement demonstrates both officials' sense of their own ability compared to other Europeans, and officials' desire to manage African interactions with Europeans. Nevertheless, this view was not necessarily set in stone. Men working in industry were initially largely unknown to officials. However, if officials got to know and like such men, as occurred in the case of those working at the tin mines at Bauchi, then officials became more amenable to their endeavours.[25] Miller-Stirling was not snobbish about making money, but there may have been a different form of hostility at play in shaping his attitudes; Hesketh Bell certainly favoured the government running tin mines rather than handing them over to 'Jews and concession-mongers who have not contributed one sou to the pacification of this country'.[26]

Secondly, Miller-Stirling's statement concerning the imminent appearance of a 'Cape clerk' class in the north is apparently at odds with his assessment elsewhere that local governmental and social structures in fact guarded against the emergence of disequilibrating and undesirable alterations to the social fabric.[27] In particular, strong and able men who led the caliphates would prevent the future emergence of 'that loathsome product the Europeanised native which they have on the coast'.[28] Writing to his father, Miller-Stirling argued that the 'Coast clerk' was a product of the south because the people there were 'very backward from what one hears and the Political Organisation is nothing compared with what we have up here'.[29] Consequently, whilst in 'the Pagan countries ... they take on a veneer of civilisation at a Mission School ... there is not much fear of that in the Mohammedan States'.[30]

How can we account for Miller-Stirling's anti-rail outburst if it was not caused by a deep-seated belief that his corner of the empire was going to be significantly harmed by the impact of commercial and infrastructural development? After all, in other letters written both before and after his January 1911 complaint, he supported the expansion of travel networks.[31] The answer to this conundrum, it seems, lies in personal relationships. Due in part to absences caused by ongoing illness, Hesketh Bell frequently had to allow himself to be guided by strong-willed and well-established Residents such as Charles Temple.[32] Furthermore, much of the lobbying and planning for the railways had been undertaken in London, often thanks to Winston Churchill's efforts on behalf of the British Cotton Growing Association.[33] Nevertheless, it was Hesketh Bell who attracted hostility on the ground for his implementation of grand schemes, such as the building of the railways, without consulting officials.[34] With scant attention to punctuation imparting a somewhat breathless tone to his objection, Miller-Stirling believed that Zaria would be 'a beastly place to be in as the Governor is constantly interfering with everyone and starting new schemes, new towns being built everywhere one shortly at Kano the name suggested for it being "Bellville" this is not the official suggestion however'.[35] Furthermore, Miller-Stirling feared that the advent of rail travel would make it easier for his superiors to come and check up on his work.[36] This was not due to laziness. Indeed, Miller-Stirling was a rather austere workaholic.[37] Instead, as a 'bush' official, he enjoyed the monopoly of power and authority he felt came from being away from others.[38] Miller-Stirling's frustration with the 'opening up' of Northern Nigeria was a frustration borne of hostility over the arrival of a change over which he had had no say, to which he would have to adjust, and which threatened his opportunity to work away from 'civilisation', rather than because he genuinely feared it would undermine the region's social fabric.

Why did Miller-Stirling frame his frustration in terms of the implications of 'unfortunate' commercial and political developments for

Northern Nigeria? As we will see shortly, the notion that officials' everyday conduct was solely motivated by selflessness is inaccurate. Nevertheless, Miller-Stirling was part of both working and family environments that stressed altruism, self-sacrifice and an overriding concern for African wellbeing above all else. Like others in the region, he belonged to a family whose members, whilst not officials, had a heavy involvement in empire.[39] Miller-Stirling's father was a Commander in the Royal Navy, and his brother was a businessman in Canada. As a servant of empire writing to this family, it would have been rather unbecoming for Miller-Stirling to have expressed vehement opposition to a railway designed to affect the lives of everyone in Northern Nigeria merely because it altered how he would have to work. If he was to make any sort of protest against elites' actions, rhetorical legerdemain was required. Miller-Stirling consequently transformed his personal disgruntlement into concern about a change that, on paper at least, threatened imperial peace and stability. In attempting to win over his family to the disgust he felt for the new, his claims assumed profound proportions that surpassed his hostility to the readjustments such changes asked of him.

In keeping with the points made in Chapter Two, officials were not inherently opposed to industrialisation partly because they had not emerged from a metropolitan environment inherently hostile to industrialisation. Officials were nevertheless keener on the development of export crop agriculture than they were on industrialisation.[40] Some appear to have become genuinely interested in agronomy.[41] In Tanganyika, Bukoba DO Lionel Vickers-Haviland welcomed an increase in 'native trading' of crops, both internally and as export goods.[42] In Mbulu, further to the south, Frank Hallier wanted markets maintained because 'We want to induce them to sell regularly all the year round and so we must hold sales conveniently near'.[43]

Why might officials have shown more enthusiasm for such endeavours than for industrial ones? Here, we return to the topic of control. Officials felt they could play a significant role in the production and trading of agricultural goods. They could open and close markets.[44] They could train auctioneers. They could give advice to producers on both the best crops to grow in particular climatic and edaphic circumstances, and how to market their produce.[45] Officials spent a good deal of time destroying the locusts that threatened not only famine but also stable export levels, and therefore economic stability.[46] In contrast, even those officials who worked in close proximity to industrial operations felt their ability to get involved in such matters was limited. For example, tin mining required the operation of specialised equipment and the involvement of outsiders possessing specialist knowledge.

[128]

Officials had little to do with the actual functioning of the mines beyond occasionally having to assemble workforces for them.[47] As will be argued in Chapter Six, it is possible to overstate officials' fears that industry would 'detribalise' Africans. Nevertheless, the appearance of other Europeans in officials' districts introduced a new variable that was hard to regulate.

This is not to suggest that officials deceived themselves that their agricultural actions went uncontested by Africans and other Europeans. Regarding the latter, officials were frequently rather dismissive of the efforts of those working in agriculture and forestry departments. After all, officials appear to have been correct that these other administrators often prioritised economic gain over political stability.[48] The other principal threat to officials' sense of control was the relatively powerful trading companies.[49] Officials frequently felt that traders were insensitive to Africans. Whilst European traders had attempted to improve their image since the late nineteenth century, there was a lingering sense amongst officials that many of them were not reputable and would antagonise Africans.[50] For example, Britons on 'commercial undertakings' in Sudan were criticised for racial attitudes that were bound to antagonise Africans, their being unaware that 'natives have a point of view, and that Arabs aren't niggers'.[51] Nevertheless, as was the case with industry, once the ice had been broken, administrators were less distrustful of, and in some cases even amenable to, those working for trading companies.[52] However, officials were adamant that the development of trade be on their terms. For example, Tanganyikan officials openly opposed European 'outsiders' working in the trade in *dagaa* (a type of fish), the centre of which was Tanganyika's Kigoma District. This was a 'native' industry, and the Kigoma DCs felt better able to control it if it remained that way.[53]

Nevertheless, officials were not esoteric when it came to trade. Very few went out of their way to grapple with different models of development. Prior to the First World War, a small but diligent band of Agricultural Officers had sought to establish cooperative societies in Egypt. London was broadly supportive of such endeavours.[54] However, the development of cooperative societies was patchy across sub-Saharan Africa. Philip Mitchell, Tanganyika's Secretary for Native Affairs, called the societies the 'extension of the "indirect" principle from administration to farming'.[55] Charles Strickland, noted in Chapter Two as the principal champion of these societies, nevertheless confided to one Gold Coast official his fear that conservative elites were holding back the scheme. For Strickland, it was up to younger DCs to overcome this resistance.[56] Whether or not this is accurate, there was a low awareness of the cooperative movement amongst officials. William Walker, the official to whom Strickland wrote, was a rare convert.[57] As Walker argued, 'Unfortunately few, if any, administrative officers have the foggiest idea about the cooperative movement or the technicalities of Cooperative Societies'.[58] Others felt such societies would change Africa beyond a rate with which Africans could cope. Upon reading the literature on cooperative societies sent to him by his mother, one Tanganyikan DO wrote back saying, 'I see that we have been playing with fire and we will have to go very carefully in the future until someone comes who knows something about the subject'.[59]

In spite of a general enthusiasm for developing Africa when officials felt they could control the process, there was no single response to commercial activity. This might be surmised from the diversity of Edwardian officials' employment histories. In terms of personnel, the boundary between colonial administrations and commerce was at its most porous before the First World War.[60] As one might expect, those who had worked in the latter sector before becoming officials were invariably comfortable with Africa's closer economic integration with the wider world. They placed the promotion of trade, rather than of reformed political life, at the heart of imperial pacification and stability. J. H. Ewart had started his African career as a Royal Niger Company official in 1889. He believed that reputable trading companies engaged in rubber trading had the capacity to unlock the economic potential of an area, which would lead to development in a responsible manner.[61] In 1902, Ewart noted in his diary that Igbeti was 'a well built town and does not now bear the slightest resemblance to the broken down village I remember nine years ago. The trade is evidently increasing in this district and people seem prosperous and happy'.[62] He was not the only Edwardian official who felt sorry for those British entrepreneurs who were 'sound pioneers' but whose efforts to develop trade were hampered by poor transportation links.[63] Sydney Ormsby, the Ugandan DC noted in Chapter One who had previously worked as an ivory trader and factory manager, strongly believed that exports of some kind would help stabilise Mbale.[64] Contrary to what is normally said regarding officials' attitudes towards urbanisation, it was this type of DC that actually encouraged Africans to move to Ibadan to help develop the cocoa industry.[65]

Personnel transfers between the worlds of business and government decreased, particularly after 1918.[66] Furse's recruits were less interested in economic matters than their predecessors, and tended to place socio-political concerns at the heart of their governmental endeavours. They nevertheless felt that, in the face of the relative coercive weakness of the colonial state as a political force in certain regards, economic development had the capacity to address specific issues.

The slave trade exemplifies this.[67] In his handing over notes, one SPS official serving in a district irrigated by the Gezira scheme confronted the matter. 'My own feeling', he argued,

> is that repression without a change in education is unlikely to put down these things. The Gezira scheme has done far more to free [the] Sudanese than government, direct action, [sic] because they can make a livelihood there on their own which they could not do before.[68]

It was felt that, with patience, this transition would be smooth. The old trade networks that had supported slavery could be turned to goods.[69] If properly managed, trade could have a calming function. According to one Gold Coast official in 1924, 'It is a fine sight to see the stream of cars entering and leaving Kumawu [near Kumasi], and the road is having a very settling effect on local politics. The young men are now too busy making money'.[70]

This belief in the benefits of Africans' adoption of 'legitimate commerce' has been noted by historians before.[71] What has been neglected, however, is any assessment of how far officials' own interests shaped their attitudes to change. Historians have tended to look at realpolitik as a factor shaping imperial policy, but officials also had more prosaic concerns. Although it is not easy to separate what was driven by duty from what was driven by self-interest, it would appear as if the latter had a part to play in officials' desire for an expansion of Africans' commercial horizons. Officials valued the introduction of markets and the movement of goods in part because it improved their own quality of life. Some officials simply appear to have enjoyed the work that went into building markets and seeing to it that traders were attracted to them.[72] Often subsisting on what they felt was a fairly limited diet of tinned goods and whatever they could shoot, markets also improved officials' diets because it became easier to get hold of fresh vegetables.[73] It might seem foolhardy to ascribe much significance to such mundane concerns. However, officials had modest, austere lives in Africa and, even though many preferred to be pioneers, we must not underestimate how important minute improvements in living standards were to them. Upon officials' return from a lengthy trek, the modicum of comfort offered by their dwellings generated a palpable sense of relief.[74] It was, invariably, not long before officials once again itched to leave their station and head out into the countryside, but this does not detract from the fact that the little things in life had a tremendous impact on their morale.[75]

Whilst, as we have seen, the development of transport networks in Africa could generate hostility amongst some officials for the threat it posed to an established and self-directed way of working, self-interest also came into play in other forms. The photographic collection that forms part of the Sudan Archive in Durham indicates SPS officials felt the construction of railways, quays, dams, canals and bridges were all of sufficient interest to warrant being documented in extensive detail.[76] As Cary's *Mister Johnson* suggests, however, a passion for road building was the most commonplace and popular construction-related activity undertaken by officials.[77] At the expense of other state endeavours, officials often pushed for road building as a budgetary priority.[78] Indeed, by playing on what they felt were the secretariat's chief concerns, some officials appear to have manipulated their superiors to secure more resources for this activity. One Southern Nigerian official suggested a lack of roads meant he was not always in receipt of the latest ordinances from Lagos, which was not something about which officials were usually concerned![79]

Virtually all officials recognised the importance of roads, albeit for different reasons shaped in part by Africa's socio-political and geographical diversity. In Northern Nigeria in particular, officials found it difficult to secure the services of porters. By decreasing journey times and, it was hoped, rendering portering a less uninviting source of work, good roads might also make officials' lives easier when they wanted to go on trek.[80] Roads allowed them to be pioneers more efficiently.[81] Elsewhere, for example in parts of the Gold Coast's Western Province, officials found roads important in order to gain their bearings in otherwise 'undifferentiated' forest.[82] More commonly, roads were welcomed for making trade, troop movements and communications easier, and for enhancing the appearance of British strength. This accounts for Southern Nigerian officials' concerns about 'dreadful' roads and 'broken down' bridges.[83] According to James Elliot, who worked in western Uganda in the early 1920s, because going on tour was 'the most important part of our work', roads were crucial for the sound execution of an official's duties.[84]

However, the ways in which any road building was discussed suggests there was also something more elemental motivating some officials, causing them to put far more effort into the activity than others. Donald Cameron later claimed (perhaps disingenuously) that he encountered no 'careerists' during his time in Northern Nigeria. They 'must be the product of a later age', he wrote, 'an age in which an individual officer sometimes seems to loom larger in his own mind than the Service itself'.[85] However, during Cameron's time in Northern Nigeria, some officials were driven by a desire for promotion. George Ormsby was one such official. One of Ormsby's counterparts in Northern Nigeria suggested that promotions were few and far between even if officials were sycophantic towards their superiors.[86]

Ormsby nevertheless felt 'very glad' when told he was to be transferred from Wokkos on the Jos Plateau to Ilorin in 1908 because he thought he would have 'twice as much chance of promotion'.[87] As a result of his desire for advancement, he was keen to ascertain if there were better job opportunities on the horizon by knowing of the comings and goings of other officials.[88] Submitting an enthusiastic report suggesting the Zaria–Bauchi road be extended to where he was based was a part of Ormsby's ongoing attempt to find out what was going on in the wider world, and to get noticed for being a hard-working official.[89]

Nevertheless, not every official was after promotion. Some wanted to stay an ADC or a DC for the remainder of their careers or, at most, become a provincial governor. In the interwar Gold Coast, to have a good chance of securing promotion required the completion of a period of service in the secretariat, which was too great a disincentive for many.[90] More prosaic concerns frequently accounted for attitudes towards roads. Generally, roads improved officials' standard of living. Some simply felt it was more 'pleasant' trekking by road.[91] One official whose all-consuming interest was African flora and fauna was keen for Uganda's transportation networks to be developed because this offered him the chance of travelling around more easily to see different types of wildlife.[92] Others were supremely concerned about their health, and were therefore keen for roads to be developed in order that they could be closer to doctors.[93] George Ormsby was a devoted son, writing to his mother more frequently than most.[94] As a consequence, besides reasons of career advancement, Ormsby also wanted to have roads built so that he could receive the post quicker.[95] Furthermore, roads improved officials' quality of life because they increased access to the everyday items such as the vegetables noted above. The dilemma of wanting to serve away from an urban area whilst maintaining a certain standard of living could therefore be solved by the development of roads.

Such rational factors ran alongside more emotional ones. For one ex-Gambian official defensively rebuking anti-imperial sentiment in the late 1970s,

> We did our best, and [the roads and bridges built] carried the traffic and trade rolled across them to the advantage of the local tribes ... We are now forgotten and unwanted, but at least we did our bit, and left our mark.[96]

The desire was to leave a lasting imprint on the continent. Roads could perform a variety of functions. Whilst working in and around Ho in the Gold Coast, David Daltry noted, 'I love road work ... there is a satisfaction about making a good road which is aesthetic'.[97] Construction more broadly could also prove an escape. When Koforidua's bureau-cracy got him down, Daltry delighted in building work in a nearby village.[98] In confronting the landscape, building was a combative endeavour involving a struggle that did not endanger officials' lives. Revelling in the aesthetically transformative impact of road construc-tion, some suggested that the men of the public works department in Port Harcourt 'have excelled themselves, for the roads are like linoleum'.[99] The act of transformation was important. Building a road was 'almost defying nature'.[100]

We turn next to education in Africa. Officials felt the promotion of education was of less importance than monitoring the cut and thrust of African political life, but Africans' levels of education was one of the most important determinants of the way they were judged by Europeans.[101] Western-educated Africans were treated as a group in their own right. One administrator in the Gold Coast Secretariat felt educated Africans did not fit into his definition of the word 'native', being 'of the opinion that we should not go by descent or by blood, but by social arrangements'.[102] Some officials had a vested interest in encouraging education provision. SPS officials wanted educated young Sudanese men to replace Egyptians in junior administrative posts.[103] This is, of course, not the same as suggesting officials were reconciled to education, and so it is necessary to investigate further. For this, we turn to the Gold Coast.

Particularly under the governorship of Gordon Guggisberg between 1919 and 1927, the Gold Coast became the most 'self-consciously progressive' colony in British Africa, where governmental innovations involving 'modern' Africans were first conceptualised and put into practice.[104] For instance, the 1924 Municipal Corporations Bill intro-duced town councils with an elected majority. Guggisberg felt this would 'teach the Africans valuable lessons of local self-government and prepare them for positions of wider responsibility'.[105] Guggis-berg had two principal concerns, which turned into his two principal legacies. The first was the building of Takoradi Harbour as a means of increasing exports, so as to fund infrastructural development.[106] The second was the expansion of African education.[107] On 28 January 1927, the Prince of Wales College was opened with great fanfare at Achimota, six miles north of the centre of Accra. 2,000 people witnessed the ceremony in which Guggisberg used a gold key to open the door to the first government-run secondary school in the colony.[108]

Guggisberg believed Achimota (as the college became known) would deliver change that would not undermine Britain's control of West Africa.[109] Rejecting the Macaulay-ite assimilation that 'with honest intentions and clumsy fingers' was felt to have disrupted 'the elaborate network of tribal customs and native habits which have evolved for deep reasons through long generations', Achimota blended the 'Hampton-Tuskegee' model of industrial education then in use in the American South with a British public school emphasis upon English, history, geography, civics, and so on.[110] Teaching staff had been sent out to the Gold Coast at least a year before they were due to commence work at Achimota in order that they understood the locale and generated ideas about how to deliver universalist principles with due regard for regional specificity.[111] All in all, a great deal was riding on the £600,000 building, thanks in part to the fact that the endeavour caught the attention of *The Times*.[112] The newspaper held that the college was an 'extremely important experiment', asking, 'How can the still unspoiled West Africans be brought into a vitalizing contact with our British civilization without cutting away the deep roots of their own life? The answer is Achimota'.[113]

Gold Coast elites also propagated this progressive vision, as demonstrated by the way the Crown Colony was depicted at the Wembley Empire Exhibition of 1924.[114] These elites appear to have been genuine in their enthusiasm for change.[115] As one member of the secretariat minuted in 1918, the Great War seemed to have 'stimulated the desire for education and it is interesting and encouraging to note that the Gold Coast does not lie outside the increased activity of mind which has been awakened by the exciting times in which we are living'.[116] This goes against much of what has been written about imperial attitudes to education.[117]

However, the elites were not aggressively expansionist in this regard. The need was instead for an education system that limited the number of pupils to 'those which can be taught by thoroughly trained teachers'.[118] Gold Coast elites were nevertheless protective of Achimota because it was emblematic of the colony's progressive intentions. In 1931, the secretariat hand-picked H. S. Newlands, the Chief Commissioner of Ashanti, to write a report on Achimota's impact, already aware that he would deliver a favourable verdict.[119] The Gold Coast's Director of Education batted away concerns about the college. In 1936, he suggested that whilst 'considerable discontent' had been generated amongst Western-educated Africans because there were more of them than there were posts as clerks, this discontent was set to die away because Africans were increasingly less likely to feel that 'the sole object of education is the acquisition of clerical work in some form or other'. Educated Africans would consequently move away from the cities and assist in the running of Native Administrations.[120]

Gold Coast elites attempted to shape what might be termed a progressive 'colonial culture'. The advertised aim of the Oxford University

Summer School was to keep officials abreast of the latest thinking on governance in Africa.[121] Consequently, a higher proportion of men from the Gold Coast in attendance at Oxford than of men from elsewhere could be one indicator that an elite enthusiasm for innovation rubbed off on the rank and file. Such proof is not forthcoming. Attendance was fairly consistent across the colonies. Approximately 5–8 per cent of officials from each colony attended per year, with the exception of Sudan, for which the figure was approximately 12 per cent.[122] This was partly because SPS men had more leave in which to attend such events, and possibly also because they were, on average, more intelligent than their peers elsewhere.[123]

When considering officials' attitudes towards Achimota, we need to bear two things in mind. Firstly, of course, a European dislike of the generic trouser-wearing educated 'coastal' African felt to have no respect for his elders was common across Africa. Secondly, Achimota was only new in that it was the first of its kind to be run by the government, rather than being innovative in terms of the level to which it educated Africans in the Gold Coast. Mfantsipim, a Wesleyan-run secondary school in the Cape Coast, opened in 1876, and by 1903 there were three secondary schools in the colony.[124] In spite of these two factors, officials in the Gold Coast's Northern Territories were particularly hostile to Achimota in the 1920s (as one scholar has put it, they suffered from a bad case of 'Achimota phobia').[125] If Achimota was not the first secondary school in the Gold Coast, and if an aversion to 'coastal' Africans was not uncommon, why was hostility to Achimota particularly prominent in the Northern Territories?

There are several possible reasons for such attitudes. Firstly, Arthur Walker Leigh, the Chief Commissioner of the Northern Territories between 1924 and 1929, may have encouraged it. He was certainly hostile to anything approaching innovation, being instead a staunch supporter of the direct rule he had witnessed when he first came to the colony as a Gold Coast Constabulary Assistant Inspector in 1898. It is, however, difficult to tell how far his obduracy affected DCs' attitudes towards Achimota, because the extant testimonies are from those who sought to discredit Walker Leigh in the 1930s for not being reformist enough.[126] Barbara Bush has suggested that Walker Leigh's subordinates greatly admired him, which might have induced some to accept his arguments.[127]

Conversely, there may be something in the claim that the vehemence of Walker Leigh's hostility towards African education meant DCs were unwilling to speak up against him. Instead, they hid their own beliefs behind an acceptable distaste for change in all its forms. Officials were, after all, aware of just how uncomfortable a provincial commissioner (or equivalent) could make life for his DCs if he so wished. Few went as far as to openly accuse their provincial governors of systematically bullying their subordinates.[128] However, after witnessing the way his immediate superior had treated a new, disliked official, Tanganyikan DO William Tripe wrote 'It is awfully important to keep in with one's Provincial Commissioner'.[129]

Nevertheless, to get a fuller explanation, it is useful to look at Guggisberg's rather *laissez faire* attitude towards the Northern Territories. Some colonial elites later intimated that Guggisberg had been too weak in confronting Walker Leigh.[130] Consequently, it is possible that by keeping his distance, Guggisberg allowed Walker Leigh to perpetuate a vision of the secretariat as a wicked, distant entity, and that northern opposition to Achimota was bound up with the notion that the south was trying to push education upon the north at a rate beyond that which officials in the north felt necessary.

However, whilst the matter needs further study, it would appear more accurate to say that, for some officials, 'Achimota phobia' was rooted in a belief that the institution was part of Guggisberg's ongoing marginalisation of the Northern Territories. Guggisberg does not seem to have believed the region's importance extended much beyond a role as a source of labour for the Gold Coast Colony and Asante.[131] When it came to education, requests for funds for primary schools in the Northern Territories were turned down on the basis that the money was needed for Achimota.[132] Hostility towards Achimota may have been made more vehement because it was thought of as an institution drawing funds away from projects in the north. The idea that Accra was holding the Northern Territories back speaks of officials' frustration at their inability to control their own districts' destinies.

Upon Guggisberg and Walker Leigh's departure, a dislike of 'half-educated' Africans often remained, although anti-south animosity became less intense. Furthermore, over time new officials were drafted into the region. They were less hostile to Western-educated Africans, or even enthusiastic about pushing ahead with education.[133] Having established that opposition to particular policies was often rooted in, or at least exacerbated by, opposition to what such policies meant for officials' standing in relation to their superiors, we need to step away from this district-secretariat relationship. We turn next to processes that took place within each region, namely local education provision.

Any endorsement of local schools cannot be equated with any endorsement of Achimota, because the majority of the former were only primary schools.[134] It is nevertheless surprising to learn of officials' confidence that local schools would not destabilise the empire. One official in British Cameroon wrote in his private diary that the 'Native

Administration' school (a school paid for in part by the government, and in part by a local Native Administration) was a 'centre of light in a backward district'.[135] Even in areas officials thought more advanced, Native Administration schools were welcomed for proving capable of turning out 'intelligent and able' young men.[136] In Islamic areas of Sudan, teachers with 'tact and ability' were welcomed because they offered a genuine alternative to the 'parrotlike [sic]' or 'stultifying and deadening' education of the local *khalwas*.[137] Some officials suggested that in instances where missionaries had failed to generate enthusiasm for education, the government should step in and try to rectify the situation.[138]

Officials were particularly enthusiastic about educating chiefs' sons. Peter Acland arrived in Sudan in 1925, whereupon he took up the post of ADC in Butana, in Kassala Province. He stayed in Butana for six years. Upon his departure for Port Sudan, the handing over notes Acland left for his successor noted sadly that the peoples of Butana were generally uninterested in education, writing it 'is only by chasing the Nazir to persuade his sheikhs to send their sons to his tribal school that any real results can be hoped for. Once the sheikhs discover that a literate son is of value to them their attitude might change'.[139]

There were two principal reasons why this education was to be encouraged. Firstly, when educated sons of chiefs eventually became chiefs themselves, their education would make them improve their territory more energetically.[140] Secondly, an education that imbued future leaders of the Butana with the ability to think in a more clear-headed fashion would make them resistant to 'outside' interference. Acland had his reasons for this being at the front of his mind. At the time of writing the report, he believed the Butana tribes were being manipulated by Yusef el Hindi (a leader of a major Sufi order) into complaining about matters such as the state of the local roads when they had 'no fair cause for so doing'.[141] In spite of regional variations, the same sorts of sentiments were expressed across British Africa.[142]

Officials were happier with local education than they were with national education in part because it was closer to them. They felt they had a tighter rein on these institutions. Officials inspected these schools personally, meeting pupils and teachers and helping shape the curriculum.[143] Some even taught in Native Administration schools.[144] In certain areas, officials also put their foot down where it was thought a mission-run school's teachings clashed with officials.[145] The amenability of the White Fathers Mission to Gold Coast officials' demands explains why there was not a larger outcry when some schools were handed over to missionaries as a result of cutbacks during the depression.[146]

Of course, some officials had fractious relationships with mission-aries.[147] In spite of this, officials nevertheless felt it perfectly possible for missionary schools to turn out 'loyal' and 'useful' Western-educated Africans. There was, after all, supposedly living proof of this process. Nana Ofori Atta was a Basel Mission-educated clerk who had become a chief in the east of the Gold Coast in 1913 and a respected member of the Gold Coast Legislative Council in 1916.[148] Ofori Atta was, according to one Briton, 'without doubt the outstanding African of his generation in the Gold Coast'.[149] Other mission-educated men, such as Samwil Chiponde in Tanganyika, combined a genuine enthusiasm for European ideas with a self-interest that led them to be committed to British rule.[150]

Whilst these men were notable by their high visibility in their respective colonies, that Africans could become mission-educated and remain 'decent' was something that some officials observed firsthand. Of the Italian missions in Sudan, SPS official Thomas Owen wrote, 'I fancy the Christianity they manage to instill is mostly skin deep, though they have some 500 converts hereabouts; but they are a very useful educating influence'.[151] Another wrote home to his parents saying,

> here is a specimen on English from one of our junior clerks who sent the Reuters telegram up to my house ... 'A.D.C.. Good morning sir. Hoping and wishing that you are getting on well with your health. Herewith today's Reuters. Your humble servant, Lino Tombe Lako'. This lad's father is a naked, savage pagan (reflect). The boy is a very pleasant mannered, English speaking Italian Roman Catholic Mission trained Christian, willing and efficient in the office.[152]

It was felt that such development would not undermine the empire in the long run, provided that missionaries sympathetic to the needs of the colonial state, rather than simply the demands of their faith, were put in charge of schooling. That so many missionary-educated Africans turned out to be 'half-educated and dissatisfied' was due to the missionaries concerned, rather than something that automatically sprang from the process of education.[153]

Conclusion

Opposition to change was not an inherent feature of the colonial state. Indeed, officials wanted to alter a good deal about Africa. Officials' attitudes to change were governed by a number of factors in addition to a simple analysis as to what they felt would be of benefit to Africans. Firstly, it was important to officials that they were as content as possible with their living and working environments. Consequently, in their endorsement or rejection of certain ideas and policies, officials were influenced by calculations as to the likely impact of these ideas and policies on their ability to improve their own lot.

Secondly, responses to change were also a contingent outcome of certain struggles for power and autonomy within the ranks. These struggles were played out on two fronts: between officials and colonial elites, and between officials and Africans in their locality. Regardless of how officials subsequently framed their opposition to change, opposition to colonial elites' policies was often rooted in an objection to a diminution of officials' ability to act as they saw fit. Officials' faith in their own capacity for supervising and managing their localities meant they felt that if they were able to prevent the incursions of others into their domain, they could work as the arbiters of stable development. Contrary to certain postcolonialist claims in this regard, this meant officials were not haunted by an inherent sense of conflict between stasis and change. For example, officials were particularly amenable to African education if they were able to control access to such education. Individual Africans could be changed and yet still remain 'loyal' to the imperial project. It is to Africans as a political collectivity, and the implications of colonial rule for this collectivity, to which we now turn.

Notes

1 Willis, 'Violence, authority, and the state', 90
2 C. Ehrlich, 'Building and caretaking: economic policy in British Tropical Africa, 1890–1960', *Economic History Review* 26 (1973), 650–2; T. O. Lloyd, *The British Empire 1558–1995* (1984; Oxford: Oxford University Press, 1996), p. 273. Regarding hostility to the development of industry, see Havinden and Meredith, *Colonialism and Development*, pp. 168–9. Regarding public school culture, see M. Huggins, 'Prologue – setting the scene: second-class citizens? English middle-class culture and sport, 1850–1910 – a reconsideration', in Mangan (ed.), *A Sport-loving Society: Victorian and Edwardian Middle-class England at Play* (Abingdon: Routledge, 2006), p. 26
3 Falola and Heaton, *History of Nigeria*, p. 117
4 Lugard, 'Northern Nigeria: discussion', 165; Temple, 'Northern Nigeria', 160–1. The belief that all colonies had to balance their books and not rely on the exchequer was omnipresent in imperial thinking before, during and after the period presently under examination; see, for example, P. Burroughs, 'Imperial institutions and the government of empire', in A. Porter (ed.), *Oxford History of the British Empire: Volume III – The Nineteenth Century* (Oxford: Oxford University Press, 1999), p. 188; Berry, 'Hegemony on a shoestring', 329
5 Hesketh Bell, 'Recent progress', 390; Orr, 'Light railways for Tropical Africa', *Journal of the African Society* 10:38 (1911), 179; 'Sir Percy Girouard's new task', *Daily Express* (6 August 1907), p. 5
6 Hesketh Bell, 'Recent progress', 379–81; Hesketh Bell to family, 26 December 1909, BL Add Mss 78721/92, 98; Hesketh Bell to family, 30 April 1910, BL Add Mss 78721/132; J. S. Hogendorn, 'The cotton campaign in Northern Nigeria, 1902–1914:

an early example of a public/private planning failure in agriculture', in A. Isaacman and R. Roberts (eds), *Cotton, Colonialism, and Social History in Sub-Saharan Africa* (Portsmouth, NH: Heinemann, 1995), pp. 51–2

7 For a useful map detailing these lines, see J. M. Carland, *The Colonial Office and Nigeria, 1898–1914* (London: Macmillan, 1985), p. 136; see also C. Metcalfe, 'Railway development of Africa, present and future', *Geographical Journal* 47:1 (1916), 12–13

8 Temple, 'Northern Nigeria', 161

9 Hyam, *Britain's Imperial Century*, p. 270

10 Bell to parents, 22 September 1931, SAD 697/4/19–20

11 Orr to Leviseur, 14 October 1907, BL Add Mss 56100/50

12 Adebayo, 'Hides and skins', 276

13 Gowers, 'Notes on trade in Sokoto province', [February 1911], RHO Mss. Afr.s.662(2)/1

14 Miller-Stirling to father, 13 August 1912, RHO Mss.Afr.s.2051/100; C. R. Niven, 'Kano in 1933', *Geographical Journal* 82 (1933), 338. Those in Buganda were probably a close second; G. Portal to Rosebery, 25 May 1893, in 'Further papers relating to Uganda', *Parl. Papers 1893*, lxii (7109), p. 15

15 Miller-Stirling to mother, 3 April 1910, RHO Mss.Afr.s.2051/10; see also H. A. S. Johnston, *The Fulani Empire of Sokoto* (London: Oxford University Press, 1967), ch. 16

16 Miller-Stirling to father, 31 December 1911, RHO Mss.Afr.s.2051/78. The real reasons why little resistance was offered were naturally more complex than this; D. J. M. Muffett, 'Nigeria-Sokoto Caliphate', in Crowder (ed.), *West African Resistance*, pp. 293–4

17 Miller-Stirling to father, 3 September 1910 [incorrectly listed as 1912], RHO Mss. Afr.s.2051/106; Miller-Stirling to E. Miller-Stirling, 7 February 1911, RHO Mss. Afr.s.2051/53; Gowers, *Gazetteer of Kano Province* (London: Waterlow and Sons, 1921), pp. 50–1

18 Gowers, *Gazetteer of Kano Province*, p. 5

19 Orr, *Making of Northern Nigeria*, p. 189

20 Miller-Stirling to father, 28 January 1911, RHO Mss.Afr.s.2051/48–9

21 Miller-Stirling to father, 11 March 1912, RHO Mss.Afr.s.2051/86–7

22 See also J. E. Flint, 'Nigeria: the colonial experience from 1880 to 1914', in Gann and Duignan (eds), *Colonialism in Africa 1870–1960 Volume 1: The History and Politics of Colonialism 1870–1914* (Cambridge: Cambridge University Press, 1969), p. 253

23 Miller-Stirling to father, 11 March 1912, RHO Mss.Afr.s.2051/87

24 Miller-Stirling to father, 2 April 1912, RHO Mss.Afr.s.2051/89–90; see also Hastings, *Nigerian Days*, pp. 128–9

25 Langa Langa, *Up Against It*, p. 41; see also C. Walker, diary, 21 August 1916, RHO Mss.Afr.s.435/6

26 Hesketh Bell to family, 17 June 1910, BL Add Mss 78721/143

27 Miller-Stirling to mother, 15 January 1917, RHO Mss.Afr.s.2051/187; Miller-Stirling to mother, 15 April 1917, RHO Mss.Afr.s.2051/193

28 Miller-Stirling to father, 16 February 1911, RHO Mss.Afr.s.2051/61

29 Miller-Stirling to father, 3 April 1910, RHO Mss.Afr.s.2051/15

30 Miller-Stirling to father, 16 February 1911, RHO Mss.Afr.s.2051/61

31 Miller-Stirling to mother, 15 January 1917, RHO Mss.Afr.s.2051/187; Miller-Stirling to mother, 15 April 1917, RHO Mss.Afr.s.2051/193

32 Carland, *Colonial Office and Nigeria*, pp. 69–70

33 Hogendorn, 'The cotton campaign in Northern Nigeria', in Isaacman and Roberts (eds), *Cotton, Colonialism, and Social History*, pp. 54–5

34 G. Ormsby to mother, 11 December 1910, RHO Brit.Emp.s.287/124; G. Ormsby to mother, 15 January 1911, RHO Brit.Emp.s.287/127

35 Miller-Stirling to father, 21 November 1911, RHO Mss.Afr.s.2051/72; see also Miller-Stirling to father, 5 June 1910, RHO Mss.Afr.s.2051/23

36 Miller-Stirling to mother, 30 June 1910, RHO Mss.Afr.s.2051/41
37 Miller-Stirling to mother, 3 April 1910, RHO Mss.Afr.s.2051/10; Miller-Stirling to mother, 3 April 1910, RHO Mss.Afr.s.2051/15
38 Miller-Stirling to brother, 7 February 1911, RHO Mss.Afr.s.2051/51–4; see also Sillery, 'Working backwards', [c.1975], RHO Mss.Afr.r.207/151
39 Orr to Leviseur, 6 December 1906, BL Add Mss 56100/43–4
40 W. M. Freund, 'Labour migration to the Northern Nigerian tin mines, 1903–1945', *Journal of African History* 22:1 (1981), 73–84
41 Hallier, 'Annual report, Rufiji District, 1920', [1921], RHO Mss.Afr.s.1072/3, 7
42 L. Vickers-Haviland, 'Annual report: Bukoba 1926', 3 January 1927, RHO Mss. Afr.s.1047/4/540–1
43 Hallier to R. A. Pelham, [c.1923], RHO Mss.Afr.s.1072/2
44 R. M. Downes, 'East Tangali District report by Capt R. M. Downes ADO', 18 October 1927, RHO Mss.Afr.s.834/140
45 Hallier, 'Annual report, Rufiji District, 1920', RHO Mss.Afr.s.1072/53
46 Hallier, diary, 11 May 1931, RHO Mss.Afr.s.1072/38
47 Thomas, 'Forced labour in British West Africa: the case of the Northern Territories of the Gold Coast 1906–1927', *Journal of African History* 14:1 (1973), 88–9
48 A. T. Grove, 'The African environment', in D. Rimmer and Kirk-Greene (eds), *The British Intellectual Engagement with Africa in the Twentieth Century* (Basingstoke: Macmillan, 2000), p. 183; H. W. Moor, lecture notes, [1913], RHO Mss.Brit. Emp.s.333/33; 'Forest utilisation: reports by Mr. Cameron', NA CO 583/191/7/10–23; Martin, *Palm Oil and Protest: An Economic History of the Ngwa Region, South-eastern Nigeria, 1800–1980* (Cambridge: Cambridge University Press, 1980), pp. 64–5. On deforestation, compare E. W. Bovill, 'The encroachment of the Sahara on the Sudan', *Journal of the Royal African Society* 20:79 (1921), 174–85 to C. Hobley, 'Soil erosion: a problem in human geography', *Geographical Journal* 82:2 (1933), 139–46; E. P. Stebbing, 'The encroaching Sahara: the threat to the West African colonies', *Geographical Journal* 85:6 (1935), 506–19
49 Falola and Heaton, *History of Nigeria*, p. 121
50 Newell, 'Dirty whites: "Ruffian-Writing" in colonial West Africa', *Research in African Literatures* 29:4 (2008), 1–13
51 Lea to parents, 23 March 1927, SAD 645/7/57
52 J. B. Davies, interview with Newbury, 9 March 1971, RHO Mss.Afr.s.1428/4–5
53 D. E. McHenry, 'The underdevelopment theory: a case-study from Tanzania', *Journal of Modern African Studies* 14:4 (1976), 621–36
54 G. C. Dudgeon, 'Note on the agricultural co-operation movement with respect to Egypt', [c.1913], NA FO 141/469/4
55 Austen, 'The official mind of indirect rule: British policy in Tanganyika, 1916–1939', in Gifford and Louis (eds), *Britain and Germany in Africa*, p. 601
56 Strickland to W. Walker, 12 December 1933, RHO Mss.Afr.s.1709/1/98–102
57 W. Walker, 'Memorandum on economic development in Eastern Nzima', 26 March 1933, RHO Mss.Afr.s.1709/4/30–41; see also Passfield to Slater, 29 June 1931, PRAAD CSO 25/3/1
58 W. Walker, 'Handing over notes, Axim District', [n.d.], RHO Mss.Afr.s.1709/4/27
59 Pollock to mother, 2 February 1930, RHO Mss Afr.s.419/157; Pollock to mother, 24 April 1930, RHO Mss Afr.s.419/185
60 For instance, Edward Scott worked in Southern Nigeria from 1903, before moving to Cairo to work as a businessman (apparently for Shell) prior to his death in 1908; Scott papers, RHO Mss.Afr.s.1564
61 J. H. Ewart, diary, 28 December 1900, RHO Mss.Afr.s.1991/75; see also Ewart, diary, 31 August 1901, RHO Mss.Afr.s.1991/117
62 W. R. Reeve-Tucker, diary, 7 April 1902, RHO Mss.Afr.s.1991/166
63 S. Boni, 'Striving for resources or connecting people? Transportation in Sefwi (Ghana)', *International Journal of African Historical Studies* 32:1 (1999), 64
64 S. Ormsby to father, 15 May 1903, RHO Mss.Afr.r.105/9b; S. Ormsby to sister, 2 September 1906, RHO Mss.Afr.r.105/16; S. Ormsby to mother, 16 January 1908,

RHO Mss.Afr.r.105/22

65 Falola, 'From hospitality to hostility: Ibadan and strangers, 1830–1904', *Journal of African History* 26:1 (1985), 66–7

66 Nevertheless some examples still existed. John Morris was a DC in Uganda who then went into business, before returning to work as a DC, eventually ending up in the protectorate's education department; Elliot, 'Notes on the Kigezi District of the Western Province of Uganda for the years 1922 to 1925', 30 March 1971, RHO Mss.Afr.s.1384/15a

67 Austin, *Labour, Land and Capital*, ch. 13; P. A. Igbafe, 'Slavery and emancipation in Benin, 1897–1945', *Journal of African History* 16:3 (1975), 417–21; Lovejoy, *Slavery, Commerce and Production in the Sokoto Caliphate of West Africa* (Trenton, NJ: Africa World Press, 2005), ch. 9

68 Robertson, 'Handing over notes – Geteina and Dueim 1930', SAD 517/1/14

69 D. C. Tambo, 'The "Hill refuges" of the Jos Plateau: a historiographical examination', *History in Africa* 5 (1978), 202

70 Duncan-Johnstone, diary, 25 January 1924, RHO Mss.Afr.s.593/1/126

71 R. Law, 'Introduction', in Law (ed.), *From Slave Trade to 'Legitimate' Commerce: The Commercial Transition in Nineteenth-century West Africa* (Cambridge: Cambridge University Press, 1995), p. 1

72 Hallier papers, RHO Mss.Afr.s.1072

73 G. Ormsby to mother, 3 March 1908, RHO Mss.Brit.Emp.s.287/16; see also Mathews to M. Mathews, 18 February 1911, RHO Mss.Afr.s.783/1/1/14; Pollock to mother, 1 February 1931, RHO Mss.Afr.s.419/237; 'Irish blood', *Everyday Sudan Life*, ch. 3

74 C. Walker, diary, 28 March 1915, RHO Mss.Afr.s.433/48; C. Walker, diary, 31 March 1915, RHO Mss.Afr.s.433/51; G. Ormsby to mother, 2 July 1909, RHO Mss.Brit.Emp.s.287/79; G. Ormsby to mother, 4 October 1908, RHO Mss.Brit. Emp.s.287/63

75 C. Walker, diary, 18 January 1915, RHO Mss.Afr.s.433/9; see also C. Walker, diary, 21 August 1916, RHO Mss.Afr.s.435/6

76 E. S. Crispin, 'Making temporary quays', [1905–6], SAD 2/25/9; J. W. Crowfoot, 'The dam, Makwar', [February 1924], SAD 8/5/1; E. Jane, 'Construction of new line to Kassala 1928', SAD 2/4/7; Parker, 'Abu Deleig bridge', [January 1928], SAD 17/3/17–18; Parker, 'Plaque marking the official opening of the Kassala-Gedaref-Sennar railway', [1929], SAD 17/3/60; Parker, 'Construction work on the quays at Port Sudan', [c.1920–1932], SAD 17/3/22–3; N. R. Syme, 'Canal digging in Gezira', [1935], SAD 2/7/22–3

77 Cary, *Mister Johnson*, pp. 55–6; A. F. Bridges, photographs, RHO Mss.Afr.s.1881/2; J. M. Fremantle, 'Handing-over notes', 30 December 1927, RHO Mss.Afr.s.230; Lumley, *Forgotten Mandate*, pp. 70–4

78 Ewart, diary, 4 December 1900, RHO Mss.Afr.s.1991/71; Ewart, diary, 30 June 1901, RHO Mss.Afr.s.1991/105

79 Ewart, diary, 15 November 1900, RHO Mss.Afr.s.1991/66; Ewart, diary, 19 December 1900, RHO Mss.Afr.s.1991/73

80 On portering issues, see K. Swindell, 'The struggle for transport labor in Northern Nigeria, 1900–1912: a conflict of interests', *African Economic History* 20 (1992), 137–59

81 Too efficiently for some; car usage left elites concerned that by speeding up their own progress through their districts, DCs were reducing the efficacy of the colonial state; Duncan-Johnstone to DCs, Western Province, 19 April 1933, RHO Mss. Afr.s.593/5/4/1

82 Boni, 'Striving for resources or connecting people?', 62; see also C. Walker diary, 25 September 1915, RHO Mss.Afr.s.433/107

83 Ewart, diary, 6 November 1900, RHO Mss.Afr.s.1991/62; Ewart, diary, 13 November 1900, RHO Mss.Afr.s.1991/65

84 Elliot, 'Notes on the Kigezi District of the Western Province of Uganda for the years 1922 to 1925', [30 March 1971], RHO Mss.Afr.s.1384/2a

85 Cameron, *Tanganyika Service*, p. 273
86 Mathews to mother, 16 June 1914, RHO Mss.Afr.s.783/1/5
87 The transferral never took place; G. Ormsby to mother, 23 July 1908, RHO Mss. Brit.Emp.s.287/50; see also G. Ormsby to mother, 6 September 1908, RHO Mss. Brit.Emp.s.287/59
88 G. Ormsby to mother, 1 October 1908, RHO Mss.Brit.Emp.s.287/62
89 It is harder to assess how far his study of an African language was powered by a similar ambition; G. Ormsby, 'Some notes on the Angass language', *Journal of the African Society* 12:48 (1913), 421–4; G. Ormsby, 'Some notes on the Angass language (continued)', *Journal of the African Society* 13:49 (1913), 54–61; G. Ormsby, 'Some notes on the Angass language (continued)', *Journal of the African Society* 13:50 (1913), 204–10; G. Ormsby, 'Some notes on the Angass language (continued)', *Journal of the African Society* 13:51 (1913), 313–15
90 Kuklick, *Imperial Bureaucrat*, p. 96; Bourdillon to Secretary of State for the Colonies, 27 May 1933, NA CO 536/176/7; Mayall, memoirs, SAD 851/7/58
91 S. Ormsby to E. Ormsby, 1 September 1908, RHO Mss.Afr.r.105/25
92 W. C. Simmons, 'Uganda unspoilt', RHO Mss.Afr.s.468/5–6, 57
93 Niven, 'Along the road', pp. 287–90; Mathews to M. Mathews, 18 February 1911, RHO Mss.Afr.s.783/1/1/14; 'Irish blood', *Everyday Sudan Life*, p. 25
94 Excepting his Irish countryman, the aforementioned Maurice de Courcy Dodd
95 The railway running through the Protectorate was similarly welcomed because it would speed his passage home; G. Ormsby to mother, 7 July 1908, RHO Mss.Brit. Emp.s.287/42
96 R. G. Syme, 'The wanderings of a misfit: Gold Coast and Gambia 1928–45', [c.1977–78], RHO Mss.Afr.s.1722/46
97 Daltry, letter to mother, 22 March 1927, RHO Mss.Afr.s.2222/16
98 Daltry, letter to mother, 6 May 1927, RHO Mss.Afr.s.2222/30
99 Trinick to mother, 23 August 1922, RHO Mss.Afr.s.926/26
100 Daltry, letter to mother, 7 April 1927, RHO Mss.Afr.s.2222/19–20
101 For example, in the nineteen government primary schools in the Gold Coast Colony and Asante in 1935, 3,950 boys and 1,353 girl were enrolled; 'Annual report, 1935–36', PRAAD CSO 18/1/2/1–2
102 Comments by Acting Colonial Secretary, 'Notes on conference on Native Jurisdiction: held at Secretariat, Tuesday, 24th February, 1920', in Slater to Milner, 7 July 1920, PRAAD ADM 1/2/132/596
103 Parker, memoirs, SAD 294/2/28; see also Robertson to mother, 27 February 1923, SAD 531/2/69
104 'Future of the Gold Coast', *The Times* (18 August 1921), p. 9. Whilst Guggisberg is invariably credited with firing the interest in developing education in the Gold Coast, others had nevertheless created the environment in which subsequent heavy investment was possible; Slater to Milner, 8 July 1919, PRAAD CSO 18/1/351; Kuklick, *Imperial Bureaucrat*, p. 128
105 Bourret, *Ghana: The Road to Independence, 1919–1957* (Oxford: Oxford University Press, 1960), p. 41
106 Guggisberg, 'Takoradi', *The Times* (3 April 1928), p. 15
107 Whilst championing 'equality of opportunity' rather than 'social equality', Guggisberg's interest in this was genuine. Upon his departure from the Gold Coast in 1927, he visited the United States, where he displayed an interest in African-American education; 'The American Negro', *Observer* (15 January 1928), p. 17
108 'Achimota College opened', *The Times* (31 January 1927), p. 12
109 Guggisberg, 'Comments on Secretary for Native Affairs' Memorandum', 1 March 1926, NA CO 96/663
110 'Progress in West Africa', *The Times* (31 January 1927), p. 13; see also P. Foster, *Education and Social Change in Ghana* (Chicago, IL: University of Chicago Press, 1965), p. 166
111 *Hansard*, 5th series, vol. 191, col. 1505
112 Guggisberg was certainly unafraid to bind his legacy to Achimota; 'Gold Coast

progress', *The Times* (23 May 1925), p. xvi. Guggisberg himself noted *The Times'* attention in his speech at Achimota's opening ceremony 'Achimota College opened', *The Times* (31 January 1927), p. 12; see also 'Progress in West Africa', *The Times* (15 December 1925), p. 17

113 'Progress in West Africa', *The Times* (31 January 1927), p. 13

114 R. S. Rattray, *A Short Manual of the Gold Coast* (no publisher details provided, 1924), p. 11, in BL 7959.cc.24

115 As demonstrated by their commitment to schemes of African access to libraries; G. C. Whiteley to G. M. Rennie, 24 September 1938, PRAAD CSO 25/2/5; Minutes of Accra Public Library Committee Meeting, 19 December 1938, PRAAD CSO 25/2/5

116 C. W. Welman, minute, 10 September 1918, PRAAD CSO 18/1/350

117 C. Whitehead, 'The historiography of British imperial education policy, Part II: Africa and the rest of the colonial empire', *History of Education* 34 (2005), 447; S. J. Ball, 'Imperialism, social control and the colonial curriculum', *Journal of Curriculum Studies* 15 (1983), 237–63; see also L. Barnes, *The Duty of Empire* (London: Victor Gollancz, 1935); N. Leys, *The Colour Bar in East Africa* (London: Hogarth, 1941)

118 Slater, 'Changing problems of the Gold Coast', *Journal of the African Society* 29:117 (1930), 463

119 Newlands was already known to approve of the work of the college, and had previously instituted educational programmes of which Achimota's Principal Alexander (Alec) Fraser approved; A. G. Fraser, 'Achimota and the general education of the country around', 17 June 1931, PRAAD CSO 18/6/100, p. 7; 'Minutes of a meeting of the Board of Education held in the Council Chamber, Accra', 24 February 1930, PRAAD CSO 18/7/13; *Report of the Committee Appointed in 1932 by the Governor of the Gold Coast Colony to Inspect the Prince of Wales College and Schools, Achimota* (London: Crown Agents, 1932), p. 78

120 'Memorandum by the Honourable Director of Education', 4 April 1936, PRAAD CSO 18/1/33; S. Shaloff, 'Press controls and sedition proceedings in the Gold Coast, 1933–1939', *African Affairs* 71: 284 (1972), 241–63; R. Jenkins, 'William Ofori Atta, Nnambi Azikiwe, J. B. Danquah and the "grilling" of W. E. F. Ward of Achimota in 1935', *History in Africa* 21 (1994), 171–89

121 'The Oxford University summer school on colonial administration: 3rd–17th July 1937', *Journal of the Royal African Society* 37 (1938), 95–9

122 For example, in 1935 there were 363 officials in Nigeria, including the elite Residents. Thirty-two men from Nigeria attended the 1937 Summer School; as per Chapter One's assumption that two thirds of those in attendance were administrative officials, two thirds of 32 is 5.8 per cent of 363. Out of a total of 146 administrative officials working in Sudan including elites and those from non-administrative departments, twenty-six attended. Two thirds of 26 is 11.8 per cent of 146; see statistics in *The Dominions Office and Colonial Office List for 1935*, ed. A. J. Harding and G. E. J. Gent (London: Waterlow and Sons, 1935); *Oxford University Summer School*, pp. v–vi; *Quarterly List of the Sudan Government 1st January, 1937* (Khartoum: Sudan Government, 1937)

123 Although, as was discussed in Chapter Three, this does not mean that SPS officials were intellectually engaged enough to take an active and continued interest in what went on elsewhere in British Africa.

124 C. Coe, 'Educating an African leadership: Achimota and the teaching of African culture in the Gold Coast', *Africa Today* 49:3 (2002), 41 n.1

125 R. G. Thomas, 'Education in Northern Ghana, 1906–1940: a study in colonial paradox', *International Journal of African Historical Studies* 7:3 (1974), 465; see also P. A. Ladouceur, *Chiefs and Politicians: The Politics of Regionalism in Northern Ghana* (London: Longman, 1979), pp. 44, 53

126 Duncan-Johnstone papers, RHO Mss.Afr.s.593/1

127 Bush, *Imperialism, Race and Resistance*, p. 57

128 A rare exception is Crocker, *Nigeria*, p. 38

129 Tripe to parents, 21 September 1929, RHO Mss.Afr.s.868/1/129–35, quote at 135

130 W. Jones to Northcote, 5 November 1934, RHO Mss.Afr.s.454/1–5; see also Jones to W. Walker, 7 August 1935, RHO Mss.Afr.s.1709/1/119

131 Guggisberg, 'Northern Territories of the Gold Coast: remarks of the Governor on the Chief Commissioner's Memorandum', 1 March 1926, NA CO 96/663; Thomas, 'Forced labour', 79–103

132 Thomas, 'Education in Northern Ghana', 440

133 Humphrey Amherst was an early example of this; Amherst, diary, 10 September 1930, RHO Mss.Afr.s.1207/38; see also Duncan-Johnstone, diary, 15 May 1930, RHO Mss.Afr.s.593/1/11/10; Duncan-Johnstone, diary, 31 August 1930, RHO Mss. Afr.s.593/1/13/20

134 'Achimota: a great experiment on the Gold Coast', *Observer* (21 October 1928), p. 26

135 Childs, diary, 27 October 1934, RHO Mss.Afr.s.1861/3

136 Owen to father, 8 March 1937, SAD 414/8/19–20

137 Owen to mother, 7 October 1932, SAD 414/4/20; Robertson, 'Handing over notes on West Kordofan', SAD 517/3/41

138 Weir, 'Ogoja Province, Abakaliki Division Annual Report, 1931', 7 January 1932, RHO Mss.Afr.s.1151/63, 88

139 Acland, 'Handing over notes, A.D.C. Central District/Butana, Kassala Province', [1931], SAD 777/14/18

140 Acland, memoirs, SAD 777/14/18; see also Acland, 'Note on the Ahamda', 7 November 1931, SAD 777/14/49

141 Acland, 'Handing over notes', SAD 777/14/10; Acland, 'Note on the Khawalda in the Butana', 7 November 1931, SAD 777/14/52

142 H. Brice-Smith, 'Katagun Quarterly Report No.21 for quarter ending 30th June 1915', [July 1915], RHO Mss.Afr.s.230. This was, nevertheless, reliant on resources; Daly, *Darfur's Sorrow*, pp. 133–7

143 Duncan-Johnstone, diary, 19 January 1922, RHO Mss.Afr.s.593/1/1/4

144 Owen to father, 8 March 1937, SAD 414/8/19; see also Owen to father, 28 January 1939, SAD 414/9/5

145 G. E. London to Jones, 9 March 1937, PRAAD CSO 18/12/49

146 Cunliffe-Lister to Shenton Thomas, 23 October 1933, PRAAD CSO 18/2/5

147 A. Porter, *Religion versus Empire? British Protestant Missionaries and Overseas Expansion, 1700–1914* (Manchester: Manchester University Press, 2004), ch. 11; see also Lugard, *The Rise of Our East African Empire* (Edinburgh: Blackwood and Sons, 1893), Volume One, pp. 190–1; Gowers to Lord Lloyd, 8 May 1929, NA CO 536/158/2/5–7

148 Bourret, *Ghana*, pp. 47, 51

149 G. B. Cartland, 'The final obsequies of the late Nana Sir Ofori Atta, K.B.E. Abuakwa-hene', *Africa* 15:2 (1945), 80

150 Iliffe, *Tanganyika*, pp. 265–6

151 Owen to parents, 7 January 1927, SAD 414/1/5

152 Kenrick to parents, 23 May 1937, SAD 647/5/55

153 Mynors, memoirs, SAD 777/8/4; see also Trinick to aunt, 1 July 1925, RHO Mss. Afr.s.926/31; Willis to D. A. Willis, 2 December 1928, SAD 209/12/42; P. K. Tiben-derana, 'The Emirs and the spread of Western education in Northern Nigeria, 1910–1946', *Journal of African History* 24:4 (1983), 528

CHAPTER SIX

Managing social and political change: tradition, modernity and indirect rule

We now turn our attention to political change. The familiar tale is that officials saw in indirect rule the best chance of sustaining 'traditional' African social systems in perpetuity. 'Reformed' indigenous elites would garner the respect of Africans by governing responsibly, thereby defusing the threat of social unrest and maintaining British power. It has been customary for historians to emphasise that the appeal of indirect rule to officials lay in the conviction that African social systems were fragile. After the Great War in particular, indirect rule certainly looked attractive to a body of officials increasingly concerned about some of the supposedly deleterious effects of colonial rule upon Africa. However, this chapter will argue that officials were not perpetually besieged by anxiety as to the impending disintegration of African political order. There was a concurrent belief amongst many DCs that African societies were robust and capable of adjustment to economic and social change. There were limits to this malleability, but many of these limits, such as Africans' supposed inherent preference for traditional leaders over educated nationalists, provided further reassurance for officials. Particularly because they were not constantly beset with anxiety, the enthusiasm many officials showed for indirect rule was not solely rooted in simple calculations as to what might best strengthen the imperial state. Another factor to be considered is officials' self-interest. Officials felt the devolution of certain responsibilities would make their own work easier. Consequently, by being able to spend more time acting in accordance with the personal preferences outlined in Chapters Three and Five, indirect rule would enable officials to have a more fulfilling and varied experience of Africa.

The tale of the colonial state's relationship with African polities is well-trodden ground. The state sought the imagined 'closed, corporate, consensual systems' of Africa's past because 'dynamic' polities with 'fluid and ambiguous' boundaries were 'contrary to British expectations' and impeded routinisation and bureaucratic precision.[1] This desire for fixity and hierarchy meant it was naturally amongst the peoples lacking identifiable chiefly structures that British intervention was at its greatest. Officials created tribal leaders where none had previously existed. The best-known example of this is perhaps amongst the Igbo in south-eastern Nigeria, but there are others, such as the Lango clans of Uganda.[2] David Cannadine has rooted a British preference for such hierarchies in an enduring metropolitan obsession with class. Officials' all-consuming wish for the strengthening of hierarchical, structured societies was apparently driven by a desire to prevent the rise of the republican, meritocratic idealism they felt had the power to dissolve empires.[3] Officials sought to close the gap between reality and the hierarchical ideal, reserving the most praise for those African societies where the gap was felt smallest.[4]

However, officials' prime concern was social stability. Officials in Darfur were perfectly happy for territorial boundaries to remain undefined if it was felt that their definition would create conflict.[5] Hierarchical societies were not praised on the basis of their hierarchies *per se*, but when such structures obviated threats to peace and provided what was felt to be orderly progress. The most obvious example here is Uganda. Thanks to a British suspicion of the Banyoro that did not start to properly lift until the 1920s, officials gradually stripped away many of the powers of those who had been successful leaders within Kabaleega's chiefly hierarchy.[6] In contrast, officials' admiration for the Baganda was such that Buganda's neighbours saw in 'Gandaiza-tion' the key to their survival under European rule.[7] Quite clearly, then, officials felt there were 'good' hierarchies and 'bad' hierarchies. They were impressed when hierarchies worked, but they were not dazzled by them. Even governmental systems judged broadly effective, such as those headed by the Fulani emirs of Northern Nigeria, needed British 'supervision', their 'decadence' on the eve of British conquest supposedly justifying the colonial state's presence on the grounds that officials could introduce a state of efficient austerity.[8]

Officials were open to the reinvention of African political life. One official working in south-eastern Nigeria before the First World War noted that:

> When the Protectorate was established tribal solidarity was at a low ebb and defined in barely remembered myths, and by conventions similar to those found in other segmentary and chiefless societies ... This was the situation that prevailed in most of the Eastern Province. Each town, and there were over two hundred in the Bende district alone, consid-ered itself an autonomous, politically independent unit, on its guard against its neighbours and ready to resist by force of arms any attempts to encroach upon its territory.[9]

Now is not the place to consider the primordialist-constructionist debate concerning how far tribes or ethnic groupings were actually new.[10] Nevertheless, this quote suggests two things. Firstly, it is indicative of the belief – frequently noted by historians – that the British were saving Africans from themselves. If the 'myths' were made flesh once more, a reconstruction of 'traditional' African political structures could be added to the list of reasons justifying intervention. Secondly, running counter to the view that the imperial state was obsessed with 'divide and rule' above almost all else, the quote suggests that officials felt a plethora of local groups all looking out for themselves, rather than for a larger entity, was a nuisance.[11] In certain regions, amalgamation would reduce border tension and any resultant open conflict. A 'tendency to local confederation' was 'healthy' because it was 'infinitely preferable from every point of view to the perpetuation of bickerings and jealousies between an infinite number of small and irresponsible units'.[12]

Amalgamation schemes proliferated as a result. Under Togoland's Native Administration Ordinance of 1933, the offer of tribunals with powers of judicial decision and legal enforcement was intended to encourage the union of the mandate's small 'independent communities'.[13] It was hoped that, in time, these political unions would be cemented by social and cultural homogenisation. However, particularly in regions where resources were scarce, politically unviable entities were created with different groups herded together in ways patently not reuniting Africans by reforging ancestral links. Enthusiasm for amalgamation sometimes overrode officials' increasing commitment to understanding the nuances of African life. A notable example of this is Darfur, where a 'dog's breakfast of leftover clans and families' was brought together in various schemes of the 1920s and 1930s, such as an unsurprisingly unsuccessful attempt to amalgamate nomadic Ma'alia with sedentary Rizeigat Ma'alia.[14] The extreme lack of supervision over DOs that marked Horace Byatt's governorship of Tanganyika between 1917 and 1924 led to political innovation. As even the semi-official *Handbook of Tanganyika* later admitted, there had been a great deal of direct rule, and some officials merged small chiefdoms.[15] However, even after Byatt's departure, federating activities were attempted by means other than formal ordinances. In Kiberege in 1930, one official hoped the development of the district's transport infrastructure would facilitate intercommunication between four tribes, eventually bringing them together as one.[16] Officials' commitment to the idea of the tribe was strong, but they were flexible as to what any tribe might actually look like, and how it might reach any end point in its development.

As Carola Lentz and Paul Nugent have argued, it was only the 'more perceptive' Gold Coast DCs who understood that 'the term "tribe" did not really capture the reality of physical mobility, overlapping networks and multiple group membership'.[17] Beyond this blind spot, however, officials were invariably aware of the novelty of their endeavours to reshape African life. Britons frequently remarked that they were lifting Africa out of its equivalent of the European Middle Ages.[18] Furthermore, whilst they may have conceived of tribes as discrete entities, officials sometimes felt forces beyond their control impaired their ability to treat these tribes as such. After a portion of Uganda's Kigezi District was cut from the Kingdom of Ruanda following the International Boundary Commission of 1912, Ugandan DOs recognised that an artificial border had been created.[19] Gold Coast DCs similarly spoke of an artificial frontier established for geopolitical and strategic reasons between their colony and the Côte d'Ivoire.[20] Thanks to complaints on the part of aggrieved peoples in the Gold Coast such as the Mo, these DCs were also aware that their colony's internal boundaries, and those between the Northern Territories and Asante in particular, ran across ethnic lines.[21]

So, officials attempted to significantly alter African political life, and were aware that the very act of empire-building meant their endeavours could not be wholly 'traditional'. Officials increasingly felt such endeavours were not unmitigated blessings. This was due in part to their in-training exposure to anthropology. Even if, as Chapter Two argued, anthropologists were not in the main critical of the empire in Africa, anthropology heightened officials' awareness that British actions altered African societies. Furthermore, the longer Britain occupied Africa, the less it became possible to believe that any impediments to effective governance by African elites were merely sporadic teething troubles occasioned by conquest.[22] In 1929, SPS official G. O. Whitehead wrote a piece for *Sudan Notes and Records* about the impact of British rule on the Bari of southern Sudan. Whitehead argued that a reduction in cattle raids under British rule had allowed the Bari to settle down and increasingly turn their attention to agriculture. This reduced turbulence in one sense, but the introduction of money amongst the Bari had

> put it in the power of the servile classes to make themselves independent of their chiefs and patrons among the freemen ... when they have bought their wives with their own cows, it would seem that half the chief's claim on their services had gone. Their chief has to base his appeal to them on the other ground of traditional right.

In order to fill the void created by money, the British needed to step in and strengthen this 'traditional right'.[23]

This was symptomatic of a broader belief that economic and social change ran ahead of African political structures' capacity to absorb the impact of such change unaided. From the vantage point of 1931, one Tanganyikan DO suggested that in economic terms the country had been 'progressing rapidly, perhaps too rapidly, since the war'.[24] As has often been suggested, officials hoped indirect rule could help counteract some of these unanticipated effects of British policy. Few, after all, were really convinced that, as one anthropologist put it, 'the chief, like a piece of iron that has been in contact with a magnet, gains prestige and self-confidence from his connexion with the District Commissioner'.[25]

After the Great War in particular, officials were fed with declarations that indirect rule in a pure form was an achievable panacea for all ills. Lugard and other commentators argued indirect rule was capable of repairing those elements of African society officials felt the imperial state had damaged, and then subsequently sustaining in perpetuity a political system organised around tribal elites. Besides the observations of the relatively well-known commentators of Northern Nigeria, similar arguments were made by elites within each colony. For example, in 1925, one senior SPS official suggested that 'Native Administrations give rise to no "Intelligentsia" class. The treasurers, scribes and the rest are the humble servants of the Native Authority and their emoluments are small fractions of his. It is inconceivable that they should aspire to political power'.[26]

That indirect rule apparently made for a stable endpoint would appear a compelling reason for officials to have endorsed it. Nevertheless, some officials opposed the introduction of indirect rule. It has been suggested that Leo Amery's unsuccessful attempt to bring about a 'Closer Union' of Kenya, Uganda and Tanganyika united Tanganyikan DOs around indirect rule as a means of curbing settler influence.[27] Justin Willis has nevertheless demonstrated that in Bonde, in the north east of the Mandate, officials advocated direct rule because the 'invention of chiefs and the creation of tribes were not considered by the local administration to be effective or efficient adjuncts to colonial government'.[28]

Officials' responses to indirect rule were not merely conditioned by the region in which they worked. We also have to consider the nature of the officials themselves. Those who opposed indirect rule sometimes did so on the grounds that it would create extra work.[29] In 1926, Sir John Maffey became Governor-General of Sudan. A 'confirmed partisan' of indirect rule who argued that the system could act as 'a shield between the agitator and the bureaucracy', Maffey ended elite equivocation about its introduction to the Condominium.[30] He recognised that a particular type of official was most likely to resist this programme of reform. This type was the micro-manager, especially military officials who could not bear to act against the conviction that Europeans could run things more effectively than Africans. This explains the rhetoric with which Maffey sought to convince officials of the need to drop direct rule and 'Experiment boldly with schemes of transferred administrative control'. Maffey argued that SPS men had to change their objectives, making

> no fetish of efficiency, remembering that in the long run the temper of his own people will do more to keep a native ruler straight than alien interference, and not forgetting that our efficiency is often more apparent than real and lacks those picturesque and 'amour propre' qualities of native rule which compensate for its apparent crudities.[31]

Those who accepted indirect rule were prepared to accompany Maffey in believing it necessary to jettison a desire for administrative efficiency over all else.[32] This would suggest this consideration was key in whether officials' accepted or rejected indirect rule. One might also argue that the 'bog barons' of Sudan who opposed indirect rule either recognised that they would never be promoted to jobs in the secretariat or, more likely, had no desire for such promotion, and so felt there was no need to pay any lip service to something in which they did not believe. In addition, because they worked in an environment that, as we have already seen, was antipathetic towards Khartoum, SPS officials in the south might not have felt the peer pressure to outwardly endorse this style of government.[33]

The route to indirect rule was nevertheless paved with difficulty. Only three Native Administrations in Darfur had budgets of their own on the eve of the Second World War.[34] Darfur could be said to be an exception in certain regards. An interwar combination of poor rains, locusts, disease and low market prices created enormous hardship in what was already a particularly poverty-stricken region, and it was therefore difficult to raise the funds for the initial outlay of the scheme's introduction.[35] Conversely, in other areas, such as the Gold Coast's Western Province, officials felt difficulties had arisen because power had been devolved to chiefs too quickly without their being given time to adjust to the new roles expected of them.[36]

On occasion, difficulties such as these led officials to exceed their briefs. Humphrey Amherst was an official in the Gold Coast's Northern Territories. In Salaga in 1933, Amherst watched a tribunal consider the case of a young man who had assaulted a Native Administration policeman. This was the first time such a case had been heard in the area. The tribunal imposed a 'paltry fine', which Amherst made them increase. This gave rise to the observation that there was 'still some way to go' before a Native Administration mindset was 'properly established' amongst those in his district.[37] Amherst also intervened in Yeji, reducing some local salaries because the budget was not balanced. 'It may not be Indirect Rule', he wrote, 'but ... it would have had to be done sometime and the sooner the better. They would never have done it themselves'.[38] Similarly, education department staff in northern Nigeria and Tanganyika later suggested that some younger officials 'thought that you had so much inefficiency at times that the only way to get anything done was to be fairly direct'.[39]

For officials such as Amherst, a temporary reliance upon direct rule was justified because it would speed the establishment of Native Administrations. Some officials maintained that indirect rule offered practical benefits. One wrote home from Sokoto that in an area approximately the size of Ireland, a handful of officials did not 'pretend to do much in the nature of direct government', so an effective 'Native Administration' was a necessity.[40] Others demonstrated what appears to have been genuine pride in the system. Indirect rule allowed 'things to go along pretty smoothly', and was thought to generate economic change and social reform without undermining political stability. This would transform Africa without the need to rely on the supposedly unsatisfactory assimilationism of the French empire.[41] Furthermore, if an official was relocated to an area that he felt did not possess as sophisticated self-government as his previous posting, it was judged a retrograde step.[42]

There are of course potentially limits as to how far these sources reflected officials' true beliefs. Amherst was writing in the semi-official diary that, as a Gold Coast official, he was required to keep. He may therefore have in reality been eking out a dwindling ability to rule in a direct fashion, avoiding any intimation in his diary of displeasure at rendering his preferred *modus operandi* obsolete. Similarly, it could be that DC Harold Blair wrote that indirect rule was eminently suited to the Gold Coast Northern Territories, and that he was satisfied with how it had been introduced there, because he thought this was what his superiors wanted to hear.[43] Blair was, after all, one of a group of new DCs in the 1930s able to find elite favour in challenging the supposed torpor into which the Northern Territories had fallen under Walker Leigh in the 1920s.[44] From the middle of the 1920s onwards in particular, officials increasingly found themselves serving under elites for whom the establishment of indirect rule was of paramount importance. In John Maffey we have already noted one example of this type of figure.[45] Resistance to indirect rule from some officials exasperated elites. As a consequence, in combating the tendency of some younger officials to resort to more direct forms of rule 'when things are going wrong', the Secretary of Nigeria's Northern Provinces issued a directive in 1928 reminding them that 'as regards qualifications for promotion and passing efficiency bars I put first the question whether an officer is imbued with the true spirit of indirect rule and make my recommendations accordingly'.[46] The message could not have been clearer.

For officials who wanted to advance up the career ladder, it would consequently have been a serious cause for concern if news were to reach their superiors that 'traditional' elites' authority was being diluted by British endeavours. Even if they had unintentionally undermined indigenous elite authority, some officials were concerned that their actions risked being mistaken for direct rule. In 1931, a sheikh in Kordofan offered a bribe to an ADC, C. A. E. Lea. This angered Lea, because he was faced with the difficult task of refusing the bribe without undermining the sheikh's authority.[47] He attempted to explain to the sheikh that he was unable to accept the offer, but later feared he had inexpertly handled the situation. He was in a gloomy mood the following morning, ruminating that because he had 'probably made a mess' of the matter, 'I would never make a D.C.'[48]

Admittedly, this sort of concern was not universal. A DC could be more hopeful that a secretariat would not learn of this sort of problem if his provincial governor was 'hands-off' or had a vested interest in hiding the problem from his superiors.[49] Lea had no such luck. His provincial governor was the imposing, long-serving, hard-working and ambitious Angus Gillan, who had an excellent relationship with elites in Khartoum, and who was well known as one of the most vociferous supporters of Maffey's endeavours.[50] Elites such as Gillan certainly help explain why personnel in other departments sensed officials operated in an atmosphere of enforced ideological conformity. Two such members of staff thought that, even if officials felt indirect rule was not as effective as direct rule, they 'probably ... wouldn't have been so prepared to go into print over that, it was just a private view they had'.[51] The paradigmatic nature of indirect rule as the in-house philosophy of the colonial services sometimes led to a reluctance to speak out over differences of opinion.

However, we also need to consider the possibility that these officials would not have sanctioned indirect rule had they felt it would affect social stability in the medium- to long-term. The past would have caught up with them in the end. Their covering up cracks generated by indirect rule would have eventually incurred censure from elites, and they may have had to personally deal with the messy fallout of any major discontent and unrest.

Too much uncertainty nevertheless remains. We need to look a little more closely at the factors that underpinned this outward commitment to indirect rule in order to ascertain the extent to which it was genuine. Some academics have suggested Britons working in Africa took to indirect rule because they feared that with the advent of modernity came the inevitable unravelling of the 'social fabric' that supported traditional political structures. It has been suggested that this attitude harked back to a metropolitan affection for an imagined idyll of a pre-industrial England replete with yeomen and peasants.[52] Fears about the brittle nature of African society did indeed emerge at certain points. This tended to be during moments of crisis or transition, such as when power was being transferred from one chief to the next.[53]

However, the impact of this vision of Africa as a perpetual strain on officials was partially mitigated by another that scholars have noted less frequently. This was the idea that Africa allowed change because it was malleable and resilient, and that in time Africans would accept such changes as part of a new political reality. For one DO writing from Tanganyika in 1932, it 'is apparent that the people [of Tongwe] ... have shown to a remarkable degree their capacity for evolving laws and customs to suit the conditions under which they live'.[54] This belief derived in part from a certain reading of the continent's past. For one official, 'we are extraordinarily lucky that the black peoples have no historic past, and are practically devoid of that accumulated mass of beliefs, thoughts, and experiences which render Asiatics so impenetrable and so hostile to white influences'.[55] Widely held to be outside of history, it was felt that the closest Africa came to greatness was with the sporadic rise of kingdoms carved out by powerful chiefs.[56] The idea that it was only with the advent of the European empires that Africa had begun to 'acquire a history' was widespread. Some officials appointed in the interwar period carried this belief with them after the Second World War.[57] This sense that in certain regards Africans carried little historical baggage with them was supported by a racist attitude. Officials agreed with the belief that 'Negroes' have the 'virtues and defects of ... attractive children'. This supposedly being the case, any long-standing tribal conflict would be quickly forgotten if conditions changed, and Africa could be reshaped anew without officials being constrained by past 'tribal' animosity.[58]

The idea that Africans were malleable was not universal. Officials were frustrated when they were unable to introduce the reforms they wanted. One DC complained that social relations in Offa in southern Nigeria were 'historic', which made conflict resolution over land more difficult.[59] This did not, however, foreclose the possibility of changes being made. When one Gold Coast DC travelled around Dagomba to prepare the way for the introduction of taxation, people told him they preferred the present system of tributary labour 'since it consorted with their own custom'. The DC nevertheless suggested that 'no great weight should be attached to that reply', since it was merely that the 'natural tendency of human nature is "rather to bear those ills we have than fly to others we know not of"'.[60]

Whether they turned to Shakespeare or not, officials felt the continent was resilient. All that was needed was time to ensure Africans adjusted.[61] Ruling lineages could be broken and methods of appointment could be changed, but as long as there was eventual African acceptance of this, it did not matter. To quote one Northern Nigerian Resident, one maxim of imperial government was that the 'people care far more how they are ruled than who rules them'.[62]

An emphasis upon resilience rooted in an equanimity – which some deemed to verge at times on stolidity – increasingly replaced the idea that Africans were excitable.[63] Officials admired this, even as they felt themselves pushing against it, because they thought it dampened down the likelihood of far-reaching political upheaval.[64] A report produced in 1927 by the Gold Coast's Secretary of State for Native Affairs, C. W. Welman, demonstrates the convergence of ideas of Africa's adaptability to change, and the limits to which this change was able to destroy something quintessentially African, namely a tribal attachment to indigenous tribal leaders. Welman had asked DCs for their opinions regarding the strength of tribal affiliation in the Crown Colony, and compiled their responses. 'Tribal authority in the Gold Coast', he wrote,

> is a very sturdy growth. Within the limits of each community, among those who owe allegiance to any particular Stool, it is astonishing how little sign of decay is noticeable … Amid all the economic and social changes which have been taking place in the Colony with gathering speed and intensity during the last hundred years, it is surprising to what extent the life of each community still centres in its Stool. There is hardly such a thing as the Gold Coast – even in the Coast towns, far less in the bush, as a 'detribalised native'. The impression of detribalisation that may be received by a superficial observer in the seaport towns is very largely due to the presence of large numbers of natives of other parts of West Africa, who have no local tribal connection. Those who are natives of the place itself all know their Chief and acknowledge their Stool. Even the most highly educated, Doctors, Barristers and others, who have been to Europe and returned, are to be found among the Chief's Councillors, and there are very few, if any, natives who will not rally round their Stool, when it is in trouble or on any great occasion.[65]

Officials elsewhere felt Africans would simply filter out the elements from the outside world that did not accord with their tribal structures. Such officials suggested that it was possible to overstate the degree to which Africans were eagerly absorbing all ideas from the outside world to which they were exposed.[66]

Any emphasis upon stolidity was not universal. One SPS man in Darfur believed that the Gimr were 'noted for their fanaticism ... Many of them are Mahdiists [sic] and are very ready fuel for any religious fire'.[67] Nevertheless, we must not overstate how far officials felt change was a problem with long-term implications for British Africa. In the first instance, officials were often not reflective enough to be in a permanent state of worry or to construct a timeline of where British Africa was headed. This was for a number of reasons. Firstly, some were intellectually parochial. They were perfectly capable of responding to the often-complicated challenges of governance in the here-and-now, but evidently lacked the ability to consider broader trends.[68]

Secondly, we need to consider the parochialism that arose from the hundred and one concerns bearing down upon DCs at all hours of the day. Being task-oriented limited officials' tendency to consider macropolitics. The memoirs and diaries of Hugh Elliott, who worked in northern Nigeria, reveal a man continually busy with tax collection, locust catching and the rest of his duties. Elliott was a relative rarity in that he commenced service in the interwar period but ended up working as a permanent secretary to ministers in Eastern Nigeria after independence.[69] Nevertheless, it appears that before the Second World War, Elliott was either preoccupied with the pressing concerns of the here and now, or he was relaxing at the end of a hard day with a drink and a novel.[70] Similarly, although he had been a DO in Tanganyika since 1931, Francis Dowsett seems to have only properly considered his relationship with the bigger imperial picture when asked to give a talk at a Tanganyikan girls' school in 1955. After the talk had been delivered, he welcomed the fact that it had forced him to actually think about why the British were in Africa.[71] Those working in other departments testify to officials' overriding concern with the present and the pressing concerns of their own districts.[72]

In contrast, it generally appears to have been the case that officials who did consider Britain's future in Africa appear to have been unable, rather than unwilling, to consider a world in which their own jobs were obsolescent.[73] Some governors, such as Maffey in Sudan and Cameron in Tanganyika, certainly made explicit their aim of preventing British Africa emulating India's popular nationalism.[74] However, even allowing that interwar Britons did not believe India was inevitably headed towards independence, there were serious doubts amongst officials over whether Africans were racially capable of emulating Indians in taking on significant roles in a national government.[75] A minority of officials believed African independence was, at best, a 'remote possibility' but, for most, the introduction of indirect rule could be understood as a *quid pro quo* for the supra-tribal political rights that Africans had to be denied for their own safety.[76] This is, however, to paint with rather broad brushstrokes. We evidently need to turn next to a more detailed examination of how officials engaged with anti-colonial nationalism.

Many nationalists did not initially present themselves as opposed to British aims. Surveyor and journalist Herbert Macaulay of Lagos, who established Nigeria's first political party, the Nigerian National Democratic Party, in 1923, submerged 'nationalist rhetoric within an impeccably British framework of liberalism, constitutionalism and strong sentimental loyalty to the throne'.[77] A more hostile tone nevertheless emerged from some, particularly towards the end of the 1930s.[78] Many officials would doubtless have smiled with grim amusement upon reading the claim of one commentator that most Nigerian officials had 'a pleasant collection of Lagos [newspaper] cuttings accusing them of every malpractice from embezzlement to high treason'.[79] One example of anti-colonial activity of nationalist origin took place in Sudan in 1924. This case study will be looked into in some detail so that we might better understand officials' attitudes to nationalism.

To begin with, some context is required. In the wake of Egypt's attainment of only partial independence in 1922, the ensuing frustration amongst nationalists in both Egypt and Sudan sparked an intensification of their claim that the two nations were bound together. This call for the 'Unity of the Nile Valley' was vague in all aspects barring its demand that the British leave.[80] In the first few months of 1924, most towns in northern Sudan witnessed some form of anti-colonial protest. These protests were usually led by Sudanese clerks and artisans, but were dispersed by police with relative ease, and the ring-leaders were arrested. The protests were invariably organised by the White Flag League, led by 'Ali 'Abd al-Latif, an ex-army officer of Dinka extraction.[81] In early July 1924, Latif and his deputy 'Ubaid Haj al-Amin were arrested and imprisoned. These arrests crippled the White Flag League, but anti-British activity continued courtesy of soldiers stationed in urban areas. In August, cadets at the Military School in Khartoum mutinied and marched to the prison where Latif was incarcerated, before being arrested themselves. This intermittent protest climaxed following the assassination of Lee Stack, the Governor-General of Sudan, in Cairo on 19 November. Britain issued an ultimatum to

Cairo, demanding that all Egyptian troops be withdrawn from Sudan. In protest, on the night of 27 November around seventy Sudanese soldiers, predominantly of the 11th Battalion, revolted in Khartoum. They had been given assurances that Egyptian forces nearby would join them in protest, but this support was not forthcoming, and the majority of the mutineers retreated to the Khartoum Military Hospital. The hospital was shelled and reduced to ruins by the British, and all of the mutineers were killed. Of those leaders not involved in this siege, three were executed by firing squad and the rest, including Latif, were given long prison sentences.

Peter Woodward has suggested that the event was a turning point, a 'severe shock' that transformed SPS officials' attitudes towards the Sudanese.[82] This is rather a generalisation. The whole affair was rather distant and of little lasting concern for officials living in rural areas. After having been surrounded by supposedly 'simple and primitive' peoples such as those in Roseires in Fung, one DC who started work in 1922 later argued that it was only after the Second World War that the 'first stirrings of political interest and excitement' emerged in the Condominium.[83] Officials with firsthand experience of the uprisings felt it significant, but publically responded to it in a very particular manner. In a letter to his parents soon after witnessing the mutiny in Khartoum, one SPS man recounted that he had been shopping with his wife when they had spotted the mutineers marching along a road parallel to theirs. They went to look for the Governor of Khartoum,

Figure 6 The aftermath of rebellion: bodies of Sudanese soldiers in the compound of the Khartoum Military Hospital, November 1924

were told that he had already been called for, and so carried on with what they had been doing, first stopping off at a hotel to say hello to the wife of another British official, and then on to finish their shopping trip.[84] When the fighting finally broke out, another official wrote soon after the event that he had 'had the time of his life' helping out manning the guns used to fire on mutineers.[85] 'It was rather like a pheasant drive', one SPS man wrote a couple of days later, 'and great fun listening to the shelling and machine-gun fire next morning'.[86]

It is not unfeasible that officials derived some enjoyment from the break from routine administrative work that the skirmish offered. However, it is fair to assume that officials included these anecdotes and references in letters home to reassure loved ones that the situation had been met and contained with true British pluck, rather than because they were themselves convinced that all was well. After all, the British had been taken by surprise, and concern that not enough had been done to predict the uprising was the major factor in accounting for C. A. Willis' eventual removal from his post in Sudan's Intelligence Department.[87]

However, in this instance, the gap between what officials said and what they felt was not great. Officials' responses were representative of a confidence that the mutiny was not indicative of bigger problems inevitably headed their way. Upon reading the declarations of confidence discussed below, the natural response will be that these were merely colonial whitewash. It is consequently important to bear in mind the simple fact that officials had a vested interest in not dying. At times like these, the British genuinely sought to understand the likely roots of anti-colonial activity so that it could be ended for good.

Firstly, uprisings in general were treated as forms of insubordination that arose only when Africans' basic needs were not met, and when they were given the opportunity to reflect on this.[88] Some SPS officials agreed that 'the old adage about the Devil finding mischief for idle hands to do, is very applicable to the denizens of fertile Africa'.[89] The 1924 uprising was judged the product of personal disaffection rather than genuine ideological conviction. Officials looked to the fact that the majority of the members of the White Flag League were public employees aged between seventeen and twenty-five working in the two lowest bands of clerical employment, and naturally concluded that the rebellion was only made up of the 'disgruntled ones who were not making a success of their jobs'.[90] This belief found widespread purchase thanks in no small part to the story circulated around the SPS that 'Ali 'Abd al-Latif himself had only become anti-British when he was sacked from the army following a personal spat with an English officer. As a consequence, officials felt many with anti-colonial tendencies would be won over once they truly realised what the British were doing for them and their country.[91]

Officials believed a 'Unity of the Nile Valley' alliance was unsustainable because the majority in Sudan harboured longstanding anti-Egyptian sentiments.[92] As one official wrote in 1940, 'please don't call the Sudan part of Egypt, the Sudanese don't like it'.[93] Instead, one SPS official suggested that 'the majority of the mutineers were ignorant, simple souls ... [and] they were merely obeying orders. Had their officers been British, the mutiny would never have happened'.[94] This created an environment in which mutineers' retrospective attempts at exoneration could be accepted. One example of this is the story heard by one SPS official that the rebels 'had not been told [by Egyptians] that they were going to fight the "Inglese", that was carefully avoided, and they were told that they were turned out to fight some strange and savage foreigners called the "Scotch"'.[95]

Such an acceptance helps explain why officials responded to the Egyptian failure to assist the Sudanese rebels with the suggestion that the 'poor [Sudanese] devils had been led down the garden path as a result of Egyptian propaganda and didn't rightly know what was going on'.[96] SPS officials' paternalism led to a belief that Egyptians and Sudanese were completely different in nature. Egyptians were viewed as scheming crooks.[97] Any sympathy directed towards Egyptians had dried up by the early 1920s, thanks to intelligence that they were actively circulating seditious material in the Condominium.[98] The externalisation of the threats posed to British rule in Sudan had a healthy precedent. In order to gain officials' assent for the conquest of Darfur, Wingate successfully played on fears that 'Turco-German' agents were manipulating Sultan Ali Dinar.[99] Use of the term 'coastal Africans' elsewhere in British Africa was a different way of externalising the threat. These Africans were either not of the place in which they resided, or they had sought to detach themselves from what they actually were. They were either interlopers or perversions.

As a result of a belief that those living outside urban areas were inherently attached to 'traditional' leaders, and not nationalist figures, officials felt that if the former remained content, then so would the rural masses. Of course, this would have been less comforting to those officials actually living in the urban regions in which 'coastal Africans' were felt to proliferate. Fear of urbanisation might have persisted in spite of colonial elites' declarations that the majority of urban Africans would eventually return to the land rather than go into clerical jobs.[100]

However, there were important reasons why SPS officials did not anticipate that their actions were causing nationalist discontent amongst the majority of the urban masses. Two different – and seemingly conflicting – stereotypes were created in an attempt to understand Sudanese behaviour. Firstly, Sudan's urban dwellers were 'entirely individualistic'.[101] Secondly, they were loyal to a factional leader. Given that factional leaders in and around Khartoum and Omdurman supported the British during 1924, this was reassuring.[102] In areas judged hotbeds of nationalism by rural DCs, urban officials had grounds for thinking that nationalism was not a natural outcome of urbanisation.

Furthermore, as late as 1948, one SPS official still maintained that, 'I doubt there will ever evolve out of Africa a government that can really be called a democracy. The vast majority of the people do not know what it means, and if they did, would probably say that they think the present type of government is quite good enough'.[103] If officials were indeed genuine in this belief, it would explain two things. Firstly, it would explain the tone of those memoirs written during or after the quickening of decolonisation from the middle of the 1950s onwards. As one such official lamented in 1955, before 1939 it had not been foreseen that eventually the 'greater rights' of a part in central government would be 'granted, nay, thrust upon the native'.[104]

Secondly, it would explain why some Africans believed that officials consistently failed to appreciate the changes taking place around them. In Southern Rhodesia in the early 1930s, Thompson Samkange, who would later become President of the Bantu Congress, wrote in his private notebook that the European has 'changed our world ... He has aroused in us the stirring of divine discontent... [Yet] it is amazing how little the white man really knows of the stirring of new life in native peoples living in his midst'.[105] Viewed in this light, interwar officials' enthusiasm for indirect rule does not appear to have been rooted in the belief that it was the last stand in protecting a fragile traditional order from a strong anti-colonial nationalist movement.

If colonial officials' belief that imperial edifices and African tribal societies were about to crumble was not as pronounced as some historians have suggested, we might turn to other factors in explaining such officials' enthusiasm for indirect rule. It is this study's contention that officials' personal reasons for supporting indirect rule have been sidelined. We will now examine the role that officials' workloads might have played in their attitudes towards governance, turning to the example of C. A. E. Lea and Sheikh Ali el Tom of the Kababish in particular. To reiterate the point made in Chapter Four, as one Foreign Office official noted, under the British el Tom had amassed power 'vastly in excess of anything allowed' under Sudan's The Power of Sheikhs Ordinance of 1927.[106] It has been suggested that SPS officials were 'genuinely spellbound' by el Tom.[107] Yet enthusiasm for a leader is not conjured out of thin air. In accounting for the esteem in which el Tom was held, we need to consider the physical and emotional impact of work on officials. Lea was never the happiest of young men. He felt it worrying when Europeans (whose company he appears not to have enjoyed for the most part) were optimistic about life.[108] Lea felt hard-pressed by the amount of work he had to do, and believed that it had a direct impact upon his health. 'Altogether I am tired of this trek', he wrote in his diary in 1932, 'and have got to the stage where all food makes me feel slightly sick and I dislike the sight of my best riding camel'.[109] In Kordofan in February 1933, Lea complained of overwork, which was 'aggravated by depression in myself which was not the fault of Bara or of its litigious natives'.[110] He was doubtlessly frustrated in part because working long hours meant he could not spend as much time with his wife, who had recently joined him in Sudan, as he had hoped.[111] It is therefore reasonable to assume that Ali el Tom found approval in part because of his willingness to 'sift' through complaints, ensuring only the 'important' ones reached Lea.[112] This led to the belief that, as one official put it, no other tribe 'so completely and with such apparent success administered its own affairs'.[113] That el Tom was felt such a 'low maintenance' leader makes it unsurprising that officials working with him were sometimes willing to both turn a blind eye when he used his position for personal profit, and ignore the idea that Kababish customary law had be excised of all that was supposedly repugnant to morality.[114]

Work did not always create stress. In fact, the opposite was sometimes true. In the early years of the twentieth century, when officials were more likely to complain about their job, one DC wrote home saying that there was 'not enough work to do, and plenty of work is the only thing that makes life bearable out here'.[115] Nevertheless, even as officials became more contented with their lot, the need to remain busy remained. One official in interwar northern Nigeria wrote that 'being fully occupied I am fully contented'.[116] For such men, there were other concerns. A repetition of the same routine activities induced boredom. For example, although it provided insights into 'quaint beliefs and interesting items of tribal lore' when officials were new to Africa, routine court work invariably soon palled.[117] One SPS official argued that, when amongst the Dinka in Yirol in 1935, he had to deal with 'the interminable cases of the vexed ownership of cattle which was their only interest and support'.[118] Elsewhere in British Africa, complicated court cases drove officials to distraction.[119]

To such officials, indirect rule appealed because it afforded them the opportunity to keep an eye on, and occasionally overturn, Native Court decisions, whilst avoiding sitting through innumerable cases. Of course, this was in part borne of a desire for a more efficacious colonial state. Officials sought to maintain power whilst divesting themselves of those duties they felt were both beneath them and impaired their ability to conduct more important work. However, being away from an environment where 'Every [court] case was brought before me, from murders down to a hen claimed by two old women' also meant a chance to get on trek and undertake a greater variety of activities.[120] Life was simply a lot more fun away from the courtroom. The idea that direct rule led to officials spending 'hours daily in dealing with routine matters many of which are of secondary or even trivial importance' was one with which colonial elites concurred.[121]

It was a similar situation when it came to tax assessments. For one official serving in Kassala in Sudan in the years before indirect rule and the Great War,

> Assessing the cultivation taxes was part of my job ... There was a tax of a few pence on each date tree. There were about a hundred thousand date trees and their owners trusted no one but an Englishman to count them. One counted them all over again by night. This intensely paternal rule could not possibly last: but until enough boys had been educated and grown up, it was necessary.[122]

Officials had a variety of interests, but counting trees was never one of them. In addition, they felt that it was in the role of tax collector when they would face Africans at their most taciturn and obdurate. If a local African could be trusted to collect tax instead, so much the better, provided that the official retained the power to check and rectify matters if these were patently inaccurate. Indirect rule enthusiasts felt it allowed them to be autocratic more effectively, playing the enlightened despot without the commensurate tedious legwork.[123]

Conclusion

Support for indirect rule was not simply rooted in an obsession with the idea that Africa was fragile and unable to cope with the changes Britain was inflicting upon it, and that the continent was consequently bound to rupture into nationalist discontent unless something were done. Instead, Africa was thought able to adapt to much, and would even eventually accommodate certain governmental innovations to which it was not naturally predisposed. Officials found it difficult to envisage a world in which the empire did not exist, and in which African nationalism ever constituted more than a minority concern of a few educated Africans whose basic, non-political needs had not been met.

At any rate, the intellectual and operational environments in which officials operated kept them focused on the present and impeded their ability to envisage an empire radically different to that in their own time. Nevertheless, it would seem that the appeal of indirect rule to officials lay partly in the promise that it would be restorative (in that it had the capacity to repair some of the damage already done by social and economic change) rather than preventative (in that it was needed to forestall the empire's collapse).

At the same time, historians have not done enough to consider officials as individuals who had personal reasons for endorsing or rejecting indirect rule. A minority of officials opposed it, but a majority publically acceded to elite demands for its implementation. That colonial administrations placed pressures on officials suggests their commitment to indirect rule might have been only skin-deep. After all, those who opposed indirect rule, such as many of the 'bog barons' of southern Sudan, were often officials who had relinquished, or who did not entertain, any thought of rising rapidly through the ranks. Furthermore, it could be argued that officials who expressed their approval of indirect rule did so in an attempt to convince themselves and others that they were somehow controlling a process they were in fact powerless to counter. However, besides the genuine concerns they had regarding the efficacy of the colonial state, it would appear that officials had good reasons for supporting indirect rule that were rooted in self-interest. In addition to the very basic self-interest of ensuring they did not do anything that led to their getting killed in a rebellion, officials were motivated by prosaic concerns. Indirect rule had the capacity to make life more varied and interesting, providing greater opportunity to be on the move, seeing more of the country in which they worked. If they were prepared to let go of some of their more tedious duties, indirect rule appealed to officials' self-interest at the same time as it appealed to their wish for a more effective colonial administration. It was thus the conjunction of state and personal interests that account for indirect rule's emergence as the orthodoxy of the interwar period.

Notes

1   T. Ranger, 'The invention of tradition in Colonial Africa', in E. Hobsbawm and Ranger (eds), *The Invention of Tradition* (1983; Cambridge: Cambridge University Press, 1992), p. 249; Berry, 'Hegemony on a shoestring', 330

2   J. Tosh, 'Colonial chiefs in a stateless society: a case-study from Northern Uganda', *Journal of African History* 14:3 (1973), 473–90. There is nevertheless some debate as to how far the Igbo were 'stateless'; J. F. Ade Ajayi, 'Africa at the beginning of the nineteenth century: issues and prospects', in Ade Ajayi (ed.), *General History of Africa: Volume VI Africa in the Nineteenth Century until the 1880s* (Oxford:

James Currey, 1998), p. 7; Iliffe, *Africans*, p. 143; Iliffe, *The African Poor: A History* (Cambridge: Cambridge University Press, 1987), ch. 6

3   D. Cannadine, *Ornamentalism* (London: Penguin, 2002), *passim*

4   *Ibid.*, pp. 61–9

5   C. Vaughan, 'Negotiating the state at its margins: colonial authority in Condominium Darfur, 1916–1956' (PhD dissertation, Durham University, 2011), ch. 6

6   Doyle, *Crisis & Decline*, pp. 104, 182

7   Roberts, 'The sub-imperialism of the Baganda', *Journal of African History* 3:3 (1962), 439

8   Lugard, 'Northern Nigeria', *Geographical Journal* 23:1 (1904), 7; Gowers, *Gazetteer of Kano Province*, pp. 51–4

9   *Annual Reports of Bende Division*, p. 4

10   Useful overviews are Ranger, 'The invention of tradition revisited: the case of colonial Africa', in Ranger and O. Vaughan (eds), *Legitimacy and the State in Twentieth-Century Africa* (London: Macmillan, 1993), pp. 82–101; C. Lentz, '"Tribalism" and ethnicity in Africa: a review of four decades of Anglophone research', *Cahiers des Sciences Humaines* 31:2 (1995), 303–28

11   Regarding 'divide and rule', see Bush, *Imperialism and Postcolonialism*, pp. 33, 74, 199. This is not, of course, to say that 'divide and rule' was never employed; D. E. Omissi, *The Sepoy and The Raj: The Indian Army, 1860–1940* (Basingstoke: Macmillan, 1994), ch. 1

12   MacMichael, *Anglo-Egyptian Sudan*, pp. 253, 255

13   E. J. Arnett, 'West Africa in review: Nigeria in 1933', *Journal of the African Society* 34:134 (1935), 66; see also Tripe, 'Report on Tongwe, Kigoma District', [c. May 1932], RHO Mss.Afr.s.868/2/1/30

14   Daly, *Darfur's Sorrow*, pp. 132–3

15   Sayers (ed.), *Handbook of Tanganyika*, p. 125; Iliffe, *Tanganyika*, p. 319. On the German use of the *akida* system, see Iliffe, *Tanganyika*, pp. 209–10

16   Pollock to mother, 9 July 1930, RHO Mss Afr.s.419/209

17   C. Lentz and P. Nugent, 'Ethnicity in Ghana: a comparative perspective', in Lentz and Nugent (eds), *Ethnicity in Ghana: The Limits of Invention* (New York: St Martin's Press, 1999), p. 9; Cardinall, 'The state of our present ethnographical knowledge of the Gold Coast peoples', *Africa* 2:4 (1929), 405; Iliffe, *Tanganyika*, p. 324

18   Lea to parents, 10 February 1927, SAD 645/7/36; see also G. Ormsby to sisters, 23 August 1908, RHO Mss.Brit.Emp.s.287/57; Lea to parents, 16 January 1927, SAD 645/7/22; Duncan-Johnstone, diary, 21 January 1930, RHO Mss.s.593/1/1/7/87

19   Phillips, 'The Nabingi', 31 July 1919, RHO Mss.Afr.s.1384/477

20   W. Walker, 'Report of a visit to the French Ivory Coast', [August 1933], RHO Mss. Afr.s.1064/9

21   R. Bening, 'Internal colonial boundary problems of the Gold Coast, 1907–1951', *International Journal of African Historical Studies* 17:1 (1984), 81–99

22   There are some grounds for the suggestion that indigenous identities began to stabilise in the interwar period as Africans adjusted to life under the British; T. C. McCaskie, *Asante Identities: History and Modernity in an African Village 1850–1950* (Edinburgh: Edinburgh University Press, 2000), p. 144

23   G. O. Whitehead, 'Social change among the Bari', *Sudan Notes and Records* 12:1 (1929), 91–7, quote at 95

24   Dowsett to parents, 18 August 1931, RHO Mss.Afr.s.1276/4

25   Fortes, 'Culture contact', 28

26   Davies to Lyall, 22 January 1925, NA FO 141/632/17679

27   Austen, 'British policy in Tanganyika, 1916–1939', in Gifford and Louis (eds), *Britain and Germany in Africa* p. 591

28   Willis, 'The administration of Bonde, 1920–60: a study of the implementation of indirect rule in Tanganyika', *African Affairs* 92:366 (1993), 67

29   Duncan-Johnstone, diary, 21 January 1930, RHO Mss.Afr.s.593/1/1/7/87

30   The quotes are at Daly, *Empire on the Nile*, p. 365, and Sanderson, 'The Anglo-

Egyptian Sudan', in Roberts (ed.) *Cambridge History of Africa: Volume 7*, p. 772 respectively

31 Maffey, circular to SPS officials, 25 January 1927, SAD 716/1/5
32 Parker, memoirs, SAD 294/2/27
33 In actuality, they might instead have felt peer pressure to adhere to direct rule. Such opposition was not sufficient to prevent indirect rule's introduction across the south
34 Daly, *Darfur's Sorrow*, p. 127
35 *Ibid.*, pp. 143–4
36 Duncan-Johnston, 'Native Administration', 13 July 1936, RHO Mss.Afr.s.593/5/8/1
37 Amherst, diary, 31 July 1933, RHO Mss.Afr.s.1207/148
38 Amherst, diary, 13 May 1933, RHO Mss.Afr.s.1207/123
39 F. D. Hibbert, interview with R. E. Ellison and Kirk-Greene, 4 July 1969, RHO Mss. Afr.s.1332; see also Gailey, *Sir Donald Cameron*, p. 79
40 Tomlinson to mother, 15 September 1907, RHO Mss.Afr.s.372/60
41 Quote from Trinick to aunt, 1 July 1925, RHO Mss.Afr.s.926/31; see also E. H. Macintosh, memoirs, [c.1958–62], SAD 895/3/11; Owen to mother, 17 August 1928, SAD 414/2/9; Owen to father, 18 October 1932, SAD 414/4/22; W. Walker, 'Report of a visit to the French Ivory Coast', RHO Mss.Afr.s.1064/9
42 G. W. Titherington to godmother, 4 July 1935, SAD 636/12/31; Titherington to godmother, 27 March 1936, SAD 636/12/33
43 Blair, 'A tour of the Northern Territories of the Gold Coast', [early 1937], RHO Mss. Afr.s.626/106
44 Duncan-Johnstone, diary, 6 August 1929, RHO Mss.Afr.s.593/1/7/3; Duncan-Johnstone, diary, 24 May 1930, RHO Mss.Afr.s.593/1/11/15; Jones to Northcote, 5 November 1934, RHO Mss.Afr.s.454/12
45 Witness also the change in attitudes of SPS provincial governors in Daly, *Empire on the Nile*, pp. 366–7
46 '1928: Two Secretariat Directives', in Kirk-Greene (ed.), *Principles of Native Administration in Nigeria: Selected Documents 1900–1947* (London: Oxford University Press, 1965), p. 191
47 Lea, diary, 20 May 1931, in Lea, *On Trek*, p. 85
48 Lea, diary, 21 May 1931, in *ibid.*, p. 87
49 Regarding the differences in provincial governors, see Heussler, *British Tanganyika*, p. 42; Wilks, 'Asante nationhood and colonial administrators, 1896–1935', in Lentz and Nugent (eds), *Ethnicity in Ghana*, pp. 68–95
50 Currie to Furse, 7 August 1935, RHO Mss.Brit.Emp.s.415/6/7/9; A. Gillan, 'The Sudan: past, present and future', *African Affairs* 43:172 (1944), 123–8; G. Warburg, *Islam, Sectarianism and Politics in Sudan since the Mahdiyya* (London: C. Hurst & Co., 2003), p. 110. Gillan was well known in the service for winning gold medals for rowing at the 1908 and 1912 Olympics. A respected official who had been in Sudan since 1909, in 1934 Gillan became Civil Secretary – a post second only in importance to the Governorship – and was knighted in 1939
51 Hibbert, interview with Ellison and Kirk-Greene, RHO Mss.Afr.s.1332
52 J. L. Comaroff, 'Images of empire, contests of conscience: models of colonial domination in South Africa', in Cooper and Stoler (eds), *Tensions of Empire*, pp. 172–4
53 This was particularly the case in instances, such as that of Sheikh Ali el Tom, where the current indigenous leader was judged to have done well
54 Tripe, 'Report on Tongwe', RHO Mss.Afr.s.868/2/1/30
55 F. H. Melland, 'The problem of witchcraft', *East Africa* (9 February 1933), 517. Frank Melland served as an official in Northern Rhodesia.
56 In shaping metropolitan notions of Africa's history, fictional chiefs ranked alongside real ones; the most significant of these two categories were Shaka Zulu, Prester John and Twala of *King Solomon's Mines*
57 Dowsett to parents, 29 July 1953, RHO Mss.Afr.s.1276/518
58 Quote from Lugard, *Dual Mandate*, p. 70. For agreement with this see, for instance, Parker, diary, 29 July 1918, SAD 294/9/14; Kenrick to parents, 11 April 1937, SAD

647/5/42; Robertson to mother, 12 January 1922, SAD 531/2/29

59 Childs, diary, 10 August 1933, RHO Mss.Afr.s.1861/1

60 Blair, 'A preliminary survey in Eastern Dagomba: preparatory to the introduction of taxation', [n.d.], RHO Mss.Afr.s.626/62

61 Hamilton, 'Devolutionary principles', in Hamilton (ed.), *Anglo-Egyptian Sudan from Within*, p. 184

62 Quoted in Heussler, *British in Northern Nigeria*, p. 35

63 Bell to parents, 25 March 1932, SAD 697/6/12; Bell to parents, 11 August 1933, SAD 697/10/24; Owen to mother, 26 December 1936, SAD 414/8/6

64 Lea, diary, 27 March 1931, SAD 645/9/36–7

65 Welman, 'Memorandum', [c. February 1927], NA CO 96/663

66 Weir, 'The broad outlines of the past and present organisation in the Ekiti division of the Ondo province with suggestions for administrative and judicial reform', 13 February 1934, RHO Mss.Afr.s.1151/6/390, 429

67 W. Luce, diary, 30 November 1934, SAD 829/12; see also F. W. F. Jackson, 'Annual Administrative Report: Ashanti', [1934], NA CO 96/718/4/43; Bruce-Gardyne, 'The Sudan: some native aspects', SAD 478/12/5

68 B. E. N. Lampert, '"So we used to do": British colonial civil servants in Nigeria 1921–1968' (MSc dissertation, Bristol University, 2002), pp. 15–16

69 See also H. P. Elliott, *Darkness and Dawn in Zimbabwe* (London: Grosvenor, 1978)

70 Elliott, 'Reminiscences of colonial administrative service in Nigeria, 1934–67', RHO Mss.Afr.s.1838/1; Elliott, diary for 1935–36, RHO Mss.Afr.s.1336; Letchworth interview, RHO Mss.Afr.s.2112/20

71 Dowsett to mother, 13 February 1955, RHO Mss.Afr.s.1276/547

72 Hibbert, interview with Ellison and Kirk-Greene, RHO Mss.Afr.s.1332; see also Heussler, *British Tanganyika*, p. 39

73 Lea to parents, 14 February 1927, SAD 645/7/40

74 Daly, *Empire on the Nile*, p. 366; Iliffe, *Tanganyika*, p. 322; R. Austen, *Northwest Tanzania under German and British Rule: Colonial Policy and Tribal Politics, 1889–1939* (New Haven, CT: Yale University Press, 1968), pp. 153–4

75 Regarding Indians, see P. Rich, *Race and Empire in British Politics* (Cambridge: Cambridge University Press, 1986), pp. 66–7

76 Dundas, *African Crossroads*, p. 135; see also C. Whybrow, diary, [1926], quoted in Heussler, *British Tanganyika*, p. 66

77 I. Duffield, 'John Eldred Taylor and West African opposition to indirect rule in Nigeria', *African Affairs* 70 (1971), 252–68, quote at 253; see also J. E. Flint, 'Managing nationalism: the Colonial Office and Nnamdi Azikiwe, 1932–43', in R. D. King and R. W. Wilson (eds), *The Statecraft of British Imperialism: Essays in Honour of Wm. Roger Louis* (London: Cass, 1999), pp. 143–58; see also Newell, *Literary Culture*, pp. 18–19, 22, 44

78 Iliffe, *Africans*, p. 233

79 Field, 'Verb Sap.', p. 45

80 I. Gershoni and J. P. Jankowski, *Egypt, Islam and the Arabs: The Search for Egyptian Nationhood, 1900–1930* (Oxford: Oxford University Press, 1986), pp. 53–4

81 On White Flag League ideology, see Y. Kurita, 'The concept of nationalism in the White Flag League', in M. A. Al Safi (ed.), *The Nationalist Movement in the Sudan* (Khartoum: University of Khartoum Press, 1989), pp. 14–62

82 P. Woodward, *Sudan 1898–1989: The Unstable State* (London: Lester Crook, 1990), p. 43

83 J. W. Robertson to mother, 7 December 1931, SAD 531/3/16; Robertson, interview with Perham, 11 July 1966, RHO Mss.Afr.s.802/Robertson

84 N. R. Udal to parents, 31 November 1924, SAD 780/5/10

85 C. Dupuis to Clark, 21 December 1924, SAD 780/1/14; see also Baily to father, 10 December 1924, SAD 533/2/9

86 Udal to parents, 31 November 1924, SAD 780/5/10

87 Daly, *Empire on the Nile*, p. 330

88 Robertson, 'Handing over notes – Geteina and Dueim 1930', SAD 517/1/15

89 Hesketh Bell, 'Recent progress', 379
90 Dupuis to Mrs G. Clark, 21 December 1924, SAD 780/1/4; T. Niblock, *Class and Power in the Sudan: The Dynamics of Sudanese Politics, 1898–1985* (Basingstoke: Macmillan, 1987), p. 166
91 Baily, note, [August 1970], SAD 533/3/3; see also MacMichael, *Anglo-Egyptian Sudan*, p. 257; Newbold to Perham, 23 September 1938, in Henderson, *Modern Sudan*, p. 91
92 Robertson to mother, 27 February 1923, SAD 531/2/68
93 Robertson to mother, 27 February 1923, SAD 531/2/68; see also Mayall, memoirs, [1940], SAD 851/7/6
94 C. E. Fouracres, memoirs, SAD 815/15/40; see also Baily, diary, 28 November 1924, SAD 422/13/14
95 G. R. Storrar, diary, week commencing 25 November 1924, SAD 56/1/54–5
96 Macintosh, memoirs, SAD 895/3/5
97 Bell to parents, 22 April 1932, SAD 697/6/29
98 For an earlier, more sympathetic view of Egyptians see Baily to father, 3 July 1919, SAD 533/1/39
99 J. Slight, 'British perceptions and responses to Sultan Ali Dinar of Darfur, 1915–16', *Journal of Imperial and Commonwealth History* 38:2 (2010), 237–60
100 Duncan-Johnstone, 21 June 1933, RHO Mss.Afr.s.593/2/7/20
101 Dupuis to Clark, 21 December 1924, SAD 780/1/7; 'Report on political agitation in the Sudan', [June 1925], NA FO 371/10905; see also Orde-Browne, 'Report on tour through French West Africa 1935', [n.d.], RHO Mss.Afr.s.1117/42
102 Baily, diary, 20 November 1924, SAD 422/13/4; Baily, diary, 11 December 1924, SAD 422/13/26; Baily to father, 10 December 1924, SAD 533/2/9
103 Bloss, memoirs, SAD 704/1/107
104 Dundas, *African Crossroads*, p. 135
105 Quoted in T. Ranger, *Are We Not Also Men?: The Samkange Family and African Politics in Zimbabwe 1920–64* (London: James Currey, 1995), p. 15
106 Quoted in Daly, *Empire on the Nile*, p. 374. The Ordinance had granted a good deal of judicial authority to both territorial sheikhs and the elites of sedentary tribes; *ibid.*, p. 367
107 Willis, 'Hukm', 39. There are grounds for Willis' assertion, although officials were not above criticising el Tom to his face; Davies, *Camel's Back*, p. 59; Daly, *Imperial Sudan*, p. 32
108 Lea, diary, 17 December 1931, in Lea, *On Trek*, p. 168; Lea, diary, 15 December 1931, in *ibid.*, p. 166
109 Lea, diary, 9 October 1932, in *ibid.*, p. 240
110 Lea, diary, 20 February 1933, in *ibid.*, p. 259
111 Lea, diary, 13 January 1933, in *ibid.*, p. 246
112 Lea, diary, 17 January 1933, in *ibid.*, p. 251
113 Daly, *Empire on the Nile*, p. 375
114 Willis, 'Hukm', 36
115 S. Ormsby to father, 15 May 1903, RHO Mss.Afr.r.105/9b
116 Percival, diary, 11 September 1930, RHO Mss.Brit.Emp.s.364/2/28
117 Owen to mother, [July 1927], SAD 414/1/28
118 Penn, memoirs, [February 1983], SAD 722/13/10
119 Childs, diary, 25 October 1932, RHO Mss.Afr.s.1861/1
120 Baily, 'Early recollections of the Sudan', [c.1971], SAD 533/4/20
121 Davies to Lyall, 22 January 1925, NA FO 141/632/17679
122 Baily, 'Early recollections of the Sudan', SAD 533/4/20
123 See also Cameron, 'Mwanza Province: Report', [1928], NA CO 691/100/20/11. French colonial rule was criticised by many Britons; see, for example, G. Gorer, *Africa Dances* (1935; New York: Norton, 1962), pp. 106–7

Conclusion

It is time to return to the four historiographical issues outlined in the introduction. The first of these concerns how far officials' ideas were the product of their upbringing and education, and how far they were the product of experiences of Africa. The answer to this is straightforward. When the metropole influenced officials, it was either in an imprecise or general sense, or in ways that colonial elites did not want. Chapter Two demonstrated that, in advance of their departure for Africa, officials' knowledge of the continent was low. Even after training for officials became more sophisticated in the interwar period, it did little to surmount recruits' ignorance of the specificities of empire.

Chapter Three addressed the first historiographical issue as well as the second, namely the extent to which officials were selfless or selfish, and the third, namely the extent to which wider imperial networks played a role in shaping officials' ideas. Once officials were out in Africa, a different form of ignorance to that discussed in Chapter Two was at work. An ignorance of the African world beyond one's own district was fostered by the social and operational insularity of the environments in which officials found themselves. Whilst in Africa, the most important information networks to which officials had access on a day-to-day basis were the intra-colonial informal networks of gossip. Rather than unifying all in some form of 'imagined community' of imperial brothers across Africa (to bastardise Benedict Anderson's well-known phrase), such networks tended to generate jealousy of, or superiority towards, other colonies.[1] Each colonial corps was also fragmented internally. In an environment powered by gossip and officials' sense of themselves, divergent attitudes towards imperial governance fostered envy or condescension as to the administrative procedures, opportunities and working conditions of others in their colony. This points to the relative failure of educators' attempts to inculcate *esprit de corps* on Britain's playing fields and in Britain's classrooms, a process usually seen as a success. Officials were not incapable of forming close personal relationships with other Europeans, but colonial elites' efforts to make this tendency universal were hampered by a strong counter-current in British culture that emphasised the empire was a route to an individualistic self-fulfilment untrammelled by the endeavours of other Europeans.

Officials retrospectively chuckled about the eccentricities of their peers. At the time, however, such eccentricities were felt problematic, much as they were amongst the white settler communities in Kenya and Southern Rhodesia, where those displaying morally or socially 'aberrant' behaviour were subject to hostility and threatened with social exclusion from European communities.[2] Whilst resenting its public expression in those around them, officials admired their own individuality. At the same time as recognising the need to police social norms in order to maintain white solidarity and morale, officials were frustrated at being reined in by such norms. White settlers also felt their social groups were constrictive, but such frustration was probably greater amongst officials. Both sets of individuals had left for Africa with the intention of carving out personal fiefdoms for themselves, but a typical settler's remit was more modest. Settlers' interest in Africans largely began and ended with their role as workers. Officials' ambitions were of a different order of magnitude. From the moment they decided to apply to the colonial services, would-be officials anticipated their own eventual intimate involvement in all aspects of African life, and were pleased at the prospect. On his arrival in Sudan, one newcomer to the SPS was delighted when informed that he should act as a 'genial baron'.[3] When others impinged on this, resentment emerged.

To suggest that officials were merely latent vehicles for a particular policy, conception of empire or pattern of behaviour, shaped by either the metropole or the region in which they worked, has effectively denied them agency. Whilst they increasingly shared a common social and intellectual background, officials did not respond universally to the same concerns. A hitherto heavily underexplored determinant of the ways imperial governance was played out on the ground was officials' self-interest. They were concerned with self-preservation, self-improvement and self-aggrandisement. To date, self-interest has only been considered in any significant manner in terms of officials' desire for promotion, but not every official wanted promotion.[4] Officials were young men interested in making their own lives better in a variety of ways. Chapter One demonstrated that self-interest shaped patterns of recruitment. Once recruited, officials pursued their own administrative interests in order that they could feel they had left their mark on

Africa in ways of their own choosing. Whilst officials felt the need to continually reiterate their ongoing commitment to public service, an interest in improving their own circumstances explains the level of enthusiasm some officials felt about a variety of imperial actions, such as infrastructural development and the introduction of indirect rule. A satisfactory assessment of where duty ended and self-interest began might never be achieved, but it is hoped that this study is an initial modest attempt.

We turn now to the last of the introduction's four historiographical issues, namely certain postcolonialist claims as to ambivalence and uncertainty at the heart of the imperial mission. There are two areas in which officials' views of the world may indeed have been ambivalent or uncertain. Firstly, officials may have been unsure about how they related to Africa on a personal level. Secondly, they may have been undecided about the benefits of British rule in Africa, wracked by the belief that the changes the colonial state inevitably introduced necessarily undermined that state's control over a population, or 'ruined' Africa, or both. As we have seen, officials often had fluctuating personal relationships with Africa. To pick one example, some oscillated between wanting to live in urban and rural areas. It is plausible that such fluctuations bled into uncertainty about how Africa was to be governed, particularly in light of Chapter Three's point about how, in certain important regards, the border between professional and personal life was virtually non-existent.

However, in accounting for officials' response to changes in British Africa, we need to understand the nature of their relationships with their colonial superiors. Mindful that men on the spot often operated in regions some distance from substantial coercive military force, recruiters sought out paternalistic officials who were cool under pressure and who possessed sufficient independence of mind to deal with crises. Recruiters got what they wished for, particularly after the First World War. Nevertheless, as far as colonial elites were concerned, a payroll of individualistic, intelligent and strong-willed men did have its disadvantages. One Chief Justice of northern Nigeria mischievously told one would-be official studying in Oxford, 'My boy never obey Gov[ernmen]t Instructions: always use your own common sense', but more commonly, colonial elites wanted non-emergency policies rolled out as they envisaged.[5] This caused problems; officials' responses to processes of governance and change were shaped by the degree to which they felt in control of such processes. Resentment arose when officials believed others were challenging their own ability and knowledge of what was best for 'their' district. Officials felt that if they mediated the access Africans had to modernity, change could be effected in a stable manner. When officials believed they had lost control of what was happening on the ground thanks to the intervention of other Europeans, they feared the impact of change upon African society. The belief that imperial governance was an ambivalent exercise was, therefore, not an inherent component of the colonial encounter, but the contingent outcome of certain colonial relationships.

But what of the threat of anti-colonial nationalism, which had become such a potent force by the end of the interwar period? Two crucial elements allowed officials to think of anti-colonial activity as teething troubles, rather than as an inevitable step towards the end of British rule in Africa. Firstly, in certain important political regards, the continent was felt resilient enough to remain recognisably African in the face of imperial change, such as in a continued preference for tribal leaders over educated nationalists. However, when Africans were thought susceptible to change for the worse, the second factor of importance was the officials themselves. Whilst one cannot use a collective metropolitan experience to generalise about officials' intentions, how officials sought what they wanted was rooted in something universal: each DC's sense of his own ability, or what some African nationalists viewed as 'swollen-headedness'.[6] This sense of ability would have undoubtedly come undone eventually. Post-1945 African nationalist activity, which was on a scale unimaginable to most interwar officials, would have taken care of that. Before this could happen, however, cracks in officials' confidence were opened by other Europeans, making their own plans in far-away Rome and Berlin.

Notes

1 B. Anderson, *Imagined Communities: Reflections on the Origin and Spread of Nationalism* (1983; London: Verso, 1991)
2 Kennedy, *Islands of White*, ch. 9, quote at p. 167
3 Robertson to mother, 8 December 1922, SAD 531/2/5
4 Kuklick, *Imperial Bureaucrat*, ch. 4
5 Tripe to parents, 8 September 1929, RHO Mss.Afr.s.868/1/89
6 *Lagos Standard* (17 April 1913), quoted in Duffield, 'John Eldred Taylor', 257

BIBLIOGRAPHY

Manuscript sources

British Library, London

H. Campbell-Bannerman papers, Add Mss 52516
Lord Cromer papers, Add Mss 62124
H. Hesketh Bell papers, Add Mss 78721
D. A. Macalister papers, Add Mss 49357
C. Orr letters, Add Mss 56100
W. H. Williams diaries, Add Mss 60344

National Archives, London

CO 96/476
CO 96/538
CO 96/663
CO 96/675
CO 96/718
CO 323/916
CO 323/1162
CO 536/145
CO 536/157
CO 536/158
CO 536/176
CO 583/78
CO 583/191
CO 691/100/20
CO 691/106/1
CO 691/152/13
CO 822/1/8
FO 141/469
FO 141/632/17679
FO 371/10905
FO 407/173
FO 881/10505

Public Records and Archives Administration Department, Accra

PRAAD ADM 1/1/755
PRAAD ADM 1/2/132
PRAAD CSO 16/1
PRAAD CSO 18/1/1
PRAAD CSO 18/1/2
PRAAD CSO 18/1/32

PRAAD CSO 18/1/33
PRAAD CSO 18/1/82
PRAAD CSO 18/1/83
PRAAD CSO 18/1/134
PRAAD CSO 18/1/350
PRAAD CSO 18/1/351
PRAAD CSO 18/2/5
PRAAD CSO 18/6/26
PRAAD CSO 18/6/100
PRAAD CSO 18/7/13
PRAAD CSO 18/12/33
PRAAD CSO 18/12/49
PRAAD CSO 21/1/122
PRAAD CSO 21/11/2
PRAAD CSO 21/20/44
PRAAD CSO 25/1/32
PRAAD CSO 25/1/62
PRAAD CSO 25/2/5
PRAAD CSO 25/3/1
PRAAD CSO 25/3/61
PRAAD CSO 26/4

Rhodes House Library, University of Oxford

G. Adams papers, Mss.Afr.s.375
J. Allen memoirs, Mss.Afr.s.1551
H. Amherst diaries, Mss.Afr.s.1207
M. C. Atkinson, *Nigerian Tales of the Colonial Era* (unpublished, n.d.), in Mss. Afr.s.2065
D. Bayley diaries, Mss.Afr.r.47
W. H. Beeton diaries, Mss.Afr.s.1608(9)
W. T. C. Berry papers, Mss.Afr.t.12
H. A. Blair papers, Mss.Afr.s.626
C. Boyle diaries, Mss.Afr.s.2324
H. Brice-Smith papers, Mss.Afr.s.230
A. F. Bridges photographs, Mss.Afr.s.1881(2)
C. Cardew papers, Mss.Brit.Emp.s.500
H. Childs diaries, Mss.Afr.s.1861(1)–(3)
P. A. Clearkin memoirs, Mss.Brit.r.4/1
C. Cockey papers, Mss.Afr.s.1138
Colonial Office desk diaries, 1899–1914, Mss.Brit.Emp.r.21
J. M. Coote papers, Mss.Afr.s.1383(1)
M. de Courcy Dodd papers, Mss.Afr.s.1995
D. Daltry papers, Mss.Afr.s.2222
J. B. Davies interview, Mss.Afr.s.1428
J. Dickson diaries, Mss.Afr.s.738
L. G. Dixon papers, Mss.Afr.s.356

BIBLIOGRAPHY

F. Dowsett papers, Mss.Afr.s.1276
A. Duncan-Johnstone diaries, Mss.Afr.s.593/1–5
J. R. Elliot and W. R. Reeve-Tucker papers, Mss.Afr.s.1384
H. P. Elliott papers, Mss.Afr.s.1336, 1838
R. E. Ellison papers, Mss.Afr.s.1332
J. H. Ewart diaries, Mss.Afr.s.1991
R. Furse papers, Mss.Brit.Emp.s.415
C. Gillman papers, Mss.Afr.s.999(2)
W. Gowers papers, Mss.Afr.s.1150
Mrs C. H. B. Grant papers, Mss.Afr.s.141
R. Greig diaries, Mss.Afr.s.2319
J. Griffiths diaries, Mss.Afr.r.179–80
A. Haarer memoirs, Mss.Afr.s.1144
F. Hallier papers, Mss.Afr.s.1072
L. M. Heaney papers, Mss.Afr.s.2271
K. Henderson diaries, Mss.Afr.s.1484
A. Jones papers, Mss.Afr.s.454
T. Letchworth interview, Mss.Afr.s.2112
F. Lugard papers, Mss.Lugard 9/1, 29/3
E. Lumley papers, Mss.Afr.s.785
N. Malcolm diaries, Mss.Afr.s.759
H. Mathews papers, Mss.Afr.s.783/1–2
H. Miller-Stirling papers, Mss.Afr.s.2051
A. Milverton papers, Mss.Brit.Emp.s.368
H. W. Moor papers, Mss.Brit.Emp.s.333
R. Nicholson papers, Mss.Afr.r.81
F. Oates diaries, Mss.Afr.s.603
G. Orde-Browne papers, Mss.Afr.s.1117/3/3
G. Ormsby papers, Mss.Brit.Emp.s.287
S. Ormsby papers, Mss.Afr.r.105
F. Pedler interview, Mss.Afr.s.1718
D. Percival papers, Mss.Brit.Emp.s.364
M. Perham papers, Mss.Perham.242/1
A. J. Phillips diaries, Mss.Afr.s.803
H. Pollock papers, Mss.Afr.s.419
G. D. Popplewell memoirs, Mss.Afr.s.2156
R. K. Rice papers, Mss.Afr.r.1511
E. Richardson papers, Mss.Afr.s.580
R. A. Roberts papers, Mss.Afr.s.1348
J. W. Robertson interview, Mss.Afr.s.802/Robertson
F. Ruxton papers, Mss.Afr.s.1037
Lord Salisbury papers, Mss.Afr.s.141
A. Saunders papers, Mss.Afr.s.662, 1827(1)
E. J. Scott papers, Mss.Afr.s.1564–5
Mrs E. L. Scott interview, Mss.Afr.s.1765
J. V. Shaw diaries, Mss.Afr.s.357
A. Sheffield papers, Mss.Brit.Emp.s.310

A. Sillery memoirs, Mss.Afr.r.207
W. C. Simmons memoirs, Mss.Afr.s.468
T. Stevens papers, Mss.Afr.s.834
Lady Surridge interview, Mss.Afr.s.1480
R. G. Syme memoirs, Mss.Afr.s.1722
C. Temple papers, Mss.Afr.s.141
L. M. Thomas memoirs, Mss.Brit.Emp.s.492
G. Tomlinson papers, Mss.Afr.s.372
G. Trinick papers, Mss.Afr.s.926
W. Tripe letters, Mss.Afr.s.868/1–2
L. Vickers-Haviland papers, Mss.Afr.s.1047/4
C. R. Walker diaries, Mss.Afr.s.433–8
W. A. Walker papers, Mss.Afr.s.1064, 1709
W. Ward memoirs, Mss.Afr.r.127
A. Weatherhead diaries, Mss.Afr.s.1638
N. Weir diaries, Mss.Afr.s.1151/1–6
C. Whybrow papers, Mss.Afr.s.324
A. L. Wilkinson papers, Mss.Afr.s.713
C. Woodhouse diaries, Mss.Afr.s.236
C. Wordsworth papers, Mss.Afr.s.1373
H. Young papers, Mss.Afr.s.938

Royal Commonwealth Society Archives, University of Cambridge

Africa miscellanea, 113/89
A. R. H. Mann diaries, 116

Special Collections, University of Birmingham

J. Chamberlain papers, 9/4–5

Sudan Archives, Durham University

P. B. E. Acland papers, 707/15, 777/14
F. Addison diaries, 294/19
H. B. Arber memoirs, 736/2
R. E. H. Baily papers, 422/13, 533
E. A. Balfour papers, 606/4–5
F. Balfour papers, 303/6
G. Bell papers, 697–700
J. F. E. Bloss memoirs, 704/1
G. R. F. Bredin papers, 815/12
C. P. Browne papers, 422/14
I. M. Bruce-Gardyne papers, 478/12
L. M. Buchanan memoirs, 797/8
S. Butler letters, 304/6
C. W. M. Cox diaries, 673/4
E. S. Crispin photographs, 2/25
J. W. Crowfoot photographs, 8/5

J. Daniell diaries, 777
R. Davies papers, 627/1
A. Disney papers, 716/1
C. Dupuis papers, 780/1
W. Forbes interview, 863/3
C. E. Fouracres memoirs, 815/15
Y. Hunter memoirs, 745/4
E. Jane photographs, 2/4
J. Kenrick papers, 647/5, 815/4
C. A. E. Lea papers, 645/7
W. Luce diaries, 829/12–13
E. H. Macintosh memoirs, 895/3
R. C. Mayall memoirs, 851/7
B. McDonnell Dee diaries, 890/3
T. H. B. Mynors memoirs, 777/8
H. A. Nicholson memoirs, 777/11
T. R. H. Owen papers, 414/2–8
A. C. Parker papers, 17/3, 294/2–9
A. E. D. Penn memoirs, 722/13
W. A. Porter diaries, 700/11
J. W. Robertson papers, 517/1–3, 531/2–3
G. R. Storrar diaries, 56/1
K. C. P. Struvé papers, 212
N. R. Syme photographs, 2/7
G. W. Titherington letters, SAD 636/12
N. R. Udal papers, 780/5
M. P. Vidal-Hall papers, 727/1
C. A. Willis papers, 209/12, 212/8–13
R. Wingate papers, 180/2, 301/6

Printed sources

Primary sources

Newspapers and other periodicals

Africa
British Medical Journal
Caledonian Mercury
Cornhill Magazine
Crown Colonist
Daily Express
Daily Telegraph
East Africa
Edinburgh Review
Geographical Journal
Globe
International Affairs

Journal of the African Society [*Journal of the Royal African Society* from July 1935]
Journal of the Royal Anthropological Institute of Great Britain and Ireland
Man
Morning Post
News Chronicle
Nigerian Field Notes
Observer
Quarterly Journal of Economics
Quarterly Review
Round Table
Sudan Herald
Sudan Notes and Records
Tanganyika Notes and Records
Tanganyika Times
The Times
Uganda Journal

Parliamentary and official papers

Annual Reports of Bende Division, South Eastern Nigeria, 1905–1912, with a commentary by G. I. Jones (Cambridge: African Studies Centre, 1986)

Civil Secretary's Office, *Sudan Political Service 1899–1929* (Khartoum: Sudan Government Press, 1930)

'Correspondence respecting the retirement of the Imperial British East Africa Company', *Parl. Papers 1895*, lxxi (7646)

The Dominions Office and Colonial Office Lists [1900–39]

'Further papers relating to Uganda', *Parl. Papers 1893*, lxii (7109)

Gowers, W., *Gazetteer of Kano Province* (London: Waterlow and Sons, 1921)

Hansard, 5th series

Kaduna Secretariat Library: Catalogue of Books (Kaduna: Government Printers, 1932)

'Papers relating to Uganda', *Parl. Papers 1893*, lxxi (7708)

Quarterly/Monthly Lists of the Sudan Government [1914–39]

Report of the Committee Appointed in 1932 by the Governor of the Gold Coast Colony to Inspect the Prince of Wales College and Schools, Achimota (London: Crown Agents, 1932)

Sayers, G. F. (ed.), *The Handbook of Tanganyika* (London: Macmillan and Co., 1930)

Simpson, W., *Report to the Secretary of State for the Colonies on the Sanitary Conditions of the Mines and Mining Villages in the Gold Coast Colony and Ashanti* (London: Waterlow and Sons, 1925)

The West African Pocket Book: A Guide for Newly-Appointed Government Officers (London: Crown Agents for the Colonies, 1920)

Films

Korda, Z. (dir.), *Sanders of the River* (1935)
Korda, Z. (dir.), *The Four Feathers* (1939)

BIBLIOGRAPHY

Secondary sources

Adams, E. C., *Lyra Nigeria* (London: T. Fisher Unwin, 1911)

Ade Ajayi, J. F. (ed.), *General History of Africa: Volume VI Africa in the Nineteenth Century until the 1880s* (Oxford: James Currey, 1998)

Adebayo, A. G., 'The production of hides and skins in colonial Northern Nigeria, 1900–1945', *Journal of African History* 33:2 (1992), 273–300

Allen, C., *Plain Tales from the British Empire* (London: Abacus, 2008)

Al Safi, M. A. (ed.), *The Nationalist Movement in the Sudan* (Khartoum: University of Khartoum Press, 1989)

Anderson, B., *Imagined Communities: Reflections on the Origin and Spread of Nationalism* (1983; London: Verso, 1991)

Austen, R., *Northwest Tanzania under German and British Rule: Colonial Policy and Tribal Politics, 1889–1939* (New Haven: Yale University Press, 1968)

Austin, G., *Labour, Land and Capital in Ghana: From Slavery to Free Labour in Asante, 1807–1956* (Rochester, NY: University of Rochester Press, 2005)

Bagehot, W., *The English Constitution* (Oxford: Oxford University Press, 2001)

Baldwin, S., *This Torch of Freedom: Speeches and Addresses* (London: Hodder and Stoughton, 1935)

Ball, S. J., 'Imperialism, social control and the colonial curriculum', *Journal of Curriculum Studies* 15 (1983), 237–63

Ballantyne, R. M., *Blue Lights: Or Hot Work in the Soudan* (London: J. Nisbet & Son, 1888)

Ballhatchet, K., *Race, Sex, and Class under the Raj: Imperial Attitudes and Policies and their Critics, 1793–1905* (London: Weidenfeld and Nicolson, 1980)

Barkan, E., *The Retreat of Scientific Racism: Changing Concepts of Race in Britain and the United States Between the World Wars* (Cambridge: Cambridge University Press, 1992)

Barnes, L., *The Duty of Empire* (London: Victor Gollancz, 1935)

Barnett, C., *The Audit of War: The Illusion & Reality of Britain as a Great Nation* (London: Macmillan, 1986)

Bell, G., *Shadows on the Sand: The Memoirs of Sir Gawain Bell* (London: C. Hurst & Co., 1983)

Bell, G. and A. H. M. Kirk-Greene, *The Sudan Political Service 1902–1952: A Preliminary Register of Second Careers* (Oxford: no publisher, 1989)

Bening, R., 'Internal colonial boundary problems of the Gold Coast, 1907–1951', *International Journal of African Historical Studies* 17:1 (1984), 81–99

Berry, S., 'Hegemony on a shoestring: Indirect rule and access to agricultural land', *Africa* 62:3 (1992), 327–55

Bhabha, H. K., *The Location of Culture* (London: Routledge, 1994)

Bickers, R. (ed.), *Settlers and Expatriates: Britons over the Seas* (Oxford: Oxford University Press, 2010)

Bikle, G., 'Utopianism and social planning in the thought of Kagawa Toyohiko', *Monumenta Nipponica* 25 (1970), 447–53

Bingham, A., *Gender, Modernity, and the Popular Press in Inter-war Britain* (Oxford: Clarendon Press, 2004)

BIBLIOGRAPHY

Boni, S., 'Striving for resources or connecting people? Transportation in Sefwi (Ghana)', *International Journal of African Historical Studies* 32:1 (1999), 49–70

Bourret, F. M., *The Gold Coast: A Survey of the Gold Coast and British Togoland, 1919–1946* (Stanford, CA: Stanford University Press, 1949) [later updated as Bourret, F. M., *Ghana: The Road to Independence, 1919–1957* (Oxford: Oxford University Press, 1960)]

Bridge, C., *Holding India to the Empire: The British Conservative Party and the 1935 Constitution* (London: Oriental University Press, 1986)

Briggs, A., *The History of Broadcasting in the United Kingdom* (London: Oxford University Press, 1965), Five Volumes

British Empire Exhibition Central Committee of Tanganyika, *Tanganyika Territory Handbook* (no publisher details provided, 1925) in British Library W50/3496

Brock, M. and M. Curthoys (eds), *The History of the University of Oxford: Volume VI – Nineteenth-century Oxford* (Oxford: Oxford University Press, 1997)

Brown, J. M. and Wm. R. Louis (eds), *Oxford History of the British Empire: Volume IV – The Twentieth Century* (Oxford: Oxford University Press, 1999)

Buchan, J., *Prester John* (London: Nelson, 1910)

Burk, K., *Troublemaker: The Life and History of A. J. P. Taylor* (New Haven, CT: Yale University, 2000)

Burton, A., *African Underclass: Urbanisation, Crime & Colonial Order in Dar es Salaam* (London: BIEA and James Curry, 2005)

Bush, B., *Imperialism, Race and Resistance: Africa and Britain, 1919–1945* (London: Routledge, 1999)

Bush, B., *Imperialism and Postcolonialism* (Harlow: Pearson, 2006)

Callahan, M. D., 'NOMANSLAND: The British Colonial Office and the League of Nations Mandate for German East Africa, 1916–1920', *Albion* 25:3 (1993), 443–64

Callaway, H., *Gender, Culture and Empire: European Women in Colonial Nigeria* (Basingstoke: Macmillan, 1987)

Cameron, D., *The Principles of Native Administration and their Application* (Lagos: Government Printer, 1934)

Cameron, D., *My Tanganyika Service and some Nigeria* (London: Allen and Unwin, 1939)

Cannadine, D., *The Decline and Fall of the British Aristocracy* (1990; London: Penguin, 1992)

Cannadine, D., *Ornamentalism* (London: Penguin, 2002)

Cardinall, A. W., *The Natives of the Northern Territories of the Gold Coast: Their Customs, Religion and Folklore* (London: Routledge, 1920)

Carland, J. M., *The Colonial Office and Nigeria, 1898–1914* (London: Macmillan, 1985)

Cary, J., *An American Visitor* (1933; London: Everyman, 1995)

Cary, J., *Mister Johnson* (1939; London: J. M. Dent, 1995)

Chatteris, L., *The Holy Terror* (1932; London: Hodder and Stoughton, 1940)

Clarence-Smith, W. G. and S. Topik (eds), *The Global Coffee Economy in Africa, Asia, and Latin America, 1500–1989* (Cambridge: Cambridge University Press, 2006)

Clarkson, A., 'Pomp, circumstance, and wild Arabs: the 1912 Royal Visit to Sudan', *Journal of Imperial and Commonwealth History* 34:1 (2006), 71–85

Coe, C., 'Educating an African leadership: Achimota and the teaching of African culture in the Gold Coast', *Africa Today* 49:3 (2002), 23–44

Cohn, B., *Colonialism and its Forms of Knowledge: The British in India* (Princeton, NJ: Princeton University Press, 1996)

Collini, S., *Absent Minds: Intellectuals in Britain* (Oxford: Oxford University Press, 2006)

Collini, S. and R. Whatmore, B. Young (eds), *History, Religion and Culture: British Intellectual History, 1750–1950* (Cambridge: Cambridge University Press, 2000)

Collins, R. O., 'The Sudan Political Service: a portrait of the "Imperialists"', *African Affairs* 71:284 (1972), 293–303

Collins, R. O., *Shadows in the Grass: Britain in the Southern Sudan, 1918–1956* (London: Yale University Press, 1983)

Colquhoun, A., *The Africander Land* (London: John Murray, 1906)

Conrad, J., *Victory* (1915; Harmondsworth: Penguin, 1963)

Cook, A. R., *Uganda Memories* (Kampala: Uganda Society, 1945)

Cookey, S. J. S., 'Sir Hugh Clifford as Governor of Nigeria: an evaluation', *African Affairs* 79:317 (1980), 531–47

Cooper, F., *Colonialism in Question: Theory, Knowledge, History* (London: University of California Press, 2005)

Cooper F. and A. L. Stoler, *Tensions of Empire: Colonial Cultures in a Bourgeois World* (Berkeley, CA: University of California Press, 1997)

Crocker, W., *Nigeria: A Critique of British Colonial Administration* (London: George Allen & Unwin, 1936)

Crook, P., 'Historical monkey business: the myth of a Darwinized British imperial discourse', *History* 84:276 (1999), 633–57

Crowder, M., *West Africa under Colonial Rule* (London: Hutchinson, 1968)

Crowder, M. (ed.), *West African Resistance: The Military Response to Colonial Occupation* (London: Hutchinson, 1971)

Crozier, F. P., *Five Years Hard* (London: Jonathan Cape, 1932)

Dabydeen D. (ed.), *The Black Presence in English Literature* (Manchester: Manchester University Press, 1985)

Daly, M. W., *Empire on the Nile: The Anglo-Egyptian Sudan 1898–1934* (Cambridge: Cambridge University Press, 1986)

Daly, M. W., 'The soldier as historian: F. R. Wingate and the Sudanese Mahdia', *Journal of Imperial and Commonwealth History* 17:1 (1988), 99–106

Daly, M. W., *Imperial Sudan: The Anglo-Egyptian Condominium, 1934–1956* (Cambridge: Cambridge University Press, 1991)

Daly, M. W., *The Sirdar: Sir Reginald Wingate and the British Empire in the Middle East* (Philadelphia, PA: American Philosophical Society, 1997)

Daly, M. W., *Darfur's Sorrow: A History of Destruction and Genocide* (Cambridge: Cambridge University Press, 2009)

Darwin, B., *The English Public School* (London: Longmans, 1929)

Darwin, J., 'Imperialism in decline? Tendencies in British imperial policy between the wars', *Historical Journal* 23:3 (1980), 657–79

Davidson, B., *The Black Man's Burden: Africa and the Curse of the Nation-state* (London: Currey, 1992)

Davies, R., *The Camel's Back: Service in the Rural Sudan* (London: J. Murray, 1957)

Dewey, C., *Anglo-Indian Attitudes: The Mind of the Indian Civil Service* (London: Hambledon, 1993)

Dilke, C., *Greater Britain* (London: Macmillan, 1868)

Dixon, W. W., 'The colonial vision of Edgar Wallace', *Journal of Popular Culture* 32:1 (1998), 121–39

Dorward, D., 'The development of the British Colonial Administration among the Tiv, 1900–1949', *African Affairs* 68:273 (1969), 316–33

Doyle, S., 'Population decline and delayed recovery in Bunyoro, 1860–1960', *Journal of African History* 41:3 (2000), 429–58

Doyle, S., *Crisis & Decline in Bunyoro: Population & Environment in Western Uganda 1860–1955* (Oxford: James Currey, 2006)

Duder, C. J. D. and C. P. Youé, 'Paice's place: race and politics in Nanyuki district, Kenya, in the 1920s', *African Affairs* 93 (1994), 253–78

Duffield, I., 'John Eldred Taylor and West African opposition to indirect rule in Nigeria', *African Affairs* 70 (1971), 252–68

Duncan-Johnstone, A. C., *With the British Red Cross in Turkey 1912–1913* (London: James Nisbet & Co., 1913)

Dundas, C., *African Crossroads* (London: Macmillan, 1955)

Dunn, K., 'Lights … camera … Africa: images of Africa and Africans in Western popular films of the 1930s', *African Studies Review* 39:1 (1996), 149–75

Ehrlich, C., 'Building and caretaking: economic policy in British Tropical Africa, 1890–1960', *Economic History Review* 26 (1973), 649–67

Elliott, H. P., *Darkness and Dawn in Zimbabwe* (London: Grosvenor, 1978)

Ewing, A., 'The Indian Civil Service 1919–1924: service discontent and the response in London and Delhi', *Modern Asian Studies* 18:1 (1984), 33–53

Fabb, J., *Royal Tours of the British Empire 1860–1927* (London: B. T. Batsford, 1989)

Falola, T., 'From hospitality to hostility: Ibadan and strangers, 1830–1904', *Journal of African History* 26:1 (1985), 51–68

Falola, T. and M. Heaton, *A History of Nigeria* (Cambridge: Cambridge University Press, 2008)

Ferguson, N., *Empire: How Britain Made the Modern World* (2003; London: Penguin, 2004)

Fergusson, V. H. *et al.*, *The Story of Fergie Bey* (London: Macmillan, 1930)

Fernald, A. E., '"Out of it": alienation and coercion in D. H. Lawrence', *Modern Fiction Studies* 49:2 (2003), 183–203

Field, A., *'Verb Sap.': On Going to West Africa, Northern Nigeria, Southern, and to the Coasts* (London: Bale, Sons and Danielsson, 1913)

Foster, P., *Education and Social Change in Ghana* (Chicago, IL: University of Chicago Press, 1965)

Fox, A., *Dean Inge* (London: J. Murray, 1960)

Frank, K., *A Voyager Out: The Life of Mary Kingsley* (1986; London: I. B. Tauris, 2005)

Freund, W. M., 'Labour migration to the Northern Nigerian tin mines, 1903–1945', *Journal of African History* 22:1 (1981), 73–84

Frewen Lord, W., *The Lost Empires of the Modern World* (London: Richard Bentley and Son, 1897)

Furse, R., *Aucuparius: Recollections of a Recruiting Officer* (London: Oxford University Press, 1962)

Gailey, H. A., *Sir Donald Cameron: Colonial Governor* (Stanford, CA: Hoover Institution Press, 1974)

Gailey, H. A., *Clifford: Imperial Proconsul* (London: Collings, 1982)

Gailey, H. A., *Lugard and the Abeokuta Uprising: The Demise of Egba Independence* (London: Frank Cass, 1982)

Gann, L. and P. Duignan, *The Rulers of British Africa, 1870–1914* (London: Croom Helm, 1978)

Gann, L. and P. Duignan (eds), *Colonialism in Africa 1870–1960 Volume 1: The History and Politics of Colonialism 1870–1914* (Cambridge: Cambridge University Press, 1969)

Gann, L. and P. Duignan (eds), *Colonialism in Africa 1870–1960 Volume 2: The History and Politics of Colonialism 1914–1960* (Cambridge: Cambridge University Press, 1970)

Gann, L. and P. Duignan (eds), *African Proconsuls: European Governors in Africa* (New York: Free Press, 1978)

Geppert, D. and R. Gewarth (eds), *Wilhelmine Germany and Edwardian Britain: Essays on Cultural Affinity* (Oxford: Oxford University Press, 2008)

Gershoni, I. and J. P. Jankowski, *Egypt, Islam and the Arabs: The Search for Egyptian Nationhood, 1900–1930* (Oxford: Oxford University Press, 1986)

Getty, J. A., 'Trotsky in exile: the founding of the Fourth International', *Soviet Studies* 38 (1986), 24–35

Gibb, A. D., *Scottish Empire* (London: Alexander Maclehose & Co., 1937)

Gifford, P. and Wm. R. Louis (eds), *Britain and Germany in Africa: Imperial Rivalry and Colonial Rule* (New Haven, CT: Yale University Press, 1967)

Gillan, A., 'The Sudan: past, present and future', *African Affairs* 43:172 (1944), 123–8

Gilmour, D., *The Ruling Caste: Imperial Lives in the Victorian Raj* (2005; London: Pimlico, 2007)

Gocking, R., 'British justice and the Native Tribunals of the southern Gold Coast Colony', *Journal of African History* 34:1 (1993), 93–113

Golant, W., *Image of Empire: The Early History of the Imperial Institute* (Exeter: University of Exeter Press, 1984)

Golding, H. (ed.), *The Wonder Book of Empire for Boys and Girls* (London: Ward Lock and Co., 1925)

Gorer, G., *Africa Dances* (1935; New York: Norton, 1962)

Graham, J. D., 'Indirect rule: the establishment of "chiefs" and "tribes" in Cameron's Tanganyika', *Tanzania Notes and Records* 77 (1976), 1–9

Green, E. H. H., *The Crisis of Conservatism: The Politics, Economics and*

Ideology of the British Conservative Party, 1880–1914 (London: Routledge, 1995)

Guha, R., 'Not at home in empire', *Critical Inquiry* 23:3 (1997), 482–93

Hailey, W., *An African Survey: A Study of Problems Arising in Africa South of the Sahara* (London: Oxford University Press, 1938)

Hall, C., *Civilising Subjects: Metropole and Colony in the English Imagination, 1830–1867* (Cambridge: Polity, 2002)

Hamad, B., '*Sudan Notes and Records* and Sudanese nationalism, 1918–1956', *History in Africa* 22 (1995), 239–70

Hamilton, J. A. de C. (ed.), *The Anglo-Egyptian Sudan from Within* (London: Faber and Faber, 1935)

Hastings, A. C. G., *Nigerian Days* (London: John Lane, 1925)

Havinden, M. and D. Meredith, *Colonialism and Development: Britain and its Tropical Colonies, 1850–1960* (London: Routledge, 1993)

Henderson, K. D. D., *The Making of the Modern Sudan: The Life and Letters of Sir Douglas Newbold* (London: Faber and Faber, 1953)

Hesketh Bell, H., *A Witch's Legacy* (London: Sampson Low, Marston & Company, 1893), Two Volumes

Heussler, R., *The British in Northern Nigeria* (London: Oxford University Press, 1960)

Heussler, R., *Yesterday's Rulers: The Making of the British Colonial Service* (Syracuse, NY: Syracuse University Press, 1963)

Heussler, R., *British Tanganyika: An Essay and Documents on District Administration* (Durham, NC: Duke University Press, 1971)

Hill, R., *Slatin Pasha* (London: Oxford University Press, 1965)

Hobsbawm, E. and T. Ranger (eds), *The Invention of Tradition* (1983; Cambridge: Cambridge University Press, 1992)

Hollins, T. J., 'The Conservative Party and film propaganda between the wars', *English Historical Review* 96 (1981), 359–69

Holmes, C. and A. H. Ion, 'Bushido and the Samurai: images in British public opinion, 1894–1914', *Modern Asian Studies* 14:2 (1980), 309–29

Huxley, E., *Red Strangers* (1939; London: Penguin, 1999)

Hyam, R., *Britain's Imperial Century, 1815–1914: A Study of Empire and Expansion* (1976; Basingstoke: Macmillan, 1993)

Hyam, R., *Empire and Sexuality: The British Experience* (Manchester: Manchester University Press, 1990)

Hyslop, J., 'Cape Town Highlanders, Transvaal Scottish: military "Scottishness" and social power in nineteenth and twentieth century South Africa', *South African Historical Journal* 47 (2002), 96–114

Igbafe, P. A., 'Slavery and emancipation in Benin, 1897–1945', *Journal of African History* 16:3 (1975), 409–29

Iliffe, J., *A Modern History of Tanganyika* (Cambridge: Cambridge University Press, 1979)

Iliffe, J., *The African Poor: A History* (Cambridge: Cambridge University Press, 1987)

Iliffe, J., *Africans: The History of a Continent* (Cambridge: Cambridge University Press, 1995)

'Irish Blood', *Everyday Sudan Life* (London: Heath Cranton, 1937)

Isaacman, A. and R. Roberts (eds), *Cotton, Colonialism, and Social History in Sub-Saharan Africa* (Portsmouth, NH: Heinemann, 1995)

Isichei, E., *The Ibo People and the Europeans: The Genesis of a Relationship – to 1906* (London: Faber and Faber, 1973)

Isichei, E., *A History of Nigeria* (London: Longman, 1983)

Jaggar, P. J., 'Obituary: Frederick William Parsons', *Bulletin of the School of Oriental and African Studies* 58:1 (1995), 109–12

Jeffries, C., *The Colonial Empire and its Civil Service* (Cambridge: Cambridge University Press, 1938)

Jenkins, R., 'William Ofori Atta, Nnambi Azikiwe, J. B. Danquah and the "grilling" of W. E. F. Ward of Achimota in 1935', *History in Africa* 21 (1994), 171–89

Johnson, D., 'The death of Gordon: a Victorian myth', *Journal of Imperial and Commonwealth History* 10 (1982), 285–310

Johnson, D., 'Evans-Pritchard, the Nuer, and the Sudan Political Service', *African Affairs* 81 (1982), 231–46

Johnson, R., 'The West African medical staff and the administration of imperial tropical medicine, 1902–14', *Journal of Imperial and Commonwealth History* 38:3 (2010), 419–39

Johnston, H. A. S., *The Fulani Empire of Sokoto* (London: Oxford University Press, 1967)

Joseph, B., *Reading the East India Company, 1720–1840: Colonial Currencies of Gender* (Chicago, IL: Chicago University Press, 2004)

Kennedy, D., *Islands of White: Settler Society and Culture in Kenya and Southern Rhodesia* (Durham, NC: Duke University Press, 1987)

Killingray, D., 'Repercussions of World War I in the Gold Coast', *Journal of African History* 19:1 (1978), 39–59

Killingray, D., 'The maintenance of law and order in British Colonial Africa', *African Affairs* 85:340 (1986), 411–37

King, R. D. and R. W. Wilson (eds), *The Statecraft of British Imperialism: Essays in Honour of Wm. Roger Louis* (London: Cass, 1999)

Kingsley, M., *Travels in West Africa* (Teddington: Echo Library, 2008)

Kirk-Greene, A. H. M., 'The Thin White Line: the size of the British Colonial Service in Africa', *African Affairs* 79:314 (1980), 25–44

Kirk-Greene, A. H. M., 'Scholastic attainment and scholarly achievement in Britain's Imperial Civil Services: the case of the African governors', *Oxford Review of Education* 7:1 (1981), 11–22

Kirk-Greene, A. H. M., 'The Sudan Political Service: a profile in the sociology of imperialism', *International Journal of African Historical Studies* 15:1 (1982), 21–48

Kirk-Greene, A. H. M., 'Canada in Africa: Sir Percy Girouard, neglected colonial governor', *African Affairs* 83 (1984), 207–39

Kirk-Greene, A. H. M., *On Crown Service: A History of HM Colonial and Overseas Civil Services 1837–1997* (London: I. B. Tauris, 1999)

Kirk-Greene, A. H. M., *Britain's Imperial Administrators, 1858–1966* (Basingstoke: Macmillan, 2000)

Kirk-Greene, A. H. M., *Symbol of Authority: The British District Officer in Africa* (London: I. B. Tauris, 2006)

Kirk-Greene, A. H. M. (ed.), *Principles of Native Administration in Nigeria: Selected Documents 1900–1947* (London: Oxford University Press, 1965)

Kirk-Greene, A. H. M. (ed.), *Glimpses of Empire: A Corona Anthology* (London: I. B. Tauris, 2001)

Kisch, M., *Letters & Sketches from Northern Nigeria* (London: Chatto & Windus, 1910)

Knapman, C., *White Women in Fiji 1835–1930: The Ruin of Empire?* (Sydney: Allen & Unwin, 1986)

Knight, E. F., *Letters from the Sudan: Reprinted from* The Times *of April to October, 1896* (London: Macmillan, 1897)

Kuklick, H., *The Imperial Bureaucrat: The Colonial Administrative Service in the Gold Coast, 1920–1939* (Stanford, CA: Hoover Institution Press, 1979)

Ladouceur, P. A., *Chiefs and Politicians: The Politics of Regionalism in Northern Ghana* (London: Longman, 1979)

Lafourcade, G., *Arnold Bennett: A Study* (London: Frederick Muller, 1939)

Lambert, D. and A. Lester (eds), *Colonial Lives across the British Empire: Imperial Careering in the Long Nineteenth Century* (Cambridge: Cambridge University Press, 2006)

Lane, C., *The Ruling Passion: British Colonial Allegory and the Paradox of Homosexual Desire* (Durham, NC: Duke University, 1995)

Lane, M., *Edgar Wallace: The Biography of a Phenomenon* (London: Heinemann, 1938)

Langa Langa [H. B. Hodge], *Up Against It in Nigeria* (London: Allen and Unwin, 1922)

Law, R. (ed.), *From Slave Trade to 'Legitimate' Commerce: The Commercial Transition in Nineteenth-century West Africa* (Cambridge: Cambridge University Press, 1995)

Lawrence, D. H., *Women in Love* (1920; London: Cambridge University Press, 2002)

Lawrence, J., 'The transformation of British public politics after the First World War', *Past and Present* 190 (2006), 185–216

Lea, C. A. E., *On Trek in Kordofan: The Diaries of a British District Officer in the Sudan, 1931–1933*, ed. M. W. Daly (Oxford: Oxford University Press, 1994)

Lee, J., *Ireland 1921–1985: Politics and Society* (Cambridge: Cambridge University Press, 1989)

Lentz, C., 'A Dagara rebellion against Dagomba rule? Contested stories of origin in North-West Ghana', *Journal of African History* 35:3 (1993), 457–92

Lentz, C., '"Tribalism" and ethnicity in Africa: a review of four decades of Anglophone research', *Cahiers des Sciences Humaines* 31:2 (1995), 303–28

Lentz, C. and P. Nugent (eds), *Ethnicity in Ghana: The Limits of Invention* (New York: St Martin's Press, 1999)

Leys, N., *The Colour Bar in East Africa* (London: Hogarth, 1941)

Lloyd, T. O., *The British Empire 1558–1995* (1984; Oxford: Oxford University Press, 1996)

Longland, F., *Field Engineering* (Dar es Salaam: Government Printers, 1935)

Lovejoy, P., *Transformations in Slavery: A History of Slavery in Africa* (1983; Cambridge: Cambridge University Press, 2000)

Lovejoy, P., *Slavery, Commerce and Production in the Sokoto Caliphate of West Africa* (Trenton, NJ: Africa World Press, 2005)

Low, S. and L. C. Sanders, *The History of England during the Reign of Victoria (1837–1901)* (London: Longmans, 1907)

Lownie, A., *John Buchan: The Presbyterian Cavalier* (London: Constable, 1995)

Lucas, C., *The Partition and Colonization of Africa* (Oxford: Oxford University Press, 1922)

Lugard, F., *The Rise of Our East African Empire* (Edinburgh: Blackwood and Sons, 1893), Two Volumes

Lugard, F., *The Dual Mandate in British Tropical Africa* (Edinburgh: Blackwood and Sons, 1922)

Lugard, F., *Representative Forms of Government and 'Indirect Rule' in British Africa; Being an Extract from the Text-Book Edition of the 'Dual Mandate'* (Edinburgh: Blackwood and Sons, 1928)

Lumley, E., *Forgotten Mandate* (London: C. Hurst & Co., 1976)

Macdonald, R. H., 'Reproducing the middle-class boy: from purity to patriotism in the Boys' Magazines, 1892–1914', *Journal of Contemporary History* 24 (1989) 519–39

Mackenzie, J. M., *Propaganda and Empire: The Manipulation of British Public Opinion, 1880–1960* (Manchester: Manchester University Press, 1984)

Mackenzie, J. M., 'Essay and reflection: on Scotland and the empire', *International History Review* 14:4 (1993), 737

Mackenzie, J. M. (ed.), *Imperialism and Popular Culture* (Manchester: Manchester University Press, 1986)

Mackenzie, J. M. and N. R. Dalziel, *The Scots in South Africa: Ethnicity, Identity, Gender and Race, 1772–1914* (Manchester: Manchester University Press, 2007)

MacMichael, H., *The Tribes of Northern and Central Kordofan* (1912; London: Frank Cass, 1967)

MacMichael, H., *The Anglo-Egyptian Sudan* (London: Faber & Faber, 1934)

Macoun, M., *Wrong Place, Right Time: Policing the End of Empire* (London: Radcliffe Press, 1996)

Maddox, G., J. Giblin and I. Kimambo (eds), *Custodians of the Land: Ecology & Culture in the History of Tanzania* (Oxford: James Currey, 1996)

Mahood, M., *Joyce Cary's Africa* (London: Methuen, 1964)

Maitland, A., *Wilfred Thesiger: The Life of the Great Explorer* (2006; London: Harper Perennial, 2007)

Mangan, J. A., *Athleticism in the Victorian and Edwardian Public School: The Emergence and Consolidation of an Educational Ideology* (1981; London: Frank Cass, 2000)

Mangan, J. A., 'The education of an elite imperial administration: the Sudan Political Service and the British public school system', *International Journal of African Historical Studies* 15 (1982), 671–99

Mangan, J. A., 'Grammar schools and the games ethic in the Victorian and Edwardian eras', *Albion* 15:4 (1983), 313–35

Mangan, J. A., *The Games Ethic and Imperialism: Aspects of the Diffusion of an Ideal* (Harmondsworth: Viking, 1986)

Mangan, J. A. (ed.), *'Benefits Bestowed'? Education and British Imperialism* (Manchester: Manchester University Press, 1988)

Mangan J. A. (ed.), *The Cultural Bond: Sport, Empire, Society* (London: Frank Cass, 1992)

Mangan, J. A. (ed.), *A Sport-loving Society: Victorian and Edwardian Middle-class England at Play* (Abingdon: Routledge, 2006)

Martin, S. M., *Palm Oil and Protest: An Economic History of the Ngwa Region, South-eastern Nigeria, 1800–1980* (Cambridge: Cambridge University Press, 1980)

Martin, S. M., 'Gender and innovation: farming, cooking and palm processing in the Ngwa Region, South-Eastern Nigeria, 1900–1939', *Journal of African History* 25:4 (1984), 411–27

Mason, M., 'The history of Mr. Johnson: progress and protest in Northern Nigeria, 1900–1921', *Canadian Journal of African Studies* 27 (1993), 196–217

Maugham, W. S., *The Casuarina Tree* (New York: George H. Doran, 1926)

Maylam, P., *The Cult of Rhodes: Remembering an Imperialist in Africa* (Claremont, South Africa: David Philip, 2005)

McCaskie, T. C., *Asante Identities: History and Modernity in an African Village 1850–1950* (Edinburgh: Edinburgh University Press, 2000)

McClintock, A., 'The angel of progress: pitfalls of the term "post-colonialism"', *Social Text* 31/32 (1992), 84–98

McCormack, R., 'Airlines and empires: Great Britain and the "Scramble for Africa", 1919–1939', *Canadian Journal of African Studies* 10:1 (1976), 87–105

McHenry, D. E., 'The underdevelopment theory: a case-study from Tanzania', *Journal of Modern African Studies* 14:4 (1976), 621–36

Meinertzhagen, R., *Kenya Diary 1902–1906* (Edinburgh: Oliver & Boyd, 1957)

Morris, G. W. and L. S. Wood, *The English-speaking Nations: A Study in the Development of the Commonwealth Ideal* (1924; Oxford: Clarendon Press, 1930)

Mosse, G., *Fallen Soldiers: Reshaping the Memory of the World Wars* (1990; Oxford: Oxford University Press, 1991)

Mowat, C. L., *Britain Between the Wars, 1918–1940* (Cambridge: Cambridge University Press, 1955)

Muir, R., *A Short History of the British Commonwealth: Volume II – The Modern Commonwealth (1763 to 1919)* (London: George Philip and Son, 1922)

Neilson, B., 'D. H. Lawrence's "Dark Page": narrative primitivism in *Women in Love* and *The Plumed Serpent*', *Twentieth-Century Literature* 43 (1997), 310–25

Newbury, C., 'Accounting for power in Northern Nigeria', *Journal of African History* 45:2 (2004), 257–77

Newell, S., *Literary Culture in Colonial Ghana: How to Play the Game of Life* (Manchester: Manchester University Press, 2002)

Newell, S., 'Dirty whites: "Ruffian-writing" in colonial West Africa', *Research in African Literatures* 29:4 (2008), 1–13

Newton, A. P. and J. Ewing, *The British Empire since 1783: Its Political and Economic Development* (London: Methuen, 1929)

Niblock, T., *Class and Power in the Sudan: The Dynamics of Sudanese Politics, 1898–1985* (Basingstoke: Macmillan, 1987)

Nicolson, I. F., *The Administration of Nigeria 1900–1960: Men, Methods, and Myths* (Oxford: Clarendon Press, 1969)

Nwabughuogo, A. I., 'The role of propaganda in the development of indirect rule in Nigeria, 1890–1929', *International Journal of African Historical Studies* 14:1 (1981), 65–92

Nwauwa, A. O., *Imperialism, Academe and Nationalism: Britain and University Education for Africans 1860–1960* (London: Frank Cass, 1997)

Oakley, R., *Treks & Palavers* (London: Seeley, Service, and Co., 1938)

O'Halpin, E., *Head of the Civil Service: A Study of Sir Warren Fisher* (London: Routledge, 1989)

Omissi, D. E., *Air Power and Colonial Control: The Royal Air Force, 1919–1939* (Manchester: Manchester University Press, 1990)

Omissi, D. E., *The Sepoy and the Raj: The Indian Army, 1860–1940* (Basingstoke: Macmillan, 1994)

Orr, C., *The Making of Northern Nigeria* (1911; London: Frank Cass, 1965)

Orwell, G., *Collected Essays* (1961; London: Secker & Warburg, 1968)

Oxford University Summer School on Colonial Administration: St. Hugh's College 3–17 July 1937 (Oxford: Oxford University Press, 1937)

Pakenham, V., *The Noonday Sun: Edwardians in the Tropics* (London: Methuen, 1985)

Patterson, K. D., 'The influenza epidemic of 1918–19 in the Gold Coast', *Journal of African History* 24 (1983), 485–502

Perham, M., *Lugard: The Years of Adventure, 1858–1898* (London: Collins, 1956)

Perham, M., *Lugard: The Years of Authority, 1898–1945* (London: Collins, 1960)

Perham, M., *East African Journey* (London: Faber & Faber, 1976)

Plomer, W., *Cecil Rhodes* (London: Peter Davies, 1933)

Porter, A., *Religion versus Empire? British Protestant Missionaries and Overseas Expansion, 1700–1914* (Manchester: Manchester University Press, 2004)

Porter, A. (ed.), *Oxford History of the British Empire: Volume III – The Nineteenth Century* (Oxford: Oxford University Press, 1999)

Porter, B., *The Absent-minded Imperialists: What the British Really Thought about Empire* (Oxford: Oxford University Press, 2004)

Portman, L., *Station Studies* (London: Longmans, 1902)

Price, R., *Making Empire: Colonial Encounters and the Creation of Imperial Rule in Nineteenth-century Africa* (Cambridge: Cambridge University Press, 2008)

Ranger, T., *Are We Not Also Men? The Samkange Family and African Politics in Zimbabwe 1920–64* (London: James Currey, 1995)

Ranger, T. and O. Vaughan (eds), *Legitimacy and the State in Twentieth-century Africa* (London: Macmillan, 1993)

Rathbone, R., 'World War I and Africa: introduction', *Journal of African History* 19:1 (1978), 1–9

Rattray, R. S., *A Short Manual of the Gold Coast* (no publisher details provided, 1924) in British Library 7959.cc.24

Reader, W. J., *Professional Men: The Rise of the Professional Classes in Nineteenth-century England* (London: Weidenfeld and Nicolson, 1966)

Readman, P., 'The place of the past in English culture c.1890–1914', *Past and Present* 186 (2005), 147–99

Reid, R., *A History of Modern Africa: 1800 to the Present* (Chichester: Wiley-Blackwell, 2009)

Rich, P., *Race and Empire in British Politics* (Cambridge: Cambridge University Press, 1986)

Rieger, B., '"Modern wonders": technological innovation and public ambivalence in Britain and Germany, 1890s to 1933', *History Workshop Journal* 55 (2003), 153–171

Rimmer, D. and A. H. M. Kirk-Greene (eds), *The British Intellectual Engagement with Africa in the Twentieth Century* (Basingstoke: Macmillan, 2000)

Roberts, A., 'The sub-imperialism of the Baganda', *Journal of African History* 3:3 (1962), 435–50

Roberts, A., 'The gold boom of the 1930s in East Africa', *African Affairs* 85:341 (1986), 545–62

Roberts, A., *A History of the English-speaking Peoples since 1900* (London: Weidenfeld & Nicolson, 2006)

Roberts, A. (ed.), *Cambridge History of Africa: Volume 7 from 1905 to 1940* (Cambridge: Cambridge University Press, 1986)

Roberts, R. and M. A. Klein, 'The Banaba slave exodus of 1905 and the decline of slavery in the Western Sudan', *Journal of African History* 21:3 (1980), 375–94

Robertson, A. F., 'Anthropologists and government in Ghana', *African Affairs* 74:294 (1975), 51–9

Robinson, K. and F. Madden (eds), *Essays in Imperial Government* (Oxford: Blackwell, 1963)

Rules and Bye-laws of the Western Ridge Sports Club, Accra (Accra: Government Press, 1918)

Rush, A. S., 'Imperial identity in colonial minds: Harold Moody and the League of Coloured Peoples, 1931–50', *Twentieth Century British History* 13:4 (2002), 356–83

Rutherford, A. (ed.), *War Stories and Poems* (Oxford: Oxford University Press, 1990)

Said, E., *Orientalism* (1978; London: Penguin, 1991)

Shaloff, S., 'Press controls and sedition proceedings in the Gold Coast, 1933–1939', *African Affairs* 71:284 (1972), 241–63

Shannon, R., *Gladstone: Heroic Minister 1865–1898* (London: Penguin, 1999)

Sisman, A., *A. J. P. Taylor: A Biography* (London: Sinclair-Stevenson, 1994)

Slight, J., 'British perceptions and responses to Sultan Ali Dinar of Darfur, 1915–16', *Journal of Imperial and Commonwealth History* 38:2 (2010), 237–60

Smith, A. and M. Bull (eds), *Margery Perham and British Rule in Africa* (London: Cass, 1991)

Smith, J. (ed.), *Administering the Empire: The British Colonial Service in Retrospect* (London: University of London Press, 1999)

Snow, C. P., *The Masters* (Kelly Bray: House of Stratus, 2001)

Stigand, C. H., *Administration in Tropical Africa* (London: Constable & Co., 1914)

Stobart, J., 'Building an urban identity: cultural space and civic boosterism in a "new" industrial town: Burslem, 1761–1911', *Social History* 29:4 (2004), 485–98

Stone, D., *Breeding Superman: Nietzsche, Race and Eugenics in Edwardian and Interwar Britain* (Liverpool: Liverpool University Press, 2002)

Strachey, L., *Eminent Victorians* (1918; Harmondsworth: Penguin, 1971)

Strobel, M., *European Women and the Second British Empire* (Bloomington, IN: Indiana University Press, 1991)

Suggate, L. S., *Africa* (London: George Harrap & Co., 1929)

Surridge, K., 'More than a great poster: Lord Kitchener and the image of the military hero', *Historical Research* 74:185 (2001), 298–313

Swindell, K., 'The struggle for transport labor in Northern Nigeria, 1900–1912: a conflict of interests', *African Economic History* 20 (1992), 137–59

Symonds, R., *Oxford and Empire: The Last Lost Cause?* (Oxford: Oxford University Press, 1986)

Tambo, D. C., 'The "Hill refuges" of the Jos Plateau: a historiographical examination', *History in Africa* 5 (1978), 201–23

Temple, C. L., *Native Races and their Rulers: Sketches and Studies of Official Life and Administrative Problems in Nigeria* (Cape Town: Argus, 1918)

Thesiger, W., *Arabian Sands* (1959; Harmondsworth: Penguin, 1964)

Thesiger, W., *The Life of My Choice* (London: Collins, 1987)

Thesiger, W., *The Danakil Diary: Journeys through Abyssinia, 1930–34* (1996; London: Flamingo, 1998)

Thomas, R. G., 'Forced labour in British West Africa: the case of the Northern Territories of the Gold Coast 1906–1927', *Journal of African History* 14:1 (1973), 79–103

Thomas, R. G., 'Education in Northern Ghana, 1906–1940: a study in colonial paradox', *International Journal of African Historical Studies* 7:3 (1974), 427–67

Thompson, A., 'The language of imperialism and the meanings of empire: imperial discourse in British politics, 1895–1914', *Journal of British Studies* 36:2 (1997), 147–77

Thompson, A., *The Empire Strikes Back? The Impact of Empire on Britain from the Mid-nineteenth Century* (Harlow: Pearson Longman, 2005)

Thompson, P., *Edwardians: The Remaking of British Society* (Bloomington, IA: Indiana University Press, 1975)

Tibenderana, P. K., 'The Emirs and the spread of Western education in Northern Nigeria, 1910–1946', *Journal of African History* 24:4 (1983), 517–34

Tidrick, K., *Empire and the English Character* (1990; London: I. B. Tauris, 1992)

Tilley, H., 'Ecologies of complexity: tropical environments, African trypanosomiasis, and the science of disease control in British colonial Africa, 1900–1940', *Osiris* 19 (2004), 21–38

Tilley, H. and R. J. Gordon (eds), *Ordering Africa: Anthropology, European Imperialism, and the Politics of Knowledge* (Manchester: Manchester University Press, 2007)

Tosh, J., 'Colonial chiefs in a stateless society: a case-study from Northern Uganda', *Journal of African History* 14:3 (1973), 473–90

Tosh, J., *A Man's Place: Masculinity and the Middle-class Home in Victorian England* (London: Yale University Press, 1999)

Upward, A., *Athelstane Ford* (London: Arthur Pearson, 1899)

Wallace, E., *Sanders of the River* (1911; Kelly Bray: House of Stratus, 2001)

Wallace, E., *Again Sanders* (1928; London: Pan, 1961)

Warburg, G., *Islam, Sectarianism and Politics in Sudan since the Mahdiyya* (London: C. Hurst & Co., 2003)

Ward, S. (ed.), *British Culture and the End of Empire* (Manchester: Manchester University Press, 2001)

Westermann, D., *The African To-day* (London: Oxford University Press, 1934)

Whitehead, C., 'The historiography of British imperial education policy, Part II: Africa and the rest of the colonial empire', *History of Education* 34 (2005), 441–54

Wiener, M., *English Culture and the Decline of the Industrial Spirit 1850–1980* (1981; Harmondsworth: Penguin; 1985)

Wiener, M., *An Empire on Trial: Race, Murder, and Justice under British Rule, 1870–1935* (Cambridge: Cambridge University Press, 2009)

Wilhelm, J. J., *Ezra Pound in London and Paris, 1908–1925* (University Park, PA: Pennsylvania State University Press, 1990)

Williamson, P., *Stanley Baldwin: Conservative Leadership and National Values* (Cambridge: Cambridge University Press, 1999)

Williamson, T. and A. H. M. Kirk-Greene (eds), *Gold Coast Diaries: Chronicles of Political Officers in West Africa, 1900–1919* (London: Radcliffe Press, 2000)

Willis, J., 'The administration of Bonde, 1920–60: a study of the implementation of indirect rule in Tanganyika', *African Affairs* 92:366 (1993), 53–67

Willis, J., *Mombasa, the Swahili, and the Making of the Mijikenda* (Oxford: Clarendon, 1993)

Willis, J., 'Killing Bwana: peasant revenge and political panic in early colonial Ankole', *Journal of African History* 35:3 (1994), 379–400

Willis, J., *Potent Brews: A Social History of Alcohol in East Africa 1850–1999* (Oxford: BIEA and James Currey, 2002)

Willis, J., 'Violence, authority, and the state in the Nuba Mountains of Condominium Sudan', *Historical Journal* 46:1 (2003), 89–114

Willis, J., 'Hukm: the Creolization of authority in Condominium Sudan', *Journal of African History* 46:1 (2005), 29–50

Willis, J., '"A model of its kind": representation and performance in the Sudan self-government election of 1953', *Journal of Imperial and Commonwealth History* 35:3 (2007), 485–502

Wilson-Haffenden, J. R., *The Red Men of Nigeria* (London: Seeley, Service & Co., 1930)

Windholz, A. M., 'An emigrant and a gentleman: imperial masculinity, British magazines, and the colony that got away', *Victorian Studies* 42:4 (1999), 631–58

Woodward, P., *Sudan 1898–1989: The Unstable State* (London: Lester Crook, 1990)

Wraith, R. E., *Guggisberg* (London: Oxford University Press, 1967)

Wright, A., *The Romance of Colonisation: Being the Story of the Economic Development of the British Empire* (London: Melrose, 1923)

Wylie, D., 'Confrontation over Kenya: the Colonial Office and its critics, 1918–1940', *Journal of African History* 18 (1977), 427–47

Yearwood, P. J. and C. Hazlehurst, '"The affairs of a distant dependency": the Nigeria debate and the premiership, 1916', *Twentieth Century British History* 12:4 (2001), 397–431

Youé, C. and T. Stapleton (eds), *Agency and Action in Colonial Africa: Essays for John E. Flint* (Basingstoke: Palgrave, 2001)

Xie, S., 'Rethinking the problem of postcolonialism', *New Literary History* 28 (1997), 7–19

Unpublished theses

Gardiner, N., 'Sentinels of Empire: The British Colonial Administrative Service, 1919–1954' (PhD dissertation, Yale University, 1998)

Lampert, B. E. N., '"So we used to do": British colonial civil servants in Nigeria 1921–1968' (MSc dissertation, University of Bristol, 2002)

Vaughan, C., 'Negotiating the state at its margins: Colonial authority in Condominium Darfur, 1916–1956' (PhD dissertation, Durham University, 2011)

INDEX

Note: 'n.' after a page reference indicates the number of a note on that page.

EU authorised representative for GPSR:
Easy Access System Europe, Mustamäe tee 50,
10621 Tallinn, Estonia
gpsr.requests@easproject.com

www.ingramcontent.com/pod-product-compliance
Lightning Source LLC
Chambersburg PA
CBHW030824270326
41928CB00007B/888